THE ASSASSINATION OF NEVILLE WRAN

Milton Cockburn

Connor Court Publishing Pty Ltd

Published in 2024 by Connor Court Publishing Pty Ltd.

Copyright © Milton Cockburn

ALL RIGHTS RESERVED. This book contains material protected under International and Federal Copyright Laws and Treaties. Any unauthorised reprint or use of this material is prohibited. No part of this book may be reproduced or transmitted in any form or by any means, electronic or mechanical, including photocopying, recording, or by any information storage and retrieval system without express written permission from the publisher.

Connor Court Publishing Pty Ltd.
PO Box 7257
Redland Bay QLD 4165
sales@connorcourt.com
www.connorcourt.com

ISBN: 9781923224148

Cover illustration by Franz Kantor
Cover design by Maria Giordano

Printed in Australia.

Contents

Preface	v
1. A Few Whacks on the Coffin Lid	1
2. Minister for Corruption	19
3. Nifty and Watery	41
4. "The Premier is on the Phone"	61
5. The Ghost Train Fire Conspiracy	89
6. The Russian Tank and the Network of Influence	113
7. The Mysterious Forty Million Dollars	131
8. Media Mates	147
9. Buckets of Trouble	169
10. Riddled with Corruption	189
11. We Owe the Dead the Truth	207
Notes	225

Preface

On the evening of 30 March 2021, I watched with alarm the final episode of an ABC-TV three-part documentary 'Exposed: The Ghost Train Fire' as it unfolded a tale of tragedy and corruption at Sydney's Luna Park in June 1979. Many of the program's claims were directed at my one-time boss, former New South Wales Premier Neville Wran. My concern evaporated when a former female consort of crime boss Abe Saffron appeared on screen to tell viewers that Wran used to attend Friday night drinks at Saffron's house, in the company of others, and that the two were "really pally". I began laughing. If this was the quality of the program's findings, I had no doubt that what I had previously watched was also nonsense.

With the assistance of Nigel Stokes, a friend from our days on Wran's staff, I had already begun researching and drafting an article demolishing claims by Clarrie Briese, a former chief magistrate with whom Wran had clashed. Briese had alleged in a recently published book that Wran's exoneration by a royal commission – on claims he had perverted the course of justice – was doubtful because of "new evidence" he had uncovered. Briese's claims had been reported, at face value, on the front page of *The Australian* and *The Sydney Morning Herald* on 6 March 2021. I decided to prepare an additional article examining the allegations made by the ABC-TV documentary.

The result was two articles – 'The Revenge of Clarrie Briese' and 'Underexposed: The Ghost Train Fire Documentary' – published in my favourite journal, *The Southern Highlands Newsletter*. The instruction from my editor, Rodney Cavalier, was "write to the length you need". Any other editor would have baulked at two articles, both over 6,000 words, landing in their inbox. The publication of the articles in this privately circulating magazine prompted another old friend, Tom Kelly, to invite me, in July 2021, to present the NSW Society of Labor Lawyers' Frank Walker Memorial Lecture on the topic of 'The War on Wran'.

After the lecture, several well-meaning friends suggested it was time for a more detailed examination of the question: was Neville Wran corrupt? This was the headline of an article in the online journal *Inside Story*, prompted by the ABC documentary. This fresh examination would also need to look at events which had occurred during Wran's premiership which have cast a shadow over his reputation, such as the Rex Jackson and Bill Allen affairs. Most importantly, an examination was required of how Wran had built his wealth, since the size of his estate has also fed rumours of corruption. The result is this book.

I do not pretend to have begun this task with an open mind. In four years on Wran's staff I saw nothing to cause me to question Wran's honesty and plenty to affirm his integrity. Other former staff, including those who had a much closer personal relationship with Wran, testify the same. As one said: "Does anyone believe people such as Gerry Gleeson, Tom Fitzgerald and Graham Freudenberg would have been, and remain, so loyal to Wran if they had any suspicion that he was corrupt". Gleeson was Wran's long-serving head of the Premier's Department; Fitzgerald was the respected former Finance Editor of *The Sydney Morning Herald* (and founder of *Nation*) who became a Wran adviser; and Freudenberg was his well-known speechwriter and confidant. All three, now dead, were men of great personal integrity.

After leaving Wran's staff at the end of 1981 our relationship became rocky. I had not been part of the inner circle of staff but we had always been friendly and mutually respectful. That was tested by my transition to journalism. My job as an editorial writer and columnist for *The Sydney Morning Herald* required me to comment objectively on decisions by the Wran government. We both learned the truth of the observation that friendships are impossible between politicians and political journalists if both are doing their jobs.

Our relationship was further strained by the publication in 1986 of *Wran: An Unauthorised Biography*, co-authored with a fellow *Her-*

ald journalist Mike Steketee. Nobody has suggested this was hagiography. While we were critical of Wran's handling of some corruption incidents – criticisms which I have tempered, because of new evidence, in places in the book you are holding – we found no evidence that Wran was personally corrupt or that he had run a corrupt administration. Wran's only reaction to the book was to place an arm around my shoulders, as we were both leaving a function one night, and promising to "give it a bagging and help its sales along." He didn't criticise it but I have it on good authority that he didn't bother to read it either.

Given this history it was amusing to have been labelled a "Wran apologist" and a "member of the Saint Neville brigade" during the controversy over the ABC ghost train fire documentary. Incidentally, none of Wran's former staffers or his Labor parliamentary colleagues would nominate him for sainthood. Wran could have been speaking of himself, in his eulogy for his friend Lionel Murphy, when he said Murphy "was never cast for sainthood". Wran would have been the first to reject such a role for himself. Like most of us who fall short of exemplary virtue, however, the alternative is not a descent into villainy.

An odd thing about defending Wran against allegations of corruption is the belief by some that any evidence tendered in refutation of allegations is invalid or questionable if it is produced by his former staffers. The *Crikey* online journal, for example, was uninterested in the fact that contrary evidence was ignored by the ABC in the ghost train fire documentary. Instead, *Crikey* was obsessed that it was former Wran staffers, and *The Australian's* Troy Bramston, who had exposed the program's many flaws. Journalist Margaret Simons also found it noteworthy that the "program's most trenchant critics" were "people who built their careers in the decade 1976-86", when Wran was premier, and are "deeply invested in how history judges these times." The reality is we are all now in our 70s and our focus is our future, not our past. The only careers we worry about now are those of our children and grandchildren. Readers can make up their own minds whether those who knew Wran best are disqualified from coming to his defence.

My thanks to a small group of Wran-era Labor MPs who have willingly shared their knowledge and recollections. Some also commented on draft chapters. These are Rodney Cavalier, Terry Sheahan, Peter Anderson, Bob Carr, Michael Egan (who died before the book was completed) and Bob Debus. Thank you also to the 'Mazzaro crowd', who have been a welcome editorial committee. These are in various table settings: Brian Dale, Terry Sheahan, David Hurley, David Hill, Nigel Stokes, Tom Kelly, John Whitehouse and, not forgetting, the late Dick Smyth.

Dr David Clune, one of the pre-eminent political historians of NSW, deserves special thanks for his advice and critical comments on the draft manuscript and for suggesting this editorial feedback usually be conducted over lunch. I am also grateful to Rodney Cavalier, who has a similar passion for political history and demand for accuracy, and who also made helpful suggestions on the draft manuscript. Richard Coleman and Tom Kelly kindly cast experienced eyes over several draft chapters.

Thanks to Jill Wran and Malcolm Turnbull, both of whom shared personal information which they probably would have preferred to remain private.

Thank you also to *Quadrant* editors, Keith Windschuttle and Roger Franklin, for publishing my article, 'The Careless Journalism of Kate McClymont', in the magazine (July-August 2020) and online. This has been revised for the chapter 'Riddled With Corruption'. Rodney Cavalier willingly allowed me to mine the *Southern Highlands Newsletter* articles, referred to above, for the chapter 'The Ghost Train Fire Conspiracy' and for part of another chapter, 'The Premier Is On The Phone'.

Finally, thank you to Anthony Cappello and Connor Court Publishing, for recognising that the issue of whether one of the most prominent premiers of Australia's largest state was corrupt was deserving of a book. The cover illustration, by Frantz Kantor, originally appeared in *The Sydney Morning Herald* on 28 December 1991 and is reproduced with the permission of the artist and the newspaper. Frantz's work can be seen at www.frantzkantor.com. Thanks also to Michael Gilchrist for a quality and easy-to-read publication.

This book is dedicated to the small group of men and women who regard working for, and with, Neville Wran as a highlight of their working lives. Melbourne journalist, Andrew Rule, the leader of the 'Wran was bent' pack, has said of us: "[Wran's defenders] have no choice but to boost Wran. Otherwise, it looks too much as if they were either in on the Wran rorts or too dumb to realise that shifty Nifty had fooled them along with the voters." Again, readers can make up their own minds if we are corrupt or stupid.

1

A Few Whacks on the Coffin Lid

"No one knew better than Wran that those who live by the sword have to expect a few whacks on their coffin lid." Journalist Andrew Rule.

"After I breathe my last there will be articles and so-called learned dissertations about how I was a crook. Our law is you can defame the dead. I won't read it or hear it but my family, my friends and my colleagues will. But that's politics and there is nothing I can do about that." Neville Wran.

The page one headline in *The Sydney Morning Herald* on Saturday 6 March 2021 read, "Wran lobbied to kill legal cases for powerful friends". The story began: "Sensational evidence withheld from a royal commission throws light on the involvement of former NSW premier Neville Wran in a conspiracy to pervert the course of justice." The corresponding headline in *The Australian* that day was slightly more restrained but equally wrong: "New evidence changes Wran's role in corruption scandal". Three weeks later ABC television viewers were told in a documentary that Wran, when New South Wales premier, had nobbled a police investigation into the tragic 1979 Luna Park fire to protect his friend, crime boss Abe Saffron, and had also gifted a new lease for the site to Saffron.

Oddly neither story generated significant coverage in other mainstream media. Perhaps those charged with deciding what is newsworthy, and therefore worth following up, thought the evidence presented to justify the claims was somewhat thin. Perhaps they thought that allegations that Wran was corrupt were no longer news: there had been a steady trickle of such claims since Wran's death in 2014. Perhaps they simply made a judgment that most of their readers or audience would not even know of Wran. Nearly half of NSW residents today were not born when Wran retired as the state's premier. Given this, a brief primer is necessary before we pick up this story.

Neville Wran is the most electorally successful Labor premier in the history of NSW. In nearly 13 years leading the Australian Labor Party in Australia's largest state, Wran did not lose an election or lose a seat at a by-election. His approval rating in polls at times exceeded 80%, a stratospheric level for political leaders. Such was his electoral dominance that Labor's share of the two-party preferred vote, under NSW's preferential voting system, reached 60.7% at the 1978 election and 58.7% at the 1981 poll. The term 'Wranslide' was coined by a newspaper to describe the huge parliamentary majorities Labor gained at these elections. After the 1981 election the electorates of the last five leaders of the Liberal Party, the main opposition party, were no longer in that party's hands. Wran's electoral dominance was not confined to the metropolitan areas. By 1981 Labor held nearly one-third of the seats in country NSW, challenging the traditional dominance of the Country Party, as it was then named.

Wran did not enter Parliament until he was 43, after a successful first career in the law as a solicitor and a barrister. Despite being factionally non-aligned his talents were quickly recognised and his parliamentary rise was very rapid. He became Leader of the Opposition in the Legislative Council less than two years after his election to the upper house in 1970. In a cross-factional arrangement a safe seat was found for him in the Legislative Assembly at the 1973 election. After that election, Labor's fourth defeat in a row, he narrowly won a fiercely contested leadership ballot. Less than three years later Wran became Premier of NSW, narrowly winning government at the election on 1 May 1976. When he resigned as premier and from Parliament in July 1986 he had set a then record of 10 years of continuous service as premier, despite serving for fewer than 13 years in the Legislative Assembly, the chamber in which governments are formed.

All political careers end in tears, the old saying goes, but Wran's was an exception. Despite a year in the political doldrums after the

1984 election Wran clawed his way back in the opinion polls. When he resigned the Labor government still had a healthy 17-seat majority in the parliament, a majority that disappeared just two years later without him at the helm. Whether Wran would have recorded a fifth straight election win can never be known but many in Labor are convinced that he would.

Wran did not waste the electoral majorities he earned. Despite later claiming that he "didn't set out to achieve much", his government is acknowledged as a reformist administration. Wran democratised voting for the Legislative Council; introduced a 'one vote-one value' electoral system; a four-year parliamentary term; public funding of election campaigns and compulsory disclosure of election donations. He widened the scope of anti-discrimination legislation; repealed the draconian *Summary Offences Act;* decriminalised homosexuality and prostitution; established an Ethnic Affairs Commission and an Equal Opportunity Council; set up a Women's Co-ordination Unit in the Premier's Department to promote gender equality; widened the scope of the *Consumer Affairs Act;* pioneered an *Aboriginal Land Rights Act;* overhauled treatment of the mentally ill; implemented prison reforms; began the liberalisation of retail trading hours and liquor licensing; removed restrictions on outdoor dining and introduced random breath testing of motorists.

Wran valued environmental protection. The ground-breaking *Environmental Planning and Assessment Act* was passed, followed by the *Coastal Protection Act,* the *Historic Houses Act,* the *Royal Botanic Gardens Trust Act* and the *Centennial Park Trust Act.* His government doubled the area of the state's national parks and controlled the logging of sensitive rainforest areas. Many of these environmental protection measures came at the expense of employment. Nevertheless, and somewhat paradoxically, "jobs, jobs, jobs" became a Wran mantra. He supervised responsible state budgets and was proud his first five budgets contained no increases in taxes and charges. He placed a high priority on economic development, increased public works spending and forged good relations with the business community. He was active in seeking increased business investment in NSW, including personally driving an expansion of the aluminium smelting industry, which was only partly successful.

Wran had a strong interest in the arts and assumed the arts portfolio. He established the Sydney Theatre Company, and a permanent home at the Wharf Theatre, and the Museum of Contemporary Art; restored the Hyde Park Barracks and the Mint; set up the NSW Film Corporation; created the Powerhouse Museum as a new home for the museum of applied science and engineering; commissioned the Entertainment Centre; boosted the Art Gallery of NSW and funded regional galleries; extended the State Library; and introduced the Premier's Award for literature.

A full assessment of Wran's achievements must also acknowledge his role in restoring Labor's electoral credibility. Wran narrowly won government in NSW only six months after the comprehensive defeat of the Whitlam government at the national level, an electoral defeat which many believed would see Labor out of office for more than a decade. Wran may have been the leader of Labor in only one state but his influence extended beyond NSW's borders. His example of moderate, stable, fiscally cautious but still progressive government played a significant role in Labor's national electoral rehabilitation and the subsequent elections of Labor governments in Victoria, South Australia, Western Australia and Queensland. All deliberately adopted the 'Wran model' to entrench themselves. Political historian Dr David Clune concluded: "The Wran model was a template for a new generation of Labor state premiers such as John Bannon, John Cain and Wayne Goss: reformist, competent and, above all, electorally astute." Journalist Paul Kelly wrote: "[Wran] seized a major beachhead while the rest of the Labor Party tried to regather its strength. Wran was a beacon of reassurance when Labor felt desperate. For half a decade Wran was the only ALP incumbent who could fight the non-Labor side, a task which he performed with skill, vigour and judgment … Every senior ALP figure was influenced by the Wran model in the late 1970s."

Despite this impressive record, if Wran's name is referenced these days it is more likely to be in the context of an allegation of corruption. Journalists have openly claimed that Wran, as well as leading a corrupt administration, was also personally corrupt. One journalist has written: "The NSW Premier Neville Wran, whose administration later became a byword for graft ..." Another described the more recent Berejiklian Coalition government in NSW as "the most corrupt government since the Wran years" and wrote the Wran government was "riddled with corruption." A third journalist has said of Wran himself: "he was as bent as a three-dollar note." The same journalist has also written, without providing an example or any evidence, that in his day Wran "can nobble a murder investigation nearly as easily as Big Bill Waterhouse can nobble a horse". A commercial television program in 2022 seemed to fill in the blanks when it conveyed an allegation, again without corroboration, that Wran had interfered in the murder investigation of a horse trainer. As noted earlier an ABC television program claimed he had a friendly relationship with notorious crime boss Abe Saffron and had personally intervened to deliver the lease over Luna Park to a Saffron-linked company, following the tragic fire at the ghost train ride in 1979. The program also claimed Wran interfered in a police investigation into Saffron's alleged involvement in the fire.

Political scientist Dr Rodney Tiffen has noted "the sheer number of controversies and allegations involving Wran has persuaded some people he was corrupt". Wran, when premier, spoke of this phenomenon after his complete exoneration by a royal commission of an allegation he had perverted the course of justice. "After the findings of the Street royal commission, we were all entitled to believe that the tactic of smear and innuendo, of guilt by association, of rumours without substance, would stop. But every time some fabrication is completely disposed of, another allegation is fabricated ...The very frequency of allegations, their repetition and regurgitation, no matter how many times they are proved to be false, becomes proof that something is wrong. Innocence itself becomes a kind of presumption of guilt. Refutation after refutation of false claims becomes itself evidence of a 'log of allegations of corruption'".

Wran touches on a peculiarly Sydney characteristic. Sydney, seemingly more than any other Australian city, floats on malicious rumours and unsubstantiated gossip. This is a lesson that should quickly be learned by journalists presented with allegations about public figures. Scandalmongering is a currency for many. Few public works projects in Sydney begin, or are completed, without allegations of someone 'copping a quid', usually emanating from unsuccessful bidders or opponents of the project. Family members, unhappy with their financial lot, hurl accusations against other family members and their associates. This phenomenon is exacerbated by the law which means the dead can be defamed but their relatives cannot seek legal redress.

Melbourne journalist Andrew Rule has written: "No one knew better than Wran that those who live by the sword have to expect a few whacks on their coffin lid". Wran did expect that his name would be blackened after his death, just as it had been while in politics. In what turned out to be his last interview, he told journalist Troy Bramston in 2011: "After I breathe my last, there will be articles and so-called learned dissertations about how I was a crook. Our law is you can defame the dead. I won't read it or hear it but my family, my friends and my colleagues will. But that is politics, and there is nothing I can do about that." It is doubtful, however, if Wran anticipated those defamations would simply be printed or broadcast without any attempt at examination or corroboration.

His complaint that "every time some allegation is completely disposed of another allegation is fabricated" has continued after his death. Journalist Kate McClymont, in her book *Dead Man Walking*, wrote of a supposedly dodgy land deal in western Sydney in 1996 where the new owners of the land, pursuing a rezoning windfall, had allegedly got a cut-rate deal when buying the land from "the CSIRO under the chairmanship of the late Neville Wran, the former Labor premier of New South Wales." This claim was later repeated by a Channel 7 Crime Investigation Australia documentary *On Borrowed Time – The Michael McGurk Murder*. Simple research would have informed McClymont and the documentary makers that Wran's chairmanship of CSIRO had ended in 1991, five years before this sale occurred.

Andrew Rule has reported the uncorroborated claim of a "now-retired Sydney businessman" who "shortly after Wran became premier" supposedly witnessed Wran arrive at a popular restaurant, the Bayswater Brasserie, where prominent gangster Abe Saffron was sitting alone at a table. Wran allegedly turned on his heel and left. Rule wrote: "What the businessman could not tell is if Wran saw Saffron and didn't want the gangster to speak to him – or whether he recognised the businessman and didn't want him to witness a meeting with Saffron. Either way, it is clear that the idea of being seen mixing publicly with Saffron spooked Premier Wran." Does Rule seriously expect his readers to believe that Wran, widely acknowledged as intelligent and politically astute, would have arranged a luncheon meeting with Saffron in a popular restaurant? If Wran just happened to find himself in the same restaurant as the well-recognised Sydney crime boss, why would he not (like any sensible politician) be spooked and immediately leave?

Rule does not explain why his source has insisted on anonymity, given Wran was dead when Rule wrote this and therefore could not sue. Perhaps the answer lies in the fact that Rule reports that the businessman told him this aborted meeting took place "shortly after Wran became premier" which would make it in late 1976 or perhaps 1977. If Rule had bothered to check he would have found this restaurant did not open until 1982, at least five years after Rule's anonymous source claimed to have seen the two men there. There is a reason for the basic journalism rule requiring at least two sources for an allegation, particularly if the source is anonymous. There is always a possibility that a single source turns out to be a fantasist.

Rule's anonymous witness has also spun another yarn, almost too trivial to note. He claims he was present at the house which Wran owned with his then wife Marcia, shortly after the pair separated, when Marcia complained about a gift of a cordless phone from Abe Saffron. He claims Marcia said the phone did not work and this was typical of gifts from Saffron. If this story was true, it must have occurred around mid-1975 which was when the couple separated. Cordless phones were illegal in 1975 – they were not legalised until the early 1980s – and only began to be imported, illegally, in the late 1970s. Is it likely that Wran, a leading barrister and aspiring premier, would have risked possessing an illegal phone even if they had been available around June 1975? Incidentally Wran told Parliament in November 1977: "I do not know, I have never met, I have never eaten with and I have never been in any circumstances with a gentleman named Abe Saffron."

Rule has also claimed that the broadcaster and columnist Phillip Adams was approached by the media mogul Kerry Packer, a friend of both Adams and Wran, and asked to deliberately defame Wran in Packer's magazine *The Bulletin* as a means of disguising payments to Wran. "This was a nifty way for powerful interests to sling a politician a tax-free confidential settlement without resorting to brown paper bags," Rule claimed. Note Rule's use of the word "nifty" – Wran's nickname – and the imputation that Packer and Wran had used such a transaction. In fact, Adams had written that his conversation with Packer had come after Packer had told Adams he felt sorry for Wran and his lack of money. Adams said he offered to "write a column in next week's *Bulletin* accusing him of a sexual deviation. He sues you and you settle out of court". Adams says Packer responded, "Great", at which point Adams piped up: "Only kidding". So, a joke told by Phillip Adams becomes, in Rule's retelling, an imputation of corrupt payments from Packer to Wran.

Rule has also written that Wran "would later switch portfolios [from police] to include the one controlling mineral licences." The obvious inference of this comment is to suggest Wran was looking to line his own pockets by linking him with the scandals over coal licences in the Hunter Valley which plagued another Labor government decades later (at the time when Rule was writing). In fact, as revealed in Wran's biography, Wran "decided to take over the [mineral resources] portfolio in order to supervise what he knew would be one of his most controversial actions: the resumption of all private coal rights" in NSW. This led to a major political campaign against the government, one not confined to the coal industry, against the "nationalisation" of coal holdings. Wran had no intention of leaving this political fight in the hands of the previous Minister for Mineral Resources, Ron Mulock, a minister with whom Wran had difficulties working. (Even Wran's supporters believe those difficulties were largely of Wran's making.) Sixteen months later, after this "coal grab" was completed, Wran handed the portfolio to the affable Kevin Stewart, a minister with a reputation for being able to calm down angry constituents. *The Sydney Morning Herald* noted at the time: "Mr Wran's decision to offload the Mineral Resources portfolio was inevitable once the difficult issue of the private coal holdings had been resolved." Not for the first time Rule, a Victorian, who spent his journalistic career in Melbourne, reveals a lack of understanding of NSW political history.

Crime journalist and author Bob Bottom, who was responsible for passing the so-called 'Age tapes' to the media, has claimed that when Wran was premier there was an all-night session of the NSW Parliament, which went to 4 o'clock on Saturday morning, to debate special legislation "aimed at having me fined and jailed". He further claimed that on the following Monday the police commissioner had phoned his wife to tell her he was coming out to arrest him. Bottom says he had just flown to Melbourne "so he missed me". A check of the Hansard shows there was only one session of Parliament on a Friday between February 1984, when *The Age* transcripts were published, and July 1986, when Wran resigned from Parliament. This session was to finalise end-of-year business and adjourned at 4.38pm on Friday. There were no sessions running until the early hours of Saturday morning. Arrest warrants can be enforced in Victoria, incidentally, and there is no explanation from Bottom why he wasn't arrested in Victoria or when he arrived back in Sydney or why the police commissioner would take it upon himself to personally arrest people.

As if these false claims are not enough, Andrew Rule even finds something sinister in Wran's nickname. Rule has said: "Neville Wran was called 'Nifty' for a reason. Neville Wran was called 'Never Wrong' for a reason. Neville Wran had other nicknames as well. And he got them because there was a double-edged attitude towards him. Because some people, smart people, sharp people, savvy people – people like him in other words – realised that he was a pretty slippery customer, that he worked both sides of the fence, both sides of the room". Wran did not have a nickname 'Never Wrong'. This was a satirical name coined by broadcaster Mike Carlton as part of his biting radio political satire and mimicry, *Friday News Review*. None of Wran's former staff is aware of "other nicknames" for Wran.

While the dictionary attributes of 'nifty' – "particularly good, skilful, or effective" – certainly applied to Wran the politician, as well as Wran the barrister (as he was when he was so dubbed), the coiner of the nickname borrowed it from the well-known jockey, 'Nifty' Neville Sellwood. Many other Nevilles have since attracted the same nickname in the cause of alliteration. Wran once joked that he was sick of people taking his first name in vain to allegedly pursue criminal favours and was considering changing it to 'Marmaduke'. Perhaps that would also have stymied Rule's peculiar version of nominative determinism.

Wran could not have predicted, however, the seriousness of the two most recent "whacks on his coffin lid", both coming from apparently credible sources. In March 2021 ABC-TV broadcast a three-part program, 'Exposed: The Ghost Train Fire', which made several allegations of criminal behaviour by Wran. The program alleged that the fire at the ghost train ride at Luna Park in June 1979, which claimed seven lives, had been deliberately lit by a group of bikies at the direction of Abe Saffron. It also alleged that the cause of the fire had been covered up by corrupt police and that the cover up went all the way to Wran. The program further claimed that Wran had subsequently intervened to ensure the new lease for the site ended up with a Saffron-linked company.

These allegations followed soon after the publication of a book by a former chief magistrate, Clarrie Briese, which disputed the complete exoneration of Wran by the Street royal commission. An ABC *Four Corners* television program in 1983 had reported claims that Wran in 1977 had telephoned the then chief magistrate, Murray Farquhar, to request that fraud charges against a senior rugby league official be dismissed. Chief Justice, Sir Laurence Street, found the claim of Wran's participation to be untrue. Briese claimed to have discovered new evidence which threw doubt on Street's finding.

Before examining the validity of these and other allegations against Wran it is necessary to define what we mean by corruption. This is not as nonsensical as it sounds. Once an accusation of corruption against a politician had an unambiguous meaning. This meant the use of power or influence for illegitimate private gain, usually in the form of money. Now the definition of corruption is drawn as much broader than personal gain. It became common place for journalists and others to refer to the national Morrison Coalition government as corrupt following the revelation of the 'rorting' of various government social infrastructure schemes to favour Coalition-held electorates. None of these revelations suggested that Liberal or National politicians had personally benefited from these schemes.

An article in 2021 in the online journal *Inside Story* was headed: 'Was Neville Wran corrupt?' The author, Rodney Tiffen, concluded: "Despite gossip to the contrary, no persuasive evidence exists to support the view that Wran was corrupt in the sense of seeking personal financial gain. Nor is there persuasive evidence that Wran directly or indirectly sought to advance any criminal interests or had any direct or indirect relationships with such criminals." Tiffen further wrote: "Despite some gossip, neither during nor since Wran's years as premier, has any evidence emerged that he received bribes or sought other forms of personal enrichment." Tiffen's conclusion would seem to answer in the negative the question which framed his article. Tiffen, however, was reluctant to let Wran completely off the hook. He went on to recount several government decisions which benefited powerful media interests. He wrote that "these decisions have no hint of personal financial gain, but they do suggest that Wran was happy to use the government's prerogatives to advance Labor's interests, and that he wouldn't be inhibited by procedural niceties." By "advance Labor's interests" Tiffen presumably means boosting Labor's prospects of re-election.

If taking advantage of incumbency to enhance the chances of re-election now falls within the definition of corruption, just about every NSW premier since the beginning of responsible government would be in the dock. One of Wran's Liberal successors, Gladys Berejiklian, summed this up rather bluntly, when defending her own government's 'grants rort'. "I don't think it would be a surprise to anybody that we throw money at seats to keep them", she said. There is much truth in the old anarchist saying: 'No matter who you vote for, a politician always gets in.'

The recent widening of the definition of corruption need not unduly concern us here. When a journalist writes that Wran was "as bent as a three-dollar note", he was certainly not accusing Wran of seeking to maximise his chances of re-election. The same journalist has claimed that Wran had lined his own pockets as premier and had consorted with criminals. This book examines those specific allegations that Wran enriched himself while premier or had relationships with criminals or had made decisions which had the effect of benefiting criminal elements. One chapter, however, addresses Tiffen's claim that Wran ignored "procedural niceties" in benefiting "powerful media interests."

For several years after leaving Wran's staff, along with fellow journalist Mike Steketee, I investigated Wran's life in some detail for our book *Wran: An Unauthorised Biography*. (I have referenced this biography throughout this book as "the Wran biography".) Two chapters of the book deal with allegations of corruption during the 10 years of Wran's premiership. One of those chapters is titled: "Corruption: Recurring Themes". The heading referred to the history of NSW politics, noting that "the administration of the police force, the implementation and enforcement of laws against crime and political corruption, are recurring themes [in NSW]."

While we were critical of the Wran government's handling of some of these issues, we found no evidence to justify the claim that the government was "a byword for graft". Nor did we find any evidence that Wran was personally corrupt. My own conclusion is that the Wran government was, in many respects, much better in dealing with these recurring themes than its predecessors. The Wran government, after a very slow start and some hiccups, did more than any previous government to rid the NSW Police Force of endemic corruption, although that task was not completed until after the Wood royal commission in 1995-97. Wran would later argue that "our government has done more to fight crime and corruption, wherever it occurs, than any previous government." David Clune has cited this Wran quote and added drolly, and probably fairly, "there was not much competition".

Wran did something courageous for a supposedly corrupt or compromised premier. On 23 September 1980, following a series of allegations by the Opposition, Wran initiated a 'no restrictions' parliamentary debate on corruption. "If we are to get into the gutter or in the mud, let us all get in together," he told Parliament. "This debate will continue until there is no muck that has not been raked, no rumour that has not been regurgitated, no reputation that has not been ruined. Under the full umbrella of parliamentary privilege each and every member shall have the opportunity and the right to say whatever he wishes, however scurrilous, however repetitious …"

The debate went for around 10 hours. The government frequently moved generous extensions of time for Opposition speakers. The subsequent media reporting of the debate judged the Opposition had failed to make a case of corruption against Wran or his administration. The media verdict supported Wran's prediction at the outset of the debate: "at the end of the day no damage will have been done to the Government but great damage will have been done to this Parliament and, most of all, to the reputation and standing of the Opposition." No other premier has provided a forum for his political opponents to make their corruption allegations in such a sustained manner under the protection of parliamentary privilege. This is hardly the behaviour of a politician with skeletons in his cupboard.

The Wran government certainly made mistakes. One of Wran's successors as NSW Labor premier, Bob Carr, has revealed he learned from what he called Wran's three distinct errors. "I had seen Neville Wran's premiership tainted and compromised on probity by three distinct errors. One the elevation of a corrupt cop as assistant commissioner. Two, the extension of the term of corrupt magistrate, Murray Farquhar. Three, being too slow to shake out police corruption …. Almost every week I was to watch him struggle to ward off allegations that his administration was tainted by a laxness towards corruption." Carr could also have added a celebrated case of ministerial corruption with Wran's Minister for Corrective Services, Rex Jackson, forced to resign over allegations he accepted money for the early release of prisoners to settle gambling debts. Jackson was subsequently found guilty of conspiring to release three prisoners for money and was jailed. This may not count as an error on Wran's part, although he did appoint Jackson to the portfolio, but there is no doubt this affair helped taint the Wran administration.

The following chapters examine what Wran called "a log of allegations of corruption". They begin in chapter two, 'Minister For Corruption', with claims that Wran ignored evidence of police corruption and examines the 'Bill Allen affair' to which Bob Carr alluded: the rapid promotion of a senior policeman later forced to resign over corruption allegations. Journalist Dennis Shanahan wrote this was the beginning of the "real problems for [Wran's] administration and the commencement of a souring relationship with the media."

Wran's long-standing friendship with controversial bookmaker Bill Waterhouse is examined in chapter three 'Nifty And Watery'. This includes allegations that Wran accepted money from Waterhouse and took bribes to protect from closure an illegal casino owned by Waterhouse. Another version of this allegation is that Wran was a financial partner with Waterhouse in this illegal casino. It has also been claimed that Wran intervened, presumably on Waterhouse's behalf, to stop a police investigation into the murder of a racehorse trainer.

Wran's complete exoneration by the Street royal commission on a claim of perverting the course of justice is examined in chapter four 'The Premier Is On The Phone'. As noted earlier, a former chief magistrate, Clarrie Briese, has written that there is new evidence – supposedly uncovered by him or covered up by the royal commissioner – which throws doubt on the chief justice's finding of Wran's innocence. Central to this episode is a controversial chief magistrate, Murray Farquhar, later jailed on corruption charges. Wran had cause earlier to consider Farquhar's position as chief magistrate but did not force him off the bench.

Bill Allen, the senior policeman controversially promoted by Wran, had links to notorious Sydney crime boss Abe Saffron. Chapter five, 'The Ghost Train Fire Conspiracy', examines the allegation that Wran had a friendly relationship with Saffron, including claims that Wran helped cover up of the cause of the deadly fire at the ghost train ride at Luna Park in 1979 and had steered the new lease for the site to a Saffron-linked company.

Chapter six, 'The Russian Tank And The Network Of Influence', examines Wran's involvement in a 'network of influence', supposedly revealed by what has become known as 'the Age tapes'. This was the illegal recording by NSW police of phone conversations of Sydney solicitor, Morgan Ryan. In the Wran biography we wrote: "At worst, Wran had done Morgan Ryan a favour on one occasion – if Ryan's version of events on the tape can be believed – by appointing Bill Jegorow as Deputy Chairman of the Ethnic Affairs Commission." This allegation was examined by the Parliamentary Commission of Inquiry, established in 1986 by the Australian Parliament. The commission's report on this incident was only made public in 2017 and has not been reported until now.

Wran's wealth has also been a cause for subsequent claims that he must have been financially corrupt. When he died in April 2014, after several years battling dementia, Wran left an estate reportedly worth $40 million. The $40 million figure is a wild exaggeration but, nevertheless, he died a wealthy man. A journalist has written: "We are supposed to believe he made it legitimately after retiring from politics at 60 and before he started losing his mind in his 70s. Go figure." Wran's accumulation of his wealth is examined in chapter seven 'The Mysterious Forty Million Dollars'.

As noted earlier, Rodney Tiffen has cited several decisions made by Wran which benefited media proprietors. Tiffen said these decisions "had no hint of personal gain" but showed Wran's willingness to "use the government's prerogatives to advance Labor's interests" and that he "would not be inhibited by procedural niceties". These decisions are now seen to be examples of 'political corruption'. The decisions are examined in chapter eight 'Media Mates'.

The claims of corruption have not been confined to Wran. One journalist has written that "the Wran government was riddled with corruption." Another has claimed the Wran administration has become "a byword for graft". The only substantiated instance of corruption against a Wran government minister was the forced resignation and subsequent jailing of Rex Jackson. Chapter nine, 'Buckets Of Trouble', addresses claims that Wran was reluctant to investigate allegations against Jackson and sought to protect him, including by having the government pay his legal fees after he was charged. Corruption allegations have also been made, after their deaths, against two other ministers, Eric Bedford and Paul Landa, both known to be close to Wran. These allegations are examined in chapter ten 'Riddled With Corruption'.

Chapter eleven, 'We Owe The Dead The Truth', is the final chapter and answers the question posed by the *Inside Story* article referred to earlier: 'Was Neville Wran corrupt?'. What has the examination of various controversies in the following chapters shown about Wran? Have these various whacks on Wran's coffin lid been justified? Why has the Wran government, and Wran personally, attracted these corruption claims? Why was Wran targeted over corruption claims when he was in Parliament and why has Wran been singled out for character assassination after his death?

2

MINISTER FOR CORRUPTION

"Of course [Wran] wants to be Police Minister because to be Police Minister is to be Minister for Corruption." Bookmaker Bill Waterhouse, according to Andrew Rule.

"[Wran] tended to see the corruption issue in traditional terms relating to gambling, liquor and prostitution. If there were bad cops, it was most likely because of bad laws." Graham Freudenberg.

"The police are endeavouring to enforce a law that has long since ceased to have attached to it any question of moral turpitude. The public regards SP betting as part and parcel of the ordinary state of affairs." Neville Wran.

No-one is sure where the conversation took place. In one version it was said in Cabinet; in another it occurred in Wran's office, in front of other newly appointed ministers. There is general agreement, however, about what was said: "Let's clean up the cops". This was the advice to Wran from Frank Walker, Wran's first attorney general, shortly after the Wran government was elected. Walker, who died in 2012, confirmed in 2006 he gave this advice to Cabinet although he did not confirm the words he used: "In hindsight, if Cabinet had accepted my suggestion in 1976 to fight police corruption, Labor might have been spared much future embarrassment".

Walker's advice was seen by most colleagues as evidence of his political immaturity. The NSW Police Force in 1976 may have been regarded as overwhelmingly corrupt by journalists and political insiders but that view was not shared by the voters of NSW. A survey in 1978 of marginal seats by Labor's pollster, ANOP, found 77 per cent of respondents (and 82 per cent of swinging voters) believed the police force was a "good one". A Morgan Gallup poll, also in 1978, found 47 per cent of respondents indicated "a great deal" of respect for the NSW police and 40 per cent indicated "some" respect. Only 11 per cent said "hardly any" respect. In a confrontation between the government and the police Wran had no doubt who would carry the hearts and minds, and therefore the votes, of the public.

Picking a fight with the police force would have been a particularly courageous strategy by a new government with a one-seat majority. The subsequent campaigns by police over the repeal of the *Summary Offences Act* and the establishment of the Police Board would have paled into insignificance. Wran's much quoted comment – "We'd be regarded as great social reformers if we cut our wrists with rusty razor blades like the Whitlam ministers did" – was mainly directed at those who urged him to 'clean up the cops'. This comment was made, significantly, to a journalist from *The National Times* which was prominent in the 1980s in exposing police corruption.

If the matter of police corruption crossed the mind of the average voter, the reaction is likely to have been an assessment that, sure, there were probably some rotten apples but that was no reason for throwing out the entire barrel. It was the job of the police commissioner, wasn't it, to weed out the rotten apples so that they did not infect the entire stock? There is little evidence, however, that successive NSW police commissioners had shown much willingness to remove the rotten apples. There are credible allegations that many of the commissioners were themselves corrupt.

One commissioner who initially tackled corruption was Fred Hanson, who was commissioner from 1972 to 1976. Hanson succeeded Norman Allan whose tenure had been tarnished by claims of corruption. On taking office, Hanson sacked 28 officers allegedly on the grounds of corruption, a move which made him unpopular within the Police Force. Hanson is now alleged to have been in the pay of illegal casino operators. Hanson's behaviour in retirement – threatening to run as an independent candidate in the 1978 NSW election in protest at government moves to shut down the casinos – only served for some to give credence to the allegations.

Wran had no hesitation in appointing himself as minister for police when allocating portfolios after the May 1976 election victory. He had 'shadowed' the portfolio after his election as Leader of the Opposition in 1973 because his political opponent, Premier Sir Robert Askin, also held the police portfolio. Terry Sheahan, who had been elected to Parliament in 1973, recalls discussions and speculation after Askin's retirement that Labor's Leader in the Legislative Council, Leroy ("Lee") Serisier, a solicitor, would take the police portfolio if Labor won government in 1976. This came to nought when Serisier failed to be re-elected as leader in the Caucus ballot and was therefore not in the first Wran ministry. The largely lack-lustre Cabinet with which Wran was initially saddled had not thrown up any obvious alternative candidates as police minister.

Melbourne journalist Andrew Rule has reported an uncorroborated claim by David Waterhouse, the estranged son of controversial bookmaker, Bill Waterhouse, that his father had told him: "Of course [Wran] wants to be Police Minister because to be Police Minister is to be Minister for Corruption." This is an unlikely comment from a person who was a long-time friend of Wran. Rule added, without foundation: "To be Police Minister in Sydney in the 70s and the 80s was to be the Minister for Corruption." In one sentence Rule defames a range of police ministers, both Liberal and Labor, some of whom are still alive.

If Rule (and Waterhouse, if this hearsay is believed) had been more familiar with NSW political history he would have known, as was noted in the Wran biography, there was nothing remarkable in the premier also becoming police minister. This tradition began in the 1940s under Labor's Bill McKell when the then colonial secretary and the police commissioner had difficulties working together. Askin continued the practice when he won government in 1965. The tradition, briefly interrupted after the retirement of Askin, was only broken when Wran passed the portfolio to Bill Crabtree in 1980 and then to Peter Anderson in 1981. No NSW premier has since also held the police portfolio.

Wran's reasons for taking the portfolio were much more prosaic than the reason advanced, allegedly, by Bill Waterhouse. He knew that 'managing the police' would be one of the challenges of his government. Even Frank Walker later conceded: "The political reality of the day was that the police force was far more popular than politicians in the eyes of the electorate who had no real insight into the extent of police corruption until the Wood royal commission." Wran's speechwriter, Graham Freudenberg, wrote that "from the beginning Wran found it hard to grasp the scale of NSW police corruption." It is doubtful that such a worldly figure as Wran was under any such illusion. Freudenberg is accurate, however, in observing that Wran "tended to see the corruption issue in traditional terms related to gambling, liquor and prostitution. If there were bad cops, it was most likely because of bad laws. Thus, the way to deal with the petty corruption arising from the arbitrary powers of arrest under the *Summary Offences Act* was to repeal the Act."

Wran was aware of the general suspicion, and often outright hostility, towards Labor at the senior levels of the force. On Wran's regular visits to regional electorates a police escort was always provided for travel between venues. Wran always made a point, during one leg of the visit, to "ride with the boys" as he called it. (Women police officers were scarce in the 1970s). Wran's staff had no doubt that the Wran charm was at full throttle on these occasions. The suspicion between Labor and senior police was not one sided. According to his long-serving press secretary, Brian Dale, Wran's oft-repeated mantra when dealing with senior officers was: "Whatever they tell us, assume they are lying."

Wran inherited Fred Hanson as police commissioner. He knew Hanson only casually, having met him for the first time at Broken Hill on a visit to that city as Leader of the Opposition. He also had a formal meeting with Hanson, not long before the 1976 election. At the end of the meeting Hanson handed him an envelope with a comment along the lines that it would be best for Wran to hold this material. The envelope contained police documents concerning an alleged shoplifting incident at the David Jones department store involving a person known to Wran. The incident had come to nothing when the then chairman of David Jones, Charles Lloyd Jones junior, declined to pursue prosecution. Wran would not have been convinced, despite Hanson's gesture, that he now possessed the only copy of this police file: "whatever they tell us, assume they are lying".

Hanson's term as police commissioner was not due to expire until 1979 but he had indicated his desire to retire early provided he could nominate his successor. The candidates included the two deputy commissioners and the four assistant commissioners. Hanson wanted one of the assistant commissioners, Mervyn Wood, who was subsequently recommended by a high-level committee, including the former Chief of the General Staff, General Sir Thomas Daly and the Chairman of the Public Service Board, Sir Harold ("Jack") Dickinson. Hanson was also a member of this committee and is likely to have been influential in the committee's recommendation. Wran took the recommendation to Cabinet with an expectation it would be approved. Some of his Cabinet had other ideas. Led by Pat Hills and Kevin Stewart, the two men Wran had defeated for the Labor leadership, a group of ministers pushed for another assistant commissioner, Brian Doyle.

On the surface Wran's recommendation might have seemed evidence of the political understanding which is said to have applied for decades in NSW that a Catholic commissioner would succeed a Masonic commissioner. Norman Allan, a Mason, had recommended Hanson, a Catholic, as his successor and Hanson, in turn, was pushing for Wood, a Mason. This orderly succession of 'Mason first, Catholic next' was widely believed to operate in the police force. Peter Anderson, a former police prosecutor elected to Parliament in the 1978 'Wranslide' and later to become a reforming police minister under Wran, had no doubt when he joined the force in 1967 that this order of succession was ordained. "I clearly understood, from everything I saw and heard, that there was an apparent system of alternating between Masons or Protestants and Catholic commissioners," he told me. He jokes about an ambitious colleague who sought to cover both bases by becoming a Mason as well as joining the Catholic Club (now the Castlereagh Club).

There is superficial evidence of the operation of such a gentlemen's agreement. From 1952, when Colin Delaney became the first Catholic commissioner in NSW's history, until 1979 when Jim Lees (a Protestant, not a Mason) succeeded Mervyn Wood (a Mason), there was a strict order of succession of Masons/Protestants and Catholics in the top job. It seems unlikely, however, that this order of succession occurred by arrangement. This would require such a political understanding to have been passed on by a Labor premier to a Liberal premier (in 1965) and again to a Labor premier (in 1976) and to have been observed by successive premiers. It is more likely that this order of succession is explained by coincidence. NSW political historian David Clune is not so sure. "There are many subterranean customs, understandings and unwritten rules that operate in the bureaucracy and politics," he told me. "They need not be officially recognised but still operate by tacit understanding. Relations between Catholics and Protestants fell into this category."

Religion was certainly a factor in the appointment of the new police commissioner in 1976. Brian Doyle was a Catholic (his police nickname was 'The Cardinal'), as were Hills and Stewart. The influential and Labor-leaning Catholic archbishop James Carroll also lobbied ministers on behalf of Doyle. It was not unusual for "Jimmy" Carroll (as he was known inside the Wran government) to intervene with ministers in appointments across the public sector on behalf of Catholics in good standing. Ron Mulock, also a Catholic, was another of those pushing for Doyle in Cabinet. In his memoir Mulock denied it was a 'Catholic push': "I and others supported Doyle because we believed he was best suited to lead the State's Police". That may have been Mulock's motivation but others had no doubt Doyle's denomination was significant. There were also others in Cabinet, most notably Frank Walker, who were Wran supporters but regarded Doyle as the better prospect.

The support for Doyle led to one of the few votes in Wran's Cabinet with Wran narrowly winning the vote. Frank Walker was reported to have said that it was "too early to roll the Premier". There is no evidence, however, that Wran's motivation was a determination to maintain the Mason/Catholic order of succession. Brian Dale believes that Wran's support for Wood over Doyle occurred in the period when Wran was suspicious of anything and anyone supported by his two leadership opponents. It is also likely that a novice premier was reluctant to go against the recommendation of the heavyweight selection committee. Whether the envelope passed to him by Hanson also weighed on Wran's mind will never be known.

Whatever the reasons for Wran's preference for Wood over Doyle he very quickly had cause to regret his choice. The appointment of Wood was to prove a major error. Doyle, who first came to public notice investigating the Graeme Thorne kidnapping, had a reputation as an honest and effective policeman. "Wood quickly talked himself out of the job", was our verdict in the Wran biography and in 1979, after a series of controversies, he was persuaded to resign by Wran's departmental head, Gerry Gleeson, less than three years into the job.

The final straw for Wran appears to have been a widely circulated, anonymous document, apparently authored inside the police force, making serious corruption allegations against various senior police, including Wood, even though a police investigation subsequently cleared him. Wood had already embarrassed Wran after the Opposition produced in Parliament a Crime Investigation Unit (CIU) report into a prominent crime figure George Freeman. Wood subsequently said he had not shown this to Wran because he did not think there was anything important in the report. Wood was replaced as commissioner by Jim Lees, an assistant commissioner, widely acknowledged as an honest policeman. Lees, however, was handicapped because he was not regarded in the upper ranks as a 'real copper', having spent much of his career in Internal Affairs. "Never caught a real crook" was a common criticism of Lees, revealing the attitude in those days of senior police towards 'crooks' in their own ranks.

By the time of Lees' appointment Bill Allen had already begun his rapid rise through the senior ranks of the NSW Police, undoubtedly sponsored by Wran. Allen's first big break came while Wood was still commissioner. Wran had by then lost confidence in Wood and he chose Allen for the job of Chief Superintendent, Metropolitan Area, promoting him over 16 more senior officers. Allen was not on Wood's list of six candidates for the job. Not only did Wran not consult Wood over the appointment but Wood learned of it from a journalist and let his dissatisfaction be known publicly. We noted in the Wran biography: "Wran put Allen in the job within a few weeks of [Opposition Leader, John] Dowd producing the CIU report on Freeman. Wran had been furious with Wood for failing to pass the report on to him and he decided to put him in his place."

Andrew Rule has claimed wrongly that Allen was widely known to be corrupt. "Now he's known as a 'bent cop'. Every journalist in every pub, every other copper, every taxi driver – they could all tell you that Bill Allen was as bent as a three-dollar note," he said. In fact, Allen's reputation at the time was that of an effective policeman, not a corrupt one. Allen's controversial appointment as chief superintendent was welcomed by Opposition Leader John Dowd, who led an anti-police corruption crusade. In a personal 'Dear Bill' letter Dowd expressed "delight" in Allen's appointment: "I have been conscious of your reputation for carrying out your duties and I know you are held in very high esteem by your colleagues." The fact that Wood had opposed Allen's promotion was also considered a feather in Allen's cap. The anonymous police document which had led to Wood's demise had praised Allen's appointment and described him as an efficient and honest officer. Unlike other police who were subsequently promoted internally, Allen had not been adversely named in the Moffit royal commission into organised crime. Brian Dale, at Wran's request, had checked on Allen with a confidant in the Police Special Branch and Allen was given a tick. Sergeant Warren Molloy, who would subsequently make bribery allegations against Allen, stated he had previously admired and liked Allen. Peter Anderson says, while in the police force and later in Parliament, he had never heard any whisper that Allen was corrupt. "The first I heard any suggestion of wrongdoing was after I became police minister and had to deal with the allegations," he told me.

Wran told a media conference that Allen had come to his attention through the competent way he had conducted a recent investigation into a tow truck racket involving payoffs to police. This followed allegations that tow truck operators and panel beaters were paying police for tip offs about the location of motor vehicle accidents. The going rate was $30 for each vehicle towed from the scene. The investigation had been a controversial one as the practice was extensive and the target of the investigation was other police. The result was the suspension of 200 police and the dismissal of eight and the demotion of one.

There was another attraction for Wran. We noted in the biography: "Allen was one of the few senior officers in the police force known to have Labor Party sympathies: it was a consideration any politician would bear in mind, even though the police force under successive commissioners had shown a sensitivity to the needs of the government of the day." Not everyone close to Wran appreciated this quality. Graham Freudenberg accompanied Wran to an official dinner and found himself seated next to Allen. He told staff the next day he was offended that a senior police officer would so openly display his political sympathies.

Seven months after this promotion Allen was further promoted to assistant commissioner. Once again, he leapt over more senior officers. This was not of itself unusual since seniority no longer ruled in senior appointments. Cecil Abbott, a future commissioner, was appointed at the same time as an assistant commissioner ahead of 23 more senior officers. Abbott's appointment, not Allen's, was the lead to *The Sydney Morning Herald*'s report of the force shake up by the new commissioner, Jim Lees. Whether Wran had a hand in Allen's promotion to assistant commissioner is not known but he was certainly instrumental in Allen's appointment, two years later, as deputy commissioner, even though Wran had by then handed over the portfolio to Bill Crabtree. Allen's appointment as deputy commissioner was opposed by Jim Lees, who wanted the senior assistant commissioner, Roy Whitelaw, in the job. The appointment was a factor in Lees' later decision to resign as commissioner. Lees would regret his decision when Wran appointed Peter Anderson as police minister in October 1981, after Anderson was elected to Cabinet following the election. "If I had known you would be the minister I would not have handed in my papers," he told Anderson. By then the processes for selection of Lees' replacement were well underway.

It would later emerge that at the time of Allen's appointment as deputy commissioner, Lees had already set in train an investigation into an overseas holiday taken by Allen the previous month. Lees did not inform Wran or Crabtree of this investigation. Wran told Parliament that, although Lees had opposed Allen's appointment, he had at no stage before the appointment was finalised indicated there were question marks over Allen. This was confirmed by Lees who said he had nothing to report to Wran at that stage and preferred Whitelaw because he thought he was the better person for the job.

As deputy commissioner Bill Allen had every reason to believe he would be the next top cop. There seems little doubt this was also Wran's intention. Neither man had any idea that Allen's accelerated career, and his reputation as an honest policeman, was unravelling even before he had settled into his new office. In June 1981 Allen, his wife and a daughter, had flown to the United States for a holiday. The visit came to the attention of the Federal Police at the instigation of Jim Lees. The 'Feds' found the holiday was a 'freebie', always unwise for a policeman, particularly so when some of the benefactors were people involved in illegal casinos. The 'Feds' also found that controversial poker machine operator, Jack Rooklyn, had flown to the US at the same time and had met with Allen in Las Vegas. It would later emerge that this was Allen's second 'freebie'. The month before he had flown to Macau and Hong Kong, again courtesy of a casino operator.

Jim Lees would later also come into possession of further information about Allen. This was covert surveillance of crime figure Abe Saffron, including photographs of Saffron visiting Allen at police headquarters on at least five occasions. Astonishingly these visits had been recorded by Victorian policemen who had been sent to NSW by the Victorian police commissioner to investigate Saffron without the knowledge of the NSW police commissioner. The information was later passed to Lees, apparently via the Federal Police. Subsequent events have shown the Victorian commissioner should have been paying more attention to what was happening in his own force.

The visits were puzzling. If the meetings had been for nefarious purposes, such as handing over bribe money, the location is unlikely to have been police headquarters. Allen made no effort to disguise the meetings and Saffron even signed the visitors' book at headquarters. However, Allen failed to ensure there were police witnesses present at the meetings or to report on the meetings. Allen was later to claim the visits were to give Saffron advice to ensure his various businesses met licensing laws. This implausible explanation did not satisfy a later tribunal hearing which concluded the association "can only be regarded with serious suspicion."

The Federal Police investigation of Allen's US holiday became public on 1 November 1981 when Marian Wilkinson reported in *The National Times* that Lees had made inquiries with the assistance of the Federal Police. The 'Bill Allen affair', as it became known, had already landed on the desk of the new police minister, Peter Anderson, who was appointed by Wran on 2 October 1981. Jim Lees had sought an urgent meeting with Anderson on 26 October. They agreed on the need for Allen to be interviewed and for Lees to report back to Anderson. Lees was unsure who should conduct the interview given Allen's senior rank. Anderson advised Lees that only Lees had the seniority to conduct the interview and suggested he do so in the presence of the head of Internal Affairs, Chief Superintendent Ralph Masters. The meeting had a farcical side when Lees demurred about Masters' involvement since it was a long time since Masters had done any typing. These were the days before electronic recording of interviews. "You will have to ask your questions slowly then," Anderson told Lees. It was later revealed that Allen took the precaution of taping the interview without the knowledge of Lees or Masters.

With Labor now under sustained attack in Parliament, following Wilkinson's report, Anderson and Lees decided to use section 45 of the *Police Regulation (Allegation of Misconduct) Act,* which had been passed by the Wran government in 1979. Section 45 was a wide-ranging provision which enabled Lees to bring the matter before the President of the Police Tribunal, Justice Bill Perrignon. The section was mainly meant to be used by the tribunal to hear charges laid by the commissioner against police alleging breaches of rules and regulations. The provision also enabled the tribunal to inquire into "any matter relating to discipline in the Police Force", even when charges had not been laid. Effectively it gave Perrignon the powers of a royal commissioner. The move first had to survive an appeal to the Court of Appeal by both Allen and Saffron.

Justice Perrignon found, in April 1982, "there was no evidence that any money was paid to Mr Allen by Mr Saffron" but "the reported visits by Mr Saffron to Mr Allen is such as to disturb the confidence of the community in its Police Force." He concluded that Allen had acted in a way that brought discredit on the police force or was likely to do so, as well as adversely affecting discipline within the force. Under the relevant provision the issue of punishment was a matter for the police commissioner. This was now Cec Abbott, who had been appointed on Anderson's recommendation, and who had taken over from Lees before the tribunal hearings began. Abbott and Anderson discovered that Allen was close to his 60th birthday, on 14 May 1982. Allen was statutorily required to retire at 60. If Allen chose to challenge the findings he would be entitled to remain in his position, although still under suspension, until he turned 60 and then retire with a superannuation entitlement equivalent to the rank of deputy commissioner.

After negotiations between Abbott and Allen's solicitors a deal was struck. If Allen did not challenge the findings of the tribunal, he would be demoted to sergeant and retire on a superannuation payment equivalent to that rank. Peter Anderson announced the decision on 22 April 1982 after an Executive Council meeting that day had removed Allen's commission and demoted him to sergeant. "On legal advice I have received, any other form of action may have enabled Mr Allen, by various legal manoeuvres, to retire on May 14th with the full benefits of a Commissioned officer," Anderson announced. He added that "in terms of his salary, long service, pension and other entitlements this action represents a monetary penalty of $200,000."

Although the Government was criticised for this deal, it proved to be a sensible one since Allen had not been charged with any crime. The Solicitor General, Mary Gaudron, provided advice the following month that there were insufficient grounds to begin criminal proceedings against anyone involved in the tribunal hearing. Peter Anderson says at no stage was he told by Wran to go easy on Allen. "The decision to demote Allen and allow him to retire was entirely a pragmatic one, prompted by his rapidly approaching 60th birthday," he told me. Anderson later amended police regulations to give the commissioner discretion to prevent a police officer from resigning or retiring, either due to ill health or at the statutory age, until an investigation of alleged misconduct was concluded and where appropriate penalties had been imposed.

Andrew Rule has claimed: "Allen was let retire from the force with his pension intact after Saffron blackmailed prosecuting barrister Roger Maxwell Court QC with a secret film of him indulging in sex with an underage youth." It is difficult to know where to begin in dismantling this nonsensical sentence. The reasons for allowing Allen to retire were outlined above. His pension was not intact. His superannuation was halved: from a $77,000 lump sum and a pension of $37,248 per annum to a $38,000 lump sum and a pension of $19,300 per annum. The total financial penalty for Allen was around $200,000, the equivalent of around $800,000 today. No evidence is provided for the malicious claim of pederasty about Court, who is dead, and a perusal of the tribunal's proceedings provides no evidence Court was pulling on the reins. In any event Saffron would have needed to nobble Justice Perrignon, not Court, and Perrignon's findings show that did not happen.

Rodney Tiffen has delivered a similarly incorrect, although less salacious verdict. "In return for not contesting the charges, he was demoted to sergeant first class but allowed to retire and retain his pension. This, of course, meant that his conduct was never publicly explored," he wrote. Fia Cumming continued the error when she wrote that Allen was "allowed to retire instead of being dishonourably discharged" and was "eligible for a comfortable police pension for life." Allen did not "retain" his pension; his superannuation was halved. He was "allowed to retire" but his retirement would have been automatic (and more financially rewarding) if he had stalled for another month. His conduct was "publicly explored" in the Police Tribunal. There could only be further public exploration if Allen had been charged with a crime and the Solicitor General found there were insufficient grounds for criminal proceedings. Cumming was also critical that "Allen's legal costs for the tribunal inquiry was paid by the NSW Government", overlooking the fact that this was consistent with government guidelines, both then and today.

Allen did not escape legal punishment. He was later charged with conspiracy and bribery by the National Crime Authority (NCA) concerning the attempted bribery of a licensing policeman, Sergeant Warren Molloy. This arose from the NCA's investigation into the activities of Abe Saffron, which was jointly initiated by the Wran government and the Federal government and is discussed later in this chapter. Allen was sentenced by the District Court to 18 months in jail.

Wran's patronage of Allen was a major mistake. This compounded the mistake in initially selecting Wood over Doyle as police commissioner. He can be rightly criticised for failing to do more thorough due diligence on Allen. Brian Dale would later take this up with his contact in Special Branch and find that both he and Wran had ignored their maxim: "whatever they tell us assume they are lying". It is wrong to claim, however, that Wran knowingly bestowed patronage on a corrupt policeman. It is correct to say he favoured a policeman who was subsequently found to be corrupt. This is not a distinction without a difference. The promotion of Allen was certainly a blunder by Wran, and one that has damaged his reputation, but it is not evidence of something more sinister.

The Bill Allen affair, while it has given ammunition to Wran's critics, was a watershed in his government's relationship with the force. Anderson proved to be a reforming police minister, a rarity in NSW's history, and had Wran's full support. "Neville always backed me on anything I proposed to do," he told me. Anderson introduced a significant 'discipline package' which upgraded the Internal Affairs branch, increased the powers of the Ombudsman in dealing with police complaints and increased penalties for people offering bribes and for police accepting bribes. He also disbanded the controversial 21 Division, which had reported to Allen.

Anderson also brought back Superintendent Merv Beck in a Special Gaming Squad to shut down illegal casinos, even though Beck had only a couple of months before he was required to retire. He told me he decided to bring back Beck because he was getting reports from the police assuring him that the casinos were closed and he discovered from a journalist this was not true. He told Parliament in September 1984 of the circumstances of this decision. "Not too long after I became a Minister and perhaps at the end of 1981, at my request a meeting was held in the office of the then Commissioner Lees, former assistant commissioner Roy Whitelaw, myself and, as I recall, a member of my staff. Mr Beck was brought into the room. I told him I wished him to form a special gaming squad and that he was to be its head. He asked me how many men he could have. I said: 'How many do you want?' He told me and he got them. He said, 'Who will pick them?' I said: 'you will' and he did. He said, 'What is my charter?' I said: 'Close the casinos' and he did."

Fia Cumming has claimed that Anderson placed an obstacle in Beck's path when he appointed him. She wrote that Beck was told by Anderson that, despite giving him the freedom to select his own staff, he refused to allow him to use any of the existing gaming squad. She reports Beck claiming that Anderson told him he "wanted a clean slate". It would be understandable if Anderson had imposed such a restriction, given he believed he was misled by the claims the casinos were closed, but Anderson denies imposing such a condition. He points to his comments in Parliament in 1984. In any event it is difficult to see, if Beck's claim was true, why this would be an obstacle given Beck admits he had free rein to select his staff. Cumming reports that "most" of the police Beck approached "accepted the chance to work with an officer as strong and straight as Beck."

Anderson told me there was no evidence for the obstacle claims in the regular reports he received from Beck. He also told Parliament in September 1984: "Until his retirement on every occasion when he reported to me he was grateful for the charter he had been given and indicated to me, in his reports, that he had honoured the charter he was given. Merv Beck did what he was asked to do, and did it well, as did other police, and as Superintendent Norm West continues to do while he is in charge of the special gaming squad." In his final report before retiring Beck said: "It is with considerable pride I report in my final submission the special gaming squad has carried out the charter given to me by the Minister to close and keep close unlawful casinos."

Evan Whitton, a critical observer of the NSW Police, noted of this period: "In October 1981 the new-broom Police Minister, Peter Anderson, disbanded the 21 Division and appointed Superintendent Merv Beck head of a new Special Gaming Squad. Beck cut a swathe through the SP network and illegal casinos." The squad continued its raids after Beck's retirement and took Anderson's charter to heart. So zealous were squad members that Anderson soon found himself fielding complaints from the public about the closing of card games among ethnic communities. On 19 July 1982 *The Sydney Morning Herald* reported that Inspector (later Superintendent) Norman West, then officer-in-charge of the Special Gaming Squad, shut down a widely advertised poker marathon in Double Bay, which had attracted players from around the state. The tone of the article was unsympathetic to the police action. The squad did not only declare war on casinos. They also targeted SP operators. Whitton noted that "in one weekend in January 1983, Special Gaming Squad detectives arrested twenty-seven SP betting operators and charged another thirty people with gambling offences."

Despite the sustained efforts of Anderson, Abbott, Beck and West, illegal casinos and SP operations did not disappear from NSW. It was impossible for NSW Police to continue to commit such a large body of police to constantly combating activities which Australians of all levels of society refused to accept as criminal. In a six-month period in 1986, 87 charges were laid for SP bookmaking throughout NSW and 316 charges were laid for unlawful gaming. This was vindication of Wran's comments seven years earlier. Wran told Parliament in 1979: "With the proclivity of Australians to bet even on two flies crawling up the wall, it is well-nigh impossible to suppress SP betting. Certainly the community does not regard SP betting – that is placing a bet illegally with a starting price bookmaker – as wrong. That observation applies to knights of the realm, members of the cloth and the whole spectrum of the community. Members of the community never have any feeling of moral turpitude when they place their $5 each way bet over the telephone or their $1 each way bet in a pub. That fact must be understood. The police are endeavouring to enforce a law that has long since ceased to have attached to it any question of moral turpitude. The public regards SP betting as part and parcel of the ordinary state of affairs."

In May 1987, under Premier Barrie Unsworth, the then police minister, George Paciullo, tabled in Parliament details of "nine hard-core" illegal casinos and their operators. He said that police had advised him that "over a long period these nine casinos proved to be most difficult to close." The casinos would close for a period after raids and then reopen, often with new operators. Illegal casinos continued to operate, despite spasmodic police raids, until after Sydney's first legal casino opened in September 1995. SP betting gradually died out after the introduction of TAB telephone betting and, later, PubTAB, online betting and the explosion of other legal betting outlets. As Wran had told the Parliament on 7 March 1978: "The best way to reduce SP betting is to make the legal system so attractive that people will not want to bet illegally."

Wran only overrode Anderson once. This was over the establishment of the Police Board, announced after a Cabinet meeting in November 1983. A Police Board, introducing an element of civilian administration of the police force, had been recommended in 1979 by Justice Ted Lusher in his report on police administration. Wran had baulked at the idea because of the likely strong opposition from within the force. In the Wran biography we revealed that the person who changed Wran's mind was a trusted personal adviser, David Hill, who had left Wran's staff to head the State Rail Authority. Hill had met Wran the day before the Cabinet meeting on a transport issue. He told Wran this was the way to restore public confidence in the police force. "The day I do that, David, is the day I leave town", Wran replied. Hill was not the only Wran confidant who was pressing for this reform. Wran's influential departmental head, Gerry Gleeson, revealed in 2006 that "the Premier's Department argued strongly for the appointment of a Police Board, whose major role was the selection of senior officers". For the Premier's Department, read Gerry Gleeson.

Wran did leave town but only for a day. Cabinet met in Leeton, part of Wran's routine of holding regular Cabinet meetings in country NSW, and approved Wran's recommendation to establish a Police Board. Wran had rung Peter Anderson the night before but had ignored his protests. Anderson's view was that he was making headway in changing police culture and the fierce reaction from within the force would be a setback.

The opposition from within the force was every bit as fierce as Anderson predicted and Wran had previously feared. This was despite the quality of the civilians selected as board members and the inclusion on the board of police commissioner, Cec Abbott. As well as Abbott the board comprised former Commonwealth Solicitor General, Sir Maurice Byers, and respected business leader, Sir Gordon Jackson. Bans and work-to-rule restrictions were imposed by the Police Association. Motions of no confidence in Wran and Anderson were passed by the association representing senior police. Opportunistically the Liberal Opposition Leader, Nick Greiner, opposed the Police Board and promised to repeal it.

The resistance gradually died down, assisted by Wran giving concessions to the police. This included watering down the *Offences in Public Places Act*, one of signature reforms replacing the *Summary Offences Act*. The board did not stop police corruption but it did put distance between the government and senior police appointments. This overcame a problem identified by Gerry Gleeson: "there was no body or person to whom we could turn for alternative advice including promotions to senior police positions." Despite the pledge to abolish it the Liberal-National government, elected in 1988, maintained the Police Board. For over a decade the board recommended all senior appointments from the rank of assistant commissioner upwards and even had a hand in the appointment of superintendents. It was abolished on the recommendation of the Wood royal commission in the 1990s. Peter Anderson, who later served on the board following his departure from politics, maintains its abolition was a mistake.

Cec Abbott announced his retirement in late 1984. Anderson said it was no secret that he favoured John Avery as Abbott's successor, even though he was junior in rank to other candidates. He did not have cause for concern. Avery was the unanimous recommendation of the Police Board. Sir Gordon Jackson later said: "The three of us sought a successor who was incorruptible and who could manage change." Anderson and Avery worked harmoniously and both developed a close relationship with Ronald Grey, the Federal Police Commissioner, for whom both had a high regard. The three men were instrumental in ensuring that one of the first references of the newly established National Crime Authority in 1984 was an investigation into alleged criminal activities of controversial crime figure Abe Saffron. "I told Neville we were going after Saffron," Anderson said. "Go for it, son" was Wran's reply. In an echo of the downfall of US mobster, Al Capone, the NCA would subsequently arrest Saffron and he served 17 months in jail for tax evasion. Incidentally this NCA investigation included investigating the cause of the fatal Luna Park fire. Wran was later accused by the ABC of covering up an investigation of this fire, despite Anderson, with Wran's backing, being instrumental in establishing the NCA investigation. This is examined in chapter five.

Wran moved Anderson out of the police portfolio in February 1986. Wran was already looking ahead to his retirement – which occurred five months later – and he regarded Anderson, along with Laurie Brereton, as his only successors. "We need to soften your image", he told Anderson. Wran gave the portfolio to George Paciullo, who had eventually been elected to Cabinet in 1983 after unluckily missing out in 1976. Neither Anderson nor Brereton succeeded Wran. The NSW Labor machine moved quickly, after Wran announced his retirement in June 1986, to ensure that Barrie Unsworth, the government leader in the Legislative Council, was Wran's replacement.

Avery was commissioner for seven years and, by the time of his retirement, a Coalition government was in power. *The Sydney Morn-*

ing Herald noted on his death in 2018 that he oversaw a major effort to target corruption in police ranks. NSW, under Anderson and Abbott, and then Avery, had a police minister and a police commissioner united on rooting out corruption. Although far-reaching reforms would not be achieved until after the royal commission in the 1990s, it is still fair to say that the Wran government – after a slow start and some own goals along the way – did more than any of its predecessors to end systemic corruption in the NSW police force.

3

Nifty and Watery

"David [Waterhouse] recalls his father sending corrupt police chief Bill Allen to his illegal casino in Rockwall Crescent, Potts Point, to pick up weekly cash bribes for the then premier, Neville Wran. Sometimes young David would be sent on the errand." Andrew Rule.

"What am I supposed to do? Say suddenly he's not my friend?" Neville Wran, questioned about Bill Waterhouse in 1978.

Neville Wran was not a gambler. As premier he occasionally went to the races but usually only when obligated to by his office. There are several high-profile race meetings in Sydney a premier is expected to attend. Questioned during the Street royal commission about his gambling habits Wran said he only accepted "one or two" invitations to race meetings a year and, when he did attend, he usually only had a couple of bets. "I am just not interested in horse racing", he said.

In 2009 Wran recounted working for the Waterhouse bookmaking family in the 1940s, doing odd jobs at the racecourse to earn money while studying law full time at Sydney University. The family enterprise was run in those days by the patriarch, Charles Waterhouse. Wran said on one occasion he had handed Charles three pounds to bet on "a sure thing". Waterhouse refused to take the bet. "Son don't start punting," Charles told him. "If you do, you'll not only lose your money, you'll lose your soul." Wran took his advice, pursued a different vice, and "had a riotous night with my girlfriend." He was twice lucky that day because the "sure thing" lost.

Wran had met one of Charles' sons, William (Bill) Waterhouse, at Law School and they became friends. We noted in the Wran biography: "Waterhouse, like Wran, had style and an attractive personality. He also had plenty of money, certainly by the standards of most university students, including Wran." Wran and Waterhouse – Wran always called him 'Watery' – occasionally used the pages of the university newspaper, *Honi Soit,* to mock each other. Waterhouse once referred to Wran as a "playboy" and a "local man-about-town"; Wran used his gossip column to scold Waterhouse for "months of wayward and indulgent conduct" for missing meetings of the university law society.

Waterhouse told my co-author Mike Steketee in 1986: "We all thought we were [playboys]. We used to go out and play the field. We both liked nightclubs." The friendship survived Waterhouse sacking Wran from his race day job when Wran failed one day to turn up because it clashed with the rehearsal of a play by the university drama society. Waterhouse intended a career as a barrister and practiced for a few years while dabbling as a bookmaker. That changed following the sudden death in 1954 of his brother Charles (Charlie). Waterhouse then joined another brother, Jack, in carrying on the family business. Bill would quickly become one of the most prominent and controversial bookmakers in Australia. The brothers would also run a large SP (starting price) betting operation. SP betting was illegal but was widely overlooked by law enforcement and hypocritically tolerated by successive governments, Labor and Coalition. Bill later admitted that he had been an SP bookie. He claimed this ended after the government-run Totaliser Agency Board (TAB) was introduced in 1964, not because of the competition but because of the accompanying government threat to their bookmaking licences if they were convicted of SP betting.

Wran and Waterhouse maintained their friendship after university. Wran was best man at Waterhouse's wedding in 1952. As a solicitor, Wran advised Waterhouse, including on the handling of Charlie's estate. Waterhouse would later regret not taking Wran's advice when he and Jack, as executors, decided not to liquidate the estate but instead continue as if Charlie was still alive, supposedly gifting his estate one-third of future income. Waterhouse, in his memoir, claims this was done to protect the estate, including by avoiding death duties. "When I told Neville Wran, our solicitor, of our intentions he was aghast and earnestly tried to dissuade us. He was very firm, advising that, whilst it was an admiral motive, such an idea never worked in the long term. He said that Charlie's children were too young to realise what was being done for them, and that when they grew up there would be no gratitude. Rather, they would expect more and finish up suing us." Waterhouse admitted Wran's advice was "prophetic" but "foolishly, we ignored Neville's advice." The arrangement would later lead to long-running litigation launched by Charlie's adult children, spearheaded by Martin Waterhouse, a solicitor and nephew of Bill and Jack. The litigation eventually ended in a settlement to Charlie's children.

When Wran went to the Bar in 1957, after seven years as a solicitor, he occasionally represented Waterhouse. The most notable case was to appear for him in the bankruptcy hearing of Peter Huxley, a former secretary of the Rural Bank, who had defrauded the bank to finance his gambling. The Australian Jockey Club (AJC) later suspended Waterhouse's bookmaking licence for two years. The AJC did not give its reasons but Waterhouse said it was over the Huxley bets although he would later give a different explanation. Waterhouse had taken off course bets with Huxley but claimed, implausibly, he knew him as Peter Hunter. Wran did not represent Waterhouse in the AJC hearing. Waterhouse instead chose Sir Jack Cassidy QC because Wran "wasn't really a racing man" and Cassidy "was experienced in racing." The Waterhouse connection led to work for Wran with other bookmakers.

Wran's friendship with Waterhouse was no secret. Newspaper profiles, after Wran entered politics, mentioned it without being judgmental. Nor did we suggest anything improper or suspicious in the Wran biography. David Marr probed Wran on the relationship in a profile for *The National Times* in May 1978. "What am I supposed to do? Say suddenly he's not my friend?" Wran replied. Waterhouse was already a controversial figure. Inside the racing community rumours attached themselves to Waterhouse, particularly following the nobbling of the favourite Big Philou in the 1969 Melbourne Cup. Outside that world Waterhouse's reputation was high. This was years before the 'Fine Cotton affair', discussed later, which severely damaged Waterhouse's reputation.

The friendship came under strain following a well-publicised police raid on Waterhouse's office in North Sydney on a Saturday morning in February 1979. Waterhouse was fined over a gambling offence but this was quashed on appeal with Michael McHugh QC, later a High Court judge, successfully defending him. The raid led to a splintering of the friendship with Wran. Waterhouse let it be known he believed that Wran, as police minister, had been behind the raid and had been motivated to ensure Waterhouse would not be eligible for a licence when casinos were legalised. There is no evidence Wran was even aware the raid was going to take place but this became a popular rumour in Sydney and it reached Wran's ears. There is also a commonly recounted story that Waterhouse rang Wran's home during the raid to angrily complain and had abused Jill Wran, who was the only one at home at the time. Jill Wran told me this did not happen.

By 1984 Waterhouse had changed his tune. He was asked in a *Penthouse* magazine interview: "Well this charge in 1979 . . . What was that about? Someone said it was set up to damage you so you couldn't apply for a casino licence." Waterhouse replied: "You're wrong. Nothing to do with it." He claimed the notorious SP operator and commission agent, George Freeman, was behind the "set up". Waterhouse repeated this claim in his memoir, published in 2009, attributing it to police sources.

Brian Dale told me the incident did not end the friendship between Wran and Waterhouse but it was never again as close as it had been. Wran admitted this when he was called to give evidence in the Supreme Court in February 1990, after he had left politics, in the case against Bill Waterhouse brought by Charlie Waterhouse's family. Wran, under questioning, told the court that he and Waterhouse remained friends although "we have not been all that friendly for the last decade or so. I haven't seen much of him." Another reason for the less frequent contact between the two men was Jill Wran, who did not like Waterhouse and found him overbearing.

Wran's friendship with Waterhouse may have raised eyebrows, and led to occasional barbs in Parliament, but it was only after Wran left politics that a more sinister connection was alleged. Claims have since been made that Wran had accepted $5,000 in cash from Waterhouse just prior to the 1976 election; that Wran took bribes from Waterhouse for 'protection' of his illegal casino and the bribes were delivered by the corrupt policeman, Bill Allen. It was also alleged that Wran had a financial share in this casino. Another allegation is that Wran had nobbled a police investigation of a murdered racehorse trainer because it was getting too close to Bill Waterhouse. Some of the allegations have a source in common – Bill Waterhouse's youngest son, David Waterhouse – and these have been reported by journalist Andrew Rule without evidence of corroboration. None of the allegations emerged until after 1992 when David Waterhouse became completely alienated from his family in a dispute which began over money. Wran's name was not attached to any of these allegations until after his death and he was unable to defend himself.

David Waterhouse has dated his falling out with the rest of his family, including his mother, sister and brother, to 21 December 1992, which was the day Bill Waterhouse finally settled the long-running and complicated legal dispute launched by Charlie's adult children. David has said on that night he received a phone call from his brother Robbie and was told he was out of the family trust and that he was no longer to come to the family office in North Sydney. He also said the "turning point" in the relationship was his refusal to use a valuable Frederick McCubbin painting he owned as a guarantee in a tax debt owed by the bookmaking business. David made this claim on television on 22 January 1996, the day the AJC turned down Robbie's application to have his racing ban lifted. Robbie had been 'warned off' all racecourses by the AJC following the controversial 'Fine Cotton ring-in' scandal (discussed later). David had given damning evidence against Robbie in the AJC hearing.

Bill Waterhouse claimed in his memoir that David's refusal to use the painting as security had been hurtful to him and Robbie because in 1979, at Bill's urging, Robbie had used his family home as security to enable David to refinance a Westpac loan. At the time most of the family's assets were frozen resulting from legal action but Robbie's house was not covered by the order. Bill wrote in his memoir this later caused "great anxiety" to Robbie when Robbie's wife, the horse trainer Gai Waterhouse, received "a letter from the bank notifying her that it intended to sell her home – the home Rob put on the line to help David." The home was eventually saved. David Waterhouse said, in response, that he had refused to guarantee the tax debt because he had funded Robbie's legal cases over the Fine Cotton matter.

What are the specific allegations which have caused Rule to claim that Wran was "as bent as a three dollar note"? The first allegation, faithfully conveyed by Rule, is that Wran accepted $5,000 in cash from Bill Waterhouse just prior to Wran becoming premier in 1976. In a podcast Rule said:

> The point I'm getting to – in my own long-winded way – is this: that in 1976 when Neville Wran was already a Member of Parliament in the NSW Parliament, Neville Wran was already running to lead the Labor Party at the election of 1976. And one day, not long before the election, Neville Wran comes round to the Waterhouse office at 158 Pacific Highway, North Sydney, which is just on the other side of the Sydney Harbour Bridge. And he was a familiar figure. He was often at the office and he was often at the Waterhouse private home. He was probably Bill's best mate. And they did favours for one another. And clearly, he was a rising man by this. He was a Member of Parliament. He had been a QC by this stage for maybe nine years. And he told Bill he had come around to get some money. He didn't just want $100 because he was caught short. He wanted $5,000

cash. ... And Bill went up to the safe upstairs and he pulled out 10 $500 bundles. And David [Waterhouse] knew that they were there because it was his job to count the money at every race day and put rubber bands around it and put it in the safe. And Bill would have tens of thousands of dollars there and he just doled out $5,000 – a year's salary for a battler – and he gave it to Neville Wran. No-one is sure why Neville Wran wanted the money and, in a sense, it doesn't matter but it's interesting that he needed or wanted cash. It is interesting that there was no paperwork attached. It's interesting – and this is the most interesting thing – that he was on such close terms with Bill Waterhouse, that he had the sort of relationship with a man we know to be a crooked bookmaker at the very least and a race fixer and a thoroughly bad actor, that Neville Wran could ask him for money at any time and get it."

Rule provides no corroboration for this claim. He said that "it doesn't matter" what the money was for but, for those inclined to believe the story, there is a clue from his statement that this alleged transaction occurred "not long before the [1976] election." If such a transaction took place shortly before the election it would most likely have been an election donation and not a personal payment to Wran. In those days in NSW it was standard practice for leaders of the major political parties to maintain what was formally known in the Labor Party as "the leader's fund", irreverently called by MPs 'the slush fund', to help pay for election campaigns. The justification for such a fund was to give the state parliamentary leader discretion in how campaign funds were spent, particularly given the suspicion of these leaders that their federal colleagues were benefiting from the lion's share of the political party's fundraising. Donors, of course, also wanted the reassurance of the party leader knowing of their generosity.

Ian Hancock's history of the NSW Division of the Liberal Party records a dispute between the Liberal's State Executive and Sir Robert Askin over "the multiple methods of raising and distributing campaign funds" and that Askin "was the chief offender in selectively handing over donations paid directly to him". Hancock has further noted: "Armed with cheques from undisclosed sources made out to his own campaign fund, which he had countersigned, Askin would be driven to a meeting with a candidate. As both men sat in the back seat of the car, the Premier would ask "Son (it was always "Son"), what do you need?". On receiving an answer, Askin would produce a roll from an inside coat pocket, remove the rubber band which held them tightly together and peel off the required amount".

Gough Whitlam recounted being present in 1955 at the opening of the by-election campaign which saw Rex Jackson (later a disgraced minister) elected to the NSW Parliament. Whitlam's federal electorate in those days overlapped Jackson's state seat. Whitlam told Rodney Cavalier: "I remember when [then Premier Joe Cahill] removed a bundle of ten-pound notes from his wallet and counted out ten for Jackson. His eyes were popping. He had never seen so much money".

Cavalier, who recounted Whitlam's comment, also noted: "Joe, like all leaders of the time operated a leader's slush fund, a dangerous practice involving the direct receiving of donations by the parliamentary leader, the leader's prerogative in its disbursement. Accounting was a private affair. Public funding [of election campaigns] ended the slush funds." Public funding of itself did not end this practice; it was the associated requirement of public disclosure of election donations. The "dangerous practice" of such slush funds was ended by the Wran government when it introduced public funding of election campaigns and required the disclosure of campaign donations. This followed a Parliamentary Joint Select Committee report, mainly written by Cavalier. Public funding legislation was introduced over the objections of the ALP's Head Office which feared compulsory disclosure would function as a brake on donations. Cavalier recalls Wran telling him that the legislated disclosure obligations would put an end to leaders receiving funds directly, an outcome he desired. Brian Dale told me that soliciting campaign donations, from business and unions, was a task Wran hated.

There was a reason, apart from friendship, why Waterhouse would be donating to Wran's campaign. Rule, a Victorian journalist, seems unaware that the bookmakers' turnover tax was an issue in the 1976 NSW election campaign. The tax rate had remained at 1% for decades, including during the premiership of Sir Robert Askin, but had doubled to 2% in the first budget of Askin's Liberal successor, Tom Lewis. Part of the revenue from the tax was hypothecated to the racing authorities. The tax was unpopular with bookmakers, not just because it was a tax but because it was levied on turnover and did not take account of whether the bookie was winning or losing. It was also an inefficient tax because it was effectively paid by gamblers. Bookmakers, when framing their markets to ensure their margin, also calculated the impact of the tax. Bookmakers protested at the doubling of the tax and collectively raised money to support Labor in the campaign. Wran had promised to review the tax – the Liberal Party then matched the pledge – and he reduced it in Labor's first budget. He was persuaded by the NSW Treasury not to reinstate the previous 1% rate but to reduce the rate to 1.25%. This was announced by Treasurer, Jack Renshaw, in his Budget speech on 29 September 1976. Renshaw noted it was having an impact on employment in the racing industry, particularly outside Sydney, and that "the ordinary punter has borne much of the burden of the increase."

The next allegation, a more serious one, is that Wran took bribes from Bill Waterhouse over Waterhouse's operation of an illegal casino in Sydney. Rule wrote on 1 December 2019, after Waterhouse died (and, of course, when Wran was dead): "David [Waterhouse] recalls his father sending corrupt police chief Bill Allen to his illegal casino in Rockwall Crescent, Potts Point, to pick up weekly cash bribes for then premier, Neville Wran. Sometimes young David would be sent on the errand." Another version of this allegation – and a contradictory one – was made by an ABC *Four Corners* program 'Horses for Courses' in November 1986.

Bill Waterhouse had always fancied owning a casino. In the 1960s, having acquired the Chevron Hilton in Kings Cross, he had plans to include a casino but these never eventuated. He also sought a casino licence in Queensland but this was refused by the then premier, Joh Bjelke-Peterson. Despite this long-standing interest Waterhouse seems to have been a late entrant to the illegal casino industry which flourished in Sydney in the 1960s and 1970s. Waterhouse's name does not appear on the various lists of casino operators which were occasionally mentioned in Parliament and published in the media. The *Four Corners* program claimed the Waterhouse family operated in 1981 an illegal casino known as 'The Palace' at 22 Rockwall Crescent, Potts Point. The program resulted in legal action for defamation against the ABC by Bill and Robbie Waterhouse, as well as a controversial action for criminal defamation against the journalists. This criminal defamation litigation was long-running and was only concluded in 1988, after the election of a Coalition government, when the Liberal Attorney General, John Dowd, 'no billed' the case.

David Hickie, in his book *The Prince and the Premier*, records that in the 1970s an "illegal casino, known as The Palace, opened at 22 Rockwall Crescent, Kings Cross, across the Road from the Chevron Hotel" but he does not report any Waterhouse involvement. Confusingly the book also refers to another illegal casino in the 1970s also called 'The Palace' in Orwell Street, Kings Cross. The casino referred to in the *Four Corners* report appears to be a successor establishment to the original one at 22 Rockwall Crescent. The Waterhouses are alleged to have become involved in The Palace around the end of 1980.

The brazen operation of illegal casinos dogged the Wran government for much of its term as they had similarly plagued previous Coalition and Labor governments. Not long after he was elected in 1976, Wran had said NSW would have legal casinos "as sure as night meets day." He established an inquiry by Ted Lusher QC (later a Supreme Court judge), who reported in favour of establishing small, London club-style casinos. Lusher's report was never implemented. Wran said later he could not carry his Cabinet with him on the issue. It can now be revealed that the strongest opposition came from his economic advisers, David Hill and Nigel Stokes, supported by the NSW Treasury. Hill and Stokes were adamant that this form of casino would not generate sufficient revenue for the state. If the government was to take the bold step of legalising casino gambling, they argued it needed to be like the Tasmanian Wrest Point hotel-casino, Australia's first legal casino, which had opened in 1973. A difficulty for Wran was that he had ruled out approving "a huge legal casino in Sydney" in a meeting with the NSW Council of Churches just days before the 1976 election.

A Wrest Point-style casino would also avoid the political nightmare of illegal casino operators lining up for licences. By 1976 the illegal operators included among their ranks people whose crimes extended well beyond illegal gaming. A NSW Police Crime Intelligence Unit (CIU) report in 1977 described a meeting of casino operators at the Taiping restaurant in June 1976, shortly after Wran's comments about legalisation. At the meeting the notorious criminal Stan 'The Man' Smith urged the operators to combine to lobby for the casino licences. At least that was the interpretation of Smith's incoherent comments in a recording obtained by the CIU. As Evan Whitton later reported, Smith's speech "gives the impression that he had dined well before rising: he seems a little fatigued and emotional." The result of the impasse over the form of legalisation was a continuation of the practice of periodic police raids on the casinos, and spasmodic enforcement of the law, only for them to reopen once the heat had died down. The other result was undoubtedly the continuation of an avenue for police corruption.

Public debate over the need for a legal casino continued to bubble in NSW. In 1982 the Treasurer, Ken Booth, produced a Treasury study which recommended a large hotel-casino on tourism and revenue grounds. The NSW ALP conference, however, had reaffirmed earlier resolutions that if casinos were introduced, they should be government owned and operated. Wran, still bruised from the internal ALP brawl over Lotto (discussed in chapter eight), was unwilling to pick another fight with his party. That changed in 1985 when the government embarked on the Darling Harbour redevelopment project. Wran announced a large hotel-casino would be the financial centre piece of the project. The *Darling Harbour Casino Act* was proclaimed in May 1986, two months before Wran retired from Parliament. The consortium chosen to build and operate the casino fell over on probity grounds and the Act was repealed by the incoming Greiner Coalition government. Greiner had declared in the 1988 election campaign that there would be no legal casinos in NSW. Greiner reversed his pledge in 1991 and the *Casino Control Act* was passed in 1992. Probity issues again dogged the selection of an operator and it was not until September 1995 that Sydney's first legal casino began operation. NSW was learning a lesson, previously learned in Nevada and New Jersey, that when governments rely on casinos for revenue the integrity of those who provide such services will always be problematic. This was a lesson to be re-learned in NSW and Victoria 30 years later.

The ABC *Four Corners* program 'Horses for Courses' finally aired on 10 November 1986 after attempts by the Waterhouse family to injunct it. The legal action went as far as the High Court. The program dealt with activities of the family, including the operation of The Palace casino. The program's presenter, Tony Jones, later claimed the program, among other things, was "a story about how illegal gambling, which flourished during a period when casinos were not allowed in Australia, actively led to corruption in the highest level of government". Jones reported that the Waterhouses took over the management of The Palace in 1981. He told viewers that a Palace employee, Valerie Murphy, who was interviewed on the program, "alleges that while working in the casino office she overheard a conversation between David Waterhouse and another person in which a senior NSW politician was named by David as being paid a percentage of the casino's profits to ensure protection of its operation". Although the program did not name Wran, who had retired from Parliament four months earlier, many who watched the program would have believed Jones' use of the phrase "a senior NSW politician" was a reference to Wran.

Strangely, the *Four Corners* program did not name the other party to this reported conversation alleging Wran's financial involvement in the casino. In researching this book, I saw a copy of a later police interview with Valerie Murphy in which she named the other party referred to by Jones. That person vehemently denied to me any such conversation with Valerie Murphy and denied having been contacted by the program. For this reason I have not identified the person. That person also denied having any knowledge of Wran's involvement in the casino. "*Four Corners* did not contact me. If they had, I would not have held back. I would have widely publicised any knowledge I had of a premier getting kickbacks from a casino", the person told me. Tony Jones did not respond to emails I sent him asking whether the program had corroborated Valerie Murphy's claims with the other person. I also wanted to ask Jones why the program considered Valerie Murphy, who is now dead and who had struggled with addiction and mental health issues, a reliable uncorroborated source.

The *Four Corners*' claim of the financial involvement of "a senior NSW politician" is hearsay and would be inadmissible in any court. Indeed, it is hearsay which has been denied by one of the parties to the alleged conversation. If Wran was a part owner of the casino it raises the issue of why Bill Waterhouse would need to transmit "weekly cash bribes" to Wran, as Rule claims, whether via Bill Allen or "young David" Waterhouse (who was 22 in 1980). Andrew Rule had claimed that Bill Waterhouse had sent Bill Allen to the casino to pick up the weekly cash bribes. If the story was true Wran would have no need for such payments given his share of the takings could be arranged privately and without the risk of third-party involvement. In the later statement on 6 March 1987 to the NSW Police Major Crime Squad, Valerie Murphy said: "When I saw the Four Corners program I saw that an ex-policeman by the name of Bill Allen was mentioned and I have nerver (sic) heard his name mentioned with the protection of the 'Palace casino'". Valerie Murphy also makes no mention of Allen ever visiting the casino. She also said: "I never saw Bill Waterhouse at the Casino". We are also meant to believe that Waterhouse had the clout to command the second most senior NSW policeman to function as an errand boy. Incidentally this alleged partnership between Bill Waterhouse and Neville Wran in an illegal casino came after the splintering of the Wran-Waterhouse friendship, resulting from the police raid on Waterhouse's office in February 1979, referred to earlier.

Four Corners gave another version of this allegation attributing it to a "source close to the Waterhouse family". This anonymous person, according to Jones, "has given us a detailed account of visits to the Waterhouse North Sydney office by the then deputy police commissioner Bill Allen. This person claims to have witnessed Allen collecting money from Bill Waterhouse. He alleges he was told by Waterhouse that the money was to protect the operation of the Palace casino and that Waterhouse told him the same senior politician was receiving half of that money." According to the police statement by Valerie Murphy, Wran's ownership share was 25% and Andrew Rule reports the transactions took place at the casino. According to the anonymous "source close to the Waterhouse family", the transactions occurred at the family office in North Sydney, not at the casino, and Wran's ownership share was 50%, not 25%. Which uncorroborated version – one being uncorroborated hearsay (which has been denied by one party) and the other an uncorroborated anonymous allegation – are we expected to believe?

If Wran was a financial beneficiary of an illegal casino in 1981, why would he (as noted in the previous chapter) in the same year have appointed Peter Anderson as minister in charge of police with a remit to close the illegal casinos? Why would Wran have agreed that year to the appointment as police commissioner of Cec Abbott, widely acknowledged as an honest policeman? Why would Wran that year have given Anderson blessing to bring back Superintendent Merv Beck who, as noted by Evan Whitton in the previous chapter, "cut a swathe" through the illegal casinos. The Palace was one of those which Beck drove out of business. The statement by Valerie Murphy claims that one night the staff were advised that "Beck's Raiders were coming and to start packing everything up... Then we closed the club and I believe Beck's Raiders came either that night or the next night." The *Four Corners* program told viewers: "Late in 1981 the political climate changed and Superintendent Merv Beck, one of the few senior policemen to enforce the state's gaming laws, was given the go ahead and revive Beck's Raiders and close down all illegal casinos." In fairness the program should have pointed out this political climate change, and the go ahead for Beck, came from Peter Anderson with the blessing of Wran. Such an acknowledgement, of course, would have undermined the allegations it was making against Wran.

Further doubt about the *Four Corners*' claim is given with the recent publication of a biography – more of a memoir – of Merv Beck. In 433 pages Beck makes no allegation of corruption against Wran and no allegation of Wran being involved in an illegal casino. Beck recounts that he received praise and encouragement from Wran in his task of closing illegal casinos. He reports that in his only meeting with Wran the premier had congratulated him on his work and had told him to "watch his back." Beck was also able to use Wran's written instruction to the then police commissioner, Jim Lees, to close the illegal casinos to ward off internal police opposition to his work. This might seem an example of the 'evidence of absence' or a dog that didn't bark in the night, to cite Arthur Conan Doyle. Beck was retired from the police force in 1986, however, when *Four Corners* was doing its research and had already developed a reputation for making himself readily available to the media. It is inconceivable that *Four Corners* did not approach Beck, given Beck had spent many years living and breathing illegal casinos in NSW. It is therefore noteworthy that Beck was not interviewed on the program.

The uncorroborated claims about Wran's financial involvement in a casino are implausible and demonstrate the irresponsibility of reporting such allegations without credible corroboration. After the *Four Corners* broadcast Wran's successor as premier, Barrie Unsworth, was questioned the next day in Parliament and said police would investigate the casino allegations. That night Evan Whitton, never regarded as an admirer of Wran, was asked on ABC TV's *7.30 Report* about the allegations. The interviewer asked Whitton: "Does that mean we get a picture of an imprudent man or what sort of man?" He replied: "That doesn't give you a picture of Mr Wran at all. It gives you a picture of a lot of people who are using his name, possibly for their own end."

Whitton had, to Wran's displeasure, previously covered the Street royal commission for *The Sydney Morning Herald* (discussed in chapter four). He was aware from that experience of the dangers of the media uncritically reporting gossip from people using Wran's name for their own reasons. That lesson was not learned by *Four Corners* which was prepared to accuse Wran of corruption, this time based on an uncorroborated allegation, despite lacking the courage on this occasion of naming him. No one at the ABC appears to have asked the critical question: is it credible, given the constant political controversy over illegal casinos in NSW, that the premier of the state would risk being corruptly involved? Surely simply posing the question would cause the journalists to redouble efforts to rigorously corroborate the claims.

The final allegation made about Wran's relationship with Bill Waterhouse is the most serious: that he corrupted his responsibility as a public official to hinder a police murder investigation. The story begins with one of the most controversial and farcical Australian horse racing scandals, 'the Fine Cotton affair', which has generated books, television programs and an eight-part podcast series. To understand the allegation made against Wran it is necessary to briefly outline the scandal even though it has never been suggested that Wran, or anyone associated with his government, had any involvement in this farce.

On 18 August 1984 a poorly performing horse named Fine Cotton was entered in a race at Eagle Farm in Brisbane but was surreptitiously replaced by a better performed but ineptly disguised horse named Bold Personality. The substitute for Fine Cotton narrowly won the race but the massive betting plunge on the horse, which reduced its starting price to 7/2, had already attracted the attention of racing stewards who stopped payout of bets. A subsequent inquiry by the NSW Racing Appeal Tribunal found that, although it could not establish a link between Bill and Robbie Waterhouse and the actual substitution, it was "beyond question" that there "is some indirect link". It found that both men had knowledge of the 'ring in' and had used this to their advantage in betting on the race. The AJC banned the pair from racetracks for an indefinite period, along with others who were found to have been involved. The bans were finally lifted by the AJC 14 years later in 1998.

Claims have since been made that this was not the first planned 'ring in'. According to these claims, four months earlier, in April 1984, a minor Sydney horse trainer George Brown had taken a slow filly named Risley to Brisbane with the intention of substituting her with a better horse. It is further claimed Brown lost his nerve and refused to go through with the substitution. He supposedly saddled the real Risley instead and the horse ran second last. Risley had been heavily backed interstate despite having no obvious form and the backers lost their money. Brown's body was later found near Bulli in his burned-out car after being horribly bashed.

Andrew Rule, in his 2021 book *Chance*, wrote: "In his day Nifty can nobble a murder investigation nearly as easily as Big Bill Waterhouse can nobble a horse." This *non sequitur* must have puzzled readers. A clue is given later in the book when Rule claims Bill Waterhouse was involved in "the three worst scandals in Australian racing history", one of which was the brutal murder of George Brown. Rule wants his readers to believe that this murder remains unsolved because Wran had intervened to "nobble" the murder investigation.

Any doubt was removed in March 2022 when Channel 7 broadcast a Crime Investigation Australia documentary, *Murder and Mayhem*, about Brown's murder. In the documentary a racing form analyst, Arthur Harris, claimed: "The mail we got up here was that someone would have been arrested for the George Brown murder but for Neville Wran interfering with the investigation." Harris, now living in Queensland, once worked for the Waterhouse bookmaking business but fell out with Robbie Waterhouse and is now a bitter critic. The documentary followed a script largely based on a statutory declaration by David Waterhouse, sworn on 9 September 1997, which was reported by Rick Feneley in *The Sydney Morning Herald* on 29 November 2010. In a re-enacted scene in the documentary, based on the statutory declaration, David claims Robbie had confided to him in 1986 that he feared he would be arrested over George Brown's murder. Robbie Waterhouse has vehemently denied this and has successfully sued newspapers over the claim. No evidence has ever been produced that Robbie Waterhouse was involved. The documentary concluded with a screen shot and voice over: "Seven and the producers wish to make clear that there is no basis to suggest that Robbie Waterhouse was involved in any way in the murder of George Brown." Network 7 and the producers did not explain why the allegation about Wran was permitted to go to air given "there is no basis to suggest that Robbie Waterhouse was involved in any way in the murder of George Brown."

Neither Rule nor Harris produced any evidence for their claims. Wran was smeared by Rule without Rule citing even a primary source for his imputation, let alone corroboration. Harris smears him with hearsay, again without citing a source. Not one police source is cited, even anonymously, to back up their claims. Neither of the two former detectives involved in the murder investigation, who were interviewed on the program, made this allegation. We are meant to believe that Wran in 1984, despite having an honest police minister and honest police commissioner, and with the police now operating under an independent Police Board, was able to reach down into the police force and convince a team of homicide detectives not to do their job and without a word leaking out. At the time this supposedly occurred, Wran was dealing with a hostile police force, upset over his decision to create the Police Board. How likely is it that homicide detectives and their superiors would tolerate such an interference from Wran?

There is no credible evidence of criminality in Wran's friendship with Bill Waterhouse. The allegations rely solely on the uncorroborated claims of two men, both of whom have significant axes to grind with Bill and Robbie Waterhouse, and an anonymous source cited by *Four Corners*, whose allegation is also uncorroborated. Nor is there is any evidence of Wran using his position as premier to provide personal benefits for his old friend. Bill Waterhouse was a beneficiary of the cut in the bookmakers' tax but Wran's pledge on the tax was an opportunistic commitment made in an election campaign. Bookmakers such as Waterhouse still ended up paying more tax under the Wran government than they had under the Askin government and its Labor predecessors. Waterhouse was not an SP bookie in the 1970s and 1980s so he was not a beneficiary of the lax enforcement of the law by police during this period. He did not achieve from Wran his long-held ambition to hold a casino licence. If he did own an illegal casino, it was shut down by the actions of Wran's police minister, with Wran's blessing, after only a year or so of operation. The friendship did not prevent Waterhouse's office being raided by the police while Wran was premier and police minister. Nor did it inhibit Wran from holding a special inquiry into an allegation by a federal politician of attempted bribery by Waterhouse, which is discussed in chapter nine. The allegation was found to be false.

Disowning Waterhouse would have been a politically prudent course for Wran – as would later disowning another long-time friend, Lionel Murphy – but that would have been out of character. As Wran told David Marr in 1978: "What am I supposed to do? Say suddenly he's not my friend?" Politicians are often accused of being fair-weather friends when controversy erupts. That cannot be said of Wran: loyalty was an important virtue. In Wran's view another longtime friend, Jim McClelland, had failed to stand by their common friend, Murphy, and this was at the heart of the subsequent bitter falling out between Wran and McClelland. Wran defiantly said of Murphy at Murphy's funeral: "He was my mate." Wran's decision in 2009 to launch Waterhouse's memoir was a similarly defiant demonstration that friends would not be thrown overboard for the sake of expedience.

4

"The Premier is on the Phone"

"The Premier's contacted me. He wants Kevin Humphreys discharged." Chief magistrate Murray Farquhar, according to magistrate Kevin Jones.

"In short, try as I have with the unlimited resources and wide-ranging powers available to me in this Royal Commission, every avenue that has been followed in seeking to identify intervention by Mr Wran in the preparation or assistance of Mr Humphreys has ended, in so far as a path to Mr Wran is concerned, not merely inconclusively but specifically in his favour." Chief Justice Sir Laurence Street.

Ron Mulock believed he walked into an ambush. On 30 May 1978, with the Wran government only two years old, the Minister of Justice was summoned to a meeting with Wran. When Mulock arrived at the Premier's office, he was ushered instead to the Cabinet room, one floor above. Waiting were five members of the Cabinet's Policies and Priorities Committee (known within the government as 'P & P'): Wran, Pat Hills, Jack Renshaw, Paul Landa and Frank Walker. Absent were Jack Ferguson, who was overseas, and Peter Cox, who was ill. Mulock knew there was only one reason he could have been called: Murray Farquhar, Chairman of the Bench of Stipendiary Magistrates, a cumbersome title for the role of chief magistrate as the position would eventually be called.

Born to a poor family in Broken Hill Farquhar had, through hard work and part-time study, qualified as a magistrate in 1962. He was appointed as chairman in March 1971 by the Askin Coalition government. Hilary Golder notes in the *Australian Dictionary of Biography*: "In the early 1970s Farquhar's reputation was high: the Askin coalition government considered appointing him to the District Court bench. He improved the administration of the local courts and took several progressive initiatives, including encouraging Sydney magistrates to refer arrested alcoholics and vagrants to welfare agencies and participating in developing pre-sentence diversion programs for drink-drivers and drug users. This approach was consistent with the policies of the Wran Labor government that was elected in 1976 and in August 1977 he was appointed chairman of its interim Drug and Alcohol Authority."

Mulock had been considering Farquhar's future for several months after Andrew Clark had reported in the *National Times* on 6 March 1978 that underworld figure George Freeman was ordered from the members' enclosure of Randwick Racecourse after he had used a visitors' pass obtained on Farquhar's membership. Farquhar's explanation was that he had been asked to supply the ticket for a friend and he did not know how it ended up with Freeman. His explanation was undermined by the publication of police photos of Farquhar and Freeman sitting together at the races. Mulock had requested an investigation by the acting head of his department, Trevor Haines, a veteran public servant. The investigation was hindered by Farquhar's hospitalisation because of a serious heart complaint but Haines eventually cleared Farquhar of wrongdoing. Haines reported that Farquhar, who was on administrative duties following his illness, had committed no offence and there were no grounds to remove him or prevent him returning to the bench. Mulock instead demanded further explanation from Farquhar of his relationship, if any, with Freeman before he would agree to his return. The further investigation was still underway when Mulock walked into the P & P meeting.

Mulock had already clashed with Wran over Farquhar. In an earlier meeting, in Wran's office, Wran told Mulock that if Haines had cleared Farquhar, there was no justification for not allowing him to return to bench duties. Mulock stood his ground, arguing that might be the legal position but there were also political considerations. The P & P meeting may not have been an ambush, as Mulock believed, but Mulock found he had no supporters in the room. All five ministers argued that since Haines had cleared Farquhar he was entitled to return. According to Mulock, former Labor leader Pat Hills was the most vehement advocate of Farquhar returning to the bench. Mulock does not mention this in his version of events but Farquhar also had supporters outside the room. Kevin Stewart, the Health Minister, had been impressed by Farquhar's work in drug and alcohol rehabilitation and had appointed him as chairman of the new Drug and Alcohol Authority. The P & P meeting ended in a stalemate. Mulock refused to budge. He said the matter was now in the hands of Haines and the Chairman of the Public Service Board, Sir Harold Dickinson. "If they are satisfied Farquhar has nothing of a serious nature to answer for, and officially inform me of that effect, then he can return to bench duties," Mulock said he told the meeting.

Two weeks later, on 12 June, after consultation with Dickinson and another member of the Public Service Board, Bill Gent, Haines advised Mulock there was no reason why Farquhar should not resume duties. Mulock accepted the advice. The Chief Justice, Sir Laurence Street, was subsequently critical of the thoroughness of this Public Service Board investigation and found Farquhar's explanation of how Freeman had obtained the ticket was "false" and a "concoction." Mulock's decision was not the end of the matter, however. Farquhar was about to turn 60, the normal compulsory retirement age, but he had requested a one-year extension. Any extension had to be approved by the head of the relevant department under delegation from the Public Service Board. Since Haines, who had now been confirmed as departmental head, had just completed an investigation into Farquhar it was not surprising that he agreed to the extension. Farquhar did not serve out the full one-year extension. Wran later told the Street royal commission that at the end of 1978 he persuaded a reluctant Farquhar to retire by convincing him that the adverse publicity would continue. Farquhar finished in May 1979.

Wran's critics have suggested that Wran's support for Farquhar showed he was under an obligation to Farquhar because of the controversial Botany Council case. In 1975, in the lead up to the 1976 election which Labor won, charges were laid by police against Laurie Brereton, a Labor MP, and Geoff Cahill, Labor's general secretary. The charges were a conspiracy to corrupt and to bribe four Labor aldermen on Botany Council to vote against a proposed rezoning which would have disadvantaged News Ltd, a major newspaper publisher. The charges were heard by Farquhar who dismissed them. Farquhar found the conspiracy charge against Cahill could not be sustained. This meant the conspiracy charge against Brereton also fell away as the prosecution could not nominate other potential co-conspirators. Farquhar's dismissal of bribery charges against Brereton became controversial because Farquhar's interpretation of the relevant law conflicted with advice by the Crown Solicitor. The matter turned political after the Solicitor General, RJ Marr, issued an *ex officio* indictment against Brereton, meaning the bribery charge would proceed directly to trial. This was an unusual use of the *ex officio* indictment which was normally reserved for more serious offences. Labor claimed this indictment was engineered by the Coalition government seeking an issue in the lead up to the election. Labor accused the Premier, Sir Eric Willis, of pressuring the Solicitor General to issue the indictment, claiming the Attorney General, John Maddison, who was absent from the state, had refused to do so. Unsurprisingly, after Labor's victory in May 1976, the new Attorney General, Frank Walker, declined to proceed with the indictment. Walker said he had received advice that the prosecution was unlikely to succeed.

Mulock's account of his questioning over Farquhar's position makes no mention of Wran and the other ministers expressing an obligation to Farquhar over Brereton. Mulock's actions show he did not consider himself under any such obligation. Farquhar's main champion according to Mulock was Pat Hills, who had no reason to feel obligated since there was bad blood between Brereton and Hills. Brereton had been one of three Right faction MPs to break ranks and cast their primary votes for Wran over Hills in the 1973 leadership ballot. Hills, as leader, had opposed Brereton's preselection for the electorate of Randwick, which Brereton won at a by-election in 1970. It is also widely believed in the Labor Party that Hills had engineered the abolition of Randwick in the electoral redistribution preceding the 1971 election, tipping Brereton out of Parliament. The resourceful Brereton had returned in 1973 as the member for Heffron, which included the Botany Council area.

Even if Botany was a factor in the minds of Wran and the other ministers, they had no justification at that time for terminating Farquhar's tenure. Farquhar had been cleared of wrongdoing by three senior public servants. Subsequent events, however, vindicated Mulock's reluctance to permit Farquhar's continuing tenure on the bench. Mulock's political instincts were to prove superior to those of Wran and Wran's two predecessors as Labor leader, Hills and Renshaw. There might not have been grounds for preventing Farquhar returning to bench duties. There was, however, justification for refusing his subsequent request for a one-year extension. Wran would find that the consideration which he and the other ministers had shown to Farquhar was undeserved. Farquhar had already sewn a landmine which, when it exploded five years later, threatened Wran's political future and could have led to him facing criminal charges.

The detonation occurred on the evening of Saturday 30 April 1983. That night the ABC broadcast a *Four Corners* program called 'The Big League'. The television program had begun as an investigation into the administration of rugby league, the most popular football code in NSW and Queensland. Wran and his staff knew what was coming: the program would claim Wran had perverted the course of justice. Graham Freudenberg wrote that Wran had been informed by an ABC board member, former union official Laurie Short, who was well known to Wran and who had been appointed by the Fraser Coalition government. Brian Dale told me their main information came from Bob Carr, a former ABC journalist who was then writing for *The Bulletin,* and who would win a Labor seat at a by-election later that year. Carr confirmed to me that he had learned through legal acquaintances of program details that had been referred by the ABC for outside legal scrutiny. He passed the information on to Dale. As a result, Wran and his staff were aware that the pending program now reached well beyond the administration of rugby league. The warnings were confirmed a few days before 30 April when *Four Corners* finally approached Wran and were firmly told the allegation was false and that Wran would sue if it was broadcast.

Wran, his wife Jill, and his closest staff gathered in Wran's office that night to watch the program which, unusually, the general manager of the ABC had referred to selected ABC board members before broadcast. The program alleged that Wran, as premier, had influenced a 1977 committal hearing of fraud charges against the President of the NSW Rugby League, Kevin Humphreys, who had misappropriated money from the Balmain Leagues Club to cover gambling debts. It also included a re-enactment of a scene which had supposedly taken place on the morning that Humphreys' hearing was to begin. In the reconstruction Farquhar's secretary informs Farquhar, in front of others, that "the Premier is on the phone." This was linked to the subsequent decision by the relevant magistrate, Kevin Jones, not to commit Humphreys for trial.

Wran was outraged at the program's claim and announced he would sue for defamation. He also requested the Attorney General Paul Landa to "examine [the transcript] and consider it and if there is evidence of wrongdoing then to deal with it in accordance with the law." As part of this examination the Crown Law officers requested a report from Kevin Jones. This was received on 10 May 1983. Jones, who had refused to talk to *Four Corners*, reported that on 11 August 1977, as he was leaving Farquhar's chambers to go to court to begin hearing the Humphreys charges, Farquhar had said to him: "The Premier's contacted me. He wants Kevin Humphreys discharged."

Landa later said it was obvious to him as soon as Jones' report was received that there would need to be an official inquiry into the allegation. Wran agreed. That afternoon, 10 May, Landa announced that a royal commission would be held and that after obligatory consultation the chief justice, Sir Laurence Street, had decided to conduct the inquiry himself. Wran, against the advice of Freudenberg, Dale and his new press secretary David Hurley, announced he would stand aside as premier until the royal commission was concluded. Wran also went against the advice of Pat Hills, who argued forcefully in Cabinet that he should not stand aside.

The Street royal commission lasted nearly three months. Street found that Farquhar had influenced or attempted to influence the outcome of the committal proceedings against Humphreys. He also found that Farquhar had not been acting at the direction or request of Wran. Street concluded: "In short, try as I have with the unlimited resources and wide-ranging powers available to me in this Royal Commission, every avenue that has been followed in seeking to identify intervention by Mr Wran in the preparation or assistance of Mr Humphreys has ended, in so far as a path to Mr Wran is concerned, not merely inconclusively but specifically in his favour." Graham Freudenberg summed up Street's conclusion with greater clarity: "This is the real point of Wran's exoneration: not that he did nothing wrong in the Humphrey's affair but that he did nothing at all; he was never remotely involved."

Wran and many of his staff never forgave *Four Corners*. Wran always remained bitter that he never received an apology from the ABC. Jonathan Holmes, then executive producer of *Four Corners*, has defended the program: "Our sources, including two senior magistrates, all believed (wrongly as it turned out) that [Wran] probably was involved." Holmes has also written: "For seven years after [the committal hearing] senior members of the NSW magistracy had been convinced that the premier had perverted the course of justice. *Four Corners* could not prove – as we were well aware – that the premier had made a phone call. We could prove we believed that the chief magistrate claimed to his subordinates that Wran had done so. Our sources, though insisting on anonymity, were impeccable. It seemed to us that we had no choice but to report what we knew, and to call for a judicial inquiry. To ignore the matter was not an option. Nor was it possible for the seriousness of the allegation to be conveyed if we attempted to get around the use of the premier's name. Wran's fury, it always seemed to me, should have been directed far more at Farquhar, who used his name for nefarious purposes, and far less at the program that accurately and soberly reported what Farquhar did."

Holmes is correct that the Street royal commission had its genesis not with the ABC but in Farquhar's misuse of Wran's name. Forcing Farquhar off the bench in 1978 when ministers had probable cause would not have prevented the subsequent damage to Wran's reputation – Farquhar had already misused Wran's name – but it would have blunted subsequent suspicions that Farquhar had done Wran's bidding. The program, unlike later ABC programs blackening Wran's reputation, had reliable corroboration for its central allegation that Farquhar had used Wran's name. Nor did the program use the weasel words "a senior NSW politician" as did a later *Four Corners* program 'Horse for Courses', discussed in the previous chapter. Holmes' defence of the program stumbles, however, in saying it "soberly reported what Farquhar did". The program never contemplated the fact that Farquhar may have been using Wran's name "for nefarious purposes." The program may have called for a "full public inquiry" but to the ordinary viewer it had already convicted Wran. This was reinforced by the reconstruction.

The journalist and presenter, Chris Masters, has conceded that the program should have made the point that Farquhar may have used Wran's name without his knowledge: "I would say [Wran] did not get a fair go and I am sorry that is the case". Holmes has also conceded the program should have raised the possibility that Farquhar was not acting with Wran's authority. He admits that the program did not do this "because to be honest we thought it extraordinarily unlikely that the chief magistrate would take such a risk and because, in the climate of the times, it did not seem especially unlikely that Wran would have done what Farquhar alleged he did ... However, on the limited evidence we presented (which was all we could verify to the satisfaction of ourselves and our lawyers after weeks of sleuthing) the possibility that Farquhar was taking the premier's name in vain was a real one, and we should have made that clear." Holmes disputes that the reconstruction, which had been opposed by the ABC's legal advisers, gave the impression that the program had prejudged Wran. "Our job was to describe the events that we had been told occurred ... whether you relay that information via reconstructions, or in print, or in a reporter's soliloquy, the information is the same and implicates Wran. But we did call for a judicial inquiry to establish whether those implications were justified or not, and that is precisely what happened."

Holmes and others have made much of the fact that, following Street's exoneration, Wran criticised the ABC for the program but did not criticise Farquhar for involving him in this episode. Rodney Tiffen wrote that Wran "refused to utter a word of criticism of Farquhar." The inference seems to be that there is something suspicious in Wran's reluctance. Tiffen overlooks the fact that Street, in his report, had concluded that Farquhar had perverted the course of justice and had recommended he be charged. Farquhar was formally charged on the day after Street's report was released. It would have been improper for Wran to have made any comment about Farquhar. If he had it could have left him open to being charged for contempt as he was when he later said, in response to a journalist's question, he had a "deep conviction that Mr Justice Murphy is innocent of any wrongdoing". Wran was fined $25,000 for this contempt. It is unreasonable to suggest Wran should have also risked his bank account on this occasion by criticising Farquhar who was now facing a trial. Wran's comment about Murphy, incidentally, was not made when a trial was on foot. Wran said this after the Court of Appeal had set aside the verdict in the first trial and before the Director of Public Prosecutions, Ian Temby QC, had decided on a retrial.

Wran was rightly concerned, despite his complete exoneration by Street, that "some of the mud will stick" as he put it. Chris Masters has also conceded: "There's no doubt the program did a lot of damage to Wran." Wran knew there were those who desperately wanted the *Four Corners* allegation to be true and who would never accept Street's debunking of Wran's involvement. Wran could not have expected, however, that further mud would be thrown at him over the same allegation nearly 40 years after the *Four Corners* broadcast. On Saturday 6 March 2021 two newspapers in Sydney carried front-page articles claiming that Sir Laurence Street had got it wrong. Dennis Shanahan in *The Australian* wrote "new evidence has emerged that could have fundamentally changed the royal commission findings into the personal involvement of the then premier Neville Wran". Kate McClymont, in *The Sydney Morning Herald,* wrote: "Sensational evidence withheld from a royal commission throws light on the involvement of former NSW premier Neville Wran in a conspiracy to pervert the course of justice". Neither article would have been published if Wran had been alive.

These articles were part of a media campaign to promote a recently published book by Farquhar's successor as chief magistrate, Clarrie Briese. The book could have been written at any time after Briese retired in 1990 but did not appear until after Wran was dead and unable to personally address the allegations. Neither journalist investigated Briese's claims to evaluate their credibility. Both reported the allegations as if the allegations, having been made, established a new truth. Nor did either article provide any context for the Briese allegations. Briese had a substantial axe to grind with Wran. He is not an impartial and objective observer.

Understanding Briese's lack of objectivity about Wran requires a summary of the so-called 'Lionel Murphy affair', in which Briese was a controversial player. In 1985 High Court judge Lionel Murphy was charged with attempting corruptly to influence Briese, as a magistrate, to dismiss charges in a criminal prosecution against Murphy's dubious friend, solicitor Morgan Ryan. In the prosecution case against Murphy the principal witness was Briese, who testified that certain conversations he had with Murphy two years earlier amounted to a criminal attempt to influence him. The jury in a 1985 trial found Murphy guilty. The NSW Court of Appeal subsequently granted Murphy a new trial after it found the trial judge had misdirected the jury. In April 1986, the jury in the second trial found Murphy not guilty.

Briese's evidence against Murphy raised two issues for the jury. First, Briese testified that he had not interfered on behalf of Ryan who was, notwithstanding the alleged interference by Murphy, committed for trial and later found guilty – at least initially. There was no suggestion that Briese had sought to influence the outcome of the committal hearing. The allegation against Murphy, therefore, was that he had made an unsuccessful attempt to influence Briese. The second issue was that, despite several conversations between Briese and Murphy, Briese did not reach the conclusion that Murphy was attempting to influence him corruptly. Two years later, and only after publication of the controversial 'Age tapes', Briese apparently came to the view that his talks with Murphy amounted to an attempt to get him to intervene improperly on Ryan's behalf. (The Age tapes were illegal police wire taps of Ryan's phone, given that name because transcripts were published in *The Age* newspaper in Melbourne. These are further discussed in chapter six.)

This raised two important questions. If Murphy's attempts to influence Briese criminally were so obvious, why did Briese not reach this conclusion at the time of the conversations? Why did he not report the conversations, as he should have done, to the head of the Department of Justice, Trevor Haines? These questions have never been convincingly answered by Briese. He justifies his failure by claiming that "any official report about wrongdoing or corruption in the magistrates' court had to be made to the Under Secretary of

Justice". He believed this to be inappropriate and that "setting out my concerns" to Haines "would have been the same as reporting them to Premier Wran, one of those allegedly associated with the questionable/illegal activities with all the consequences that would entail."

This is a gratuitous smearing of the integrity of Trevor Haines, who died in 2023, a veteran of the department and widely respected by politicians on both sides and throughout the public service and judiciary. This is also spurious reasoning. The conversations occurred before publication of the Age tapes. Briese had no reason to believe questionable or illegal activities were occurring under Wran, other than the Humphreys' affair in which Wran had been completely exonerated. Briese also admits in his book that he was never asked by Wran or his government to do anything illegal or questionable so this reasoning is doubly spurious. He slides over his obligation to report such a grave conversation to Haines, whether he agreed with this obligation or not.

The verdict in the second Murphy trial meant the jury did not find Briese's sworn evidence sufficient to prove, beyond reasonable doubt, that Murphy had corruptly tried to influence Briese on Ryan's behalf. The 'not guilty' verdict obviously still rankles with Briese. His book is a long and unsuccessful attempt to justify his actions in waiting more than two years to complain about Murphy. Along the way Briese resorts to attacking the integrity and competence of anyone who raised questions about his evidence, as well as slighting a host of other players. There is room for only one morally upright person in Briese's story.

Chief among Briese's targets is Wran who was a long-standing friend of Murphy. Wran became a prominent critic of Briese, despite Briese having been appointed as Farquhar's successor by the Wran government in May 1979. Briese was later appointed chief magistrate by Wran personally, following the commencement of the *Local Courts Act* in January 1985. Wran and Briese fell out over Briese's evidence in the trials and parliamentary inquiries into Murphy's alleged behaviour. This is not simply because Briese was a witness for the prosecution. Wran made no criticism of District Court judge Paul Flannery, who was also a witness against Murphy. Wran lost confidence in Briese because he believed Briese was asserting that he was required to do favours for Wran or other members of his government.

In his statement to the first Senate Committee Inquiry into Murphy, Briese had written of a discussion he claimed he had with Farquhar when he was hoping and, as he admits, lobbying to succeed Farquhar as chairman. He claims Farquhar told him the chairman "would be asked to handle a matter sensitively for the government and what was I like on favours. I asked him what sort of favours he was talking about. He replied, 'Oh, little things like P.C.A [charges of driving with more than the prescribed concentration of alcohol]'. He then said, 'Would you handle things like that discreetly for the Premier.' I indicated that I would handle them as discreetly as I could. He said, 'Well you've got the job'".

Wran was furious that Briese, who had been recommended as chairman not by Farquhar but by an independent selection committee comprising the chief justice and very senior public servants, did not also add in his statement that he had never been asked by Wran or anyone else in the government to do such favours. Wran told Parliament: "Mr Briese allowed an atmosphere to develop that gave the public the impression that in some way the magistrates, and Mr Briese in particular, were susceptible to being influenced by members of the government, that members of the government were interfering with the work of magistrates. And yet in front of witnesses it has been recorded there was no influence and no interference."

Wran further told Parliament that he had met with Briese and had asked him if he had ever been asked to do any favours for the premier or any member of the government and that Briese had said 'no' to both questions. Briese confirms this meeting in his book and says it occurred in December 1985, which is six years after his appointment. Six years is surely a sufficient period to determine if there was any questionable conduct occurring. Briese wrote: "Yes, Wran did ask me that. And the answer I gave him was 'no'. Wran had never asked me to do a favour for him nor had I ever been asked to do any favours for other government members."

There was also concern within the government, not only Wran, that Briese had said nothing for over two years, and had reported to no one, his conversations with Murphy. If Briese believed Murphy was engaged in a criminal act he had an obligation to report that. Wran believed Briese only came forward after he found he had also been mentioned in the Age tapes, which Briese admits he obtained with the assistance of a friend, Liberal MP Bruce Baird. Briese concedes it was more than two years after the conversations with Murphy that he first saw transcripts of the Age tapes. He was alarmed, he says, "they showed misbehaviour I was aware of was not an isolated case among that group of people". More likely Briese, who admits he had already been alerted by newspaper reports that he figured on the tapes, became concerned that his conversation with Farquhar, admitting that he was willing to do favours, may have been recorded and transcribed.

Briese was obviously in a dilemma. He suddenly discovers that he has been mentioned in transcripts of illegal wire taps which are now public. He knows he has had conversations with Farquhar, Ryan and Murphy, including at an intimate dinner party. He knows that in one of those conversations he has stated he would do "discreet favours" for the premier. He fears those conversations may have been recorded. In fact, Briese's conversation with Farquhar about doing favours had not been recorded but a telephone intercept between Ryan and Murphy alludes to this conversation. Briese admits "this [intercept] can only be understood in the context of the conversation Murray Farquhar had with me" in which they discussed doing favours. In another intercept, there is a suggestion by Ryan that Farquhar had helped Briese get Farquhar's job when Farquhar retired.

Put yourself in Briese's shoes at this moment. What are your options? On one hand you could stand your ground and rely on your reputation. You could point to the fact that there was no suggestion or evidence of interference by you in Ryan's committal hearing. You could also reaffirm your appointment had been recommended by a high-powered selection committee and not by Farquhar. On the other hand you could discover, two years after the event, that the conversations with Murphy, about which you had made no complaint and which you had not reported, were really an attempt corruptly to influence you.

Wran's firm view was that Briese decided to get in front of the story and chose the second option. He could see which way the wind was blowing and decided it was every man for himself. Briese's concern about corruption, previously dormant, appears to have been born only when he found out the tapes may have caught him saying things that would not look good in the cold type of a transcript. This prompted Wran's well-publicised and adverse comments about Briese's behaviour and competence. Briese leaves no doubt his book is intended as a 'get square' with Wran. This is the relevant context for Briese's allegations in his book, a context unexplored by the two newspaper journalists who conveyed those allegations to their readers.

This brings us to the "sensational evidence" that Briese claimed, in one of the newspaper articles, "would have had a significant or, let me say, should have had a significant effect" on the findings about Wran by the Street royal commission. Briese produces only two pieces of evidence. Let us examine this evidence as if we were in a committal hearing in the Local Court, an environment in which Briese would be familiar. Let the reader place himself or herself in the role of a magistrate whose task it is to assess objectively whether evidence presented by a prosecutor could lead a jury, properly instructed at a later trial, to reach a verdict of guilty beyond all reasonable doubt.

Our imaginary committal hearing begins with the case presented by the prosecutor Clarrie Briese. He calls two witnesses. The first is former police prosecutor, Sergeant Darcy Cluff, who had presented the case against Kevin Humphreys. Briese tenders a statement by Cluff, made on 5 September 2019, about an event which had allegedly occurred 42 years earlier. Cluff recounts a conversation he had with Humphreys' solicitor, John Aston, "at about 9.40 am on 11 August 1977", the day the committal hearing began. Cluff says: "He told me that Humphreys' legal representatives were considering calling the Premier as a character witness. I said nothing, it did not concern me who they called. There was a short pause and then he asked me what my attitude would be. I asked him what he meant. He then asked me if the Premier was called would I cross examine him. I told Aston that I would and that the Premier would be treated exactly the same as any other witness. Given I knew the brief very thoroughly I thought it would be an imprudent action for the defence to take but it was not my position to offer advice. I asked Aston if the Premier was aware of the specific allegation against Humphreys. He didn't answer me, just said he would see me in court."

Briese's second witness is Sergeant Wayne Evans, another former police prosecutor, who had not been involved in the Humphreys' hearing. Evans claims that at around 3pm on 11 August he saw Wran standing beside a Ford Falcon belonging to Farquhar in the courtyard used for car parking at the Central Courts. He further claims he then saw Wran enter the building by a back entrance that was usually locked. Evans claims he made a statement at the time and handed it that afternoon to the senior prosecutor, although Evans could not recall the prosecutor's name. He claims this person undertook to get it immediately to the officer in charge of the Police Prosecution Branch but, once again, he could not recall the officer's name.

Summing up his case, Briese tells our hypothetical hearing that Cluff's statement "would have had a significant effect" on the findings of the royal commission. "The fact that Humphreys' legal team was considering [calling Wran] is indicative of a pre-existing relationship between Wran and Humphreys as well as a willingness on Wran's part to help Humphreys". On Evans' claims, Briese says "somewhere along the line, it and/or its potentially explosive contents seem to have been blocked." If Evans had been called to give evidence to the royal commission, according to Briese, "it would have demonstrated a willingness on Wran's part to help Humphreys and therefore add credence to the allegation that Wran rang Farquhar asking for Kevin Humphreys not to be committed for trial".

Briese concludes the prosecution case: "What this new information seemingly indicates is that Wran had a personal interest in seeing to it that Humphreys charges be dismissed. It is consistent with the allegation that Wran rang Farquhar at 9.30am on 11 August 1977 to ask that Humphreys not be committed for trial. It is also consistent with Humphreys' meeting Wran on 23 September 1976 and Humphreys saying that 'his main reason for wishing to see Mr Wran was to talk about the inquiry and the prosecution'. In which case, if this evidence is reliable, Wran escaped being charged for his involvement".

Before calling on the defence, our imaginary magistrate is likely to ask Briese what he means by referring to Humphreys meeting Wran on 23 September 1976 since this has not previously been tendered in evidence. Briese would be required to explain that this was a reference to evidence presented at the Street royal commission. Humphreys had sought a meeting with Wran, after Wran's election, and it took him four weeks to be granted the meeting and another two weeks before it occurred. The royal commission also heard, and this was supported by Humphreys, that as soon as Humphreys raised his case, Wran cut him short and said as police minister he could not discuss the matter. Our magistrate is likely to point out that the fact that it took Humphreys six weeks to get in to see Wran is hardly evidence of a close relationship between the two men. It also shows that Wran, a Queens Counsel, was aware of the legal proprieties of not interfering in a prosecution.

Now it is time for the defence to provide its rebuttal of the "sensational new evidence" presented by Briese. Taking the Cluff evidence first the defence points out that it is not necessary to question Cluff's memory 42 years after the event. Nothing in the reported conversation suggests Wran was willing to help Humphreys in this way. Briese or Cluff do not know if Wran had even been approached, let alone indicated he was willing to be called. There is nothing to suggest Wran was aware that this idea was being kicked around by Humphreys' legal team. Cluff conceded that Aston did not answer when he asked if Wran was aware of the allegation against Humphreys.

The defence also notes that this alleged conversation was on the same morning that the committal hearing began. Surely, the defence poses, the magistrate does not believe a premier, any premier, can simply down tools at a moment's notice and head off to Central Courts and wait around to be called as a character witness? The defence would call, as its own witness, Brian Dale, Wran's press secretary at the time. Dale has testified that Wran would never have contemplated appearing as a character witness for Humphreys without first discussing it with Dale, to assess likely media reaction, and with his department head, Gerry Gleeson and Deputy Premier, Jack Ferguson, to assess whether it is an appropriate action for a premier. Dale confirms that no such discussions were held.

The defence tells the court that Cluff's evidence should be dismissed as irrelevant. There is nothing in Cluff's statement to dispute Street's finding that the relationship between Wran and Humphreys was nothing more than "a superficial acquaintance deriving from their respective positions." Nor is there anything in this "evidence" to dispute Street's finding that the alleged phone call between Wran and Farquhar did not take place. It is important to stress this point. Street's exoneration of Wran was not based on an assumption of a relationship between Wran and Humphreys. Street found that the event which initiated the royal commission – an alleged phone call between Wran and Farquhar on the morning of the beginning of the committal hearing – never took place. Cluff's testimony has no bearing at all, one way or the other, on that finding.

Now the defence turns to the testimony of Wayne Evans. The defence ridicules Evans' claim that his evidence went missing during the Street royal commission. The defence finds it remarkable that Evans' memory is apparently excellent when it comes to seeing Wran at the Central Courts but faulty when it comes to identifying his own colleagues in the Prosecution Branch. The defence also rejects the prosecution claim that if Evans had been called before the Street royal commission "it would have demonstrated a willingness on Wran's part to help Humphreys and therefore add credence to the allegation that Wran rang Farquhar asking for Kevin Humphreys not to be committed for trial". If Evans had been called Wran could equally have had the chance to test the claim and the opportunity to prove from staff evidence, his two drivers and his secretary's diary that he was nowhere near Central Courts at that time. Wran had similarly been able to prove, from the records of a senior Treasury officer and the diary of his private secretary, Denise Darlow, that he was in a significant budget meeting with Treasury staff and his economic advisers when he was alleged to have made the phone call to Farquhar.

If Wran was at Central Courts that afternoon, surely the only reason would have been to see Farquhar. If so, why would Wran have needed to make a phone call that morning and why would Farquhar have that morning told magistrate Jones that Wran had contacted him? This was the day of the committal and by 3pm the committal hearing was nearly over. What purpose could Wran have achieved by being there on the afternoon when the case had already begun particularly if, as the prosecution claims, he had fixed the case with a phone call that morning?

The defence would pose the question whether the magistrate could accept that Wran, universally acknowledged as intelligent and politically astute, would have been so stupid and indiscreet as to come to Central Courts personally to, presumably, try to fix Humphrey's case. The defence would note there is no car entrance to the Central Courts off Liverpool Street. Wran's very recognisable LTD would have had to drive through the entrance off Central Street (in reality, a narrow laneway). The entrance was a narrow archway that bordered the former Central Police Station, where hundreds of police and administrative staff worked. Evans makes no mention of seeing Wran's official LTD in what was a small parking area, only Farquhar's Ford Falcon. How did Wran get there? Did he walk down the drive at Central Police Station, having been dropped off outside, thereby increasing the chance that he would be observed? Wran was a well-known person and could rarely go anywhere without being noticed.

The defence would note that prosecutor Briese weakened his case by telling the magistrate that "senior counsel and others with whom I have discussed this fresh evidence have questioned the veracity of the claim because Wran would have been accompanied by staff, including protection staff". Briese had sought to overcome these doubts by suggesting: "It may be that Wran dispensed with a staff member that day for his own reasons or that the accompanying staff member was in the court building seeking access for Wran via the backdoor through which he entered, so as to avoid any unnecessary media scrutiny surrounding his presence in the court building that day." In reply the defence asks: if Wran was concerned to avoid "unnecessary media scrutiny" why would he take the risk of being present in the court building, with or without staff, or by walking or having been driven through the Central Police Station grounds.

The prosecution and defence now rest their cases. How does our imaginary magistrate assess this new evidence and decide whether a jury, properly instructed, could find Wran guilty? The statement by Cluff, uncorroborated, has no bearing at all on the allegation that Wran had phoned Farquhar on the morning of the hearing. There is no evidence that Wran was even aware that Humphreys' lawyers were considering calling Wran. There is nothing in this alleged conversation which suggests a pre-existing relationship between Wran and Humphreys. Nor is there anything in this evidence to dispute Street's finding that the alleged phone call between Wran and Farquhar did not take place. Nor does the statement by Evans have any bearing on Street's finding that the phone call did not take place. Wran was not given a chance to rebut the claim that he was present at Central Courts. Why would Wran need to be at Central Courts that afternoon if he had, according to Farquhar, already fixed the case with a phone call that morning?

No sensible magistrate, after honestly and objectively assessing this "evidence", would send it off to trial. Not so former chief magistrate Briese: no need even for a trial. Briese pronounces Wran guilty. He leaps to this conclusion entirely unsupported by his own evidence. One can only assume that Briese, in his evaluation of this new evidence, has allowed his vengefulness towards Wran to swamp his objectivity.

Incidentally, nowhere in his book does Briese address one of the fundamental inconsistencies in the *Four Corners*' report and in his own "new evidence". The royal commission found that Wran's office was aware on 16 June 1977 of the date of the Humphreys' hearing, nearly two months before the committal began. Why would Wran wait until the very morning of the hearing, on 11 August, to attempt to fix the outcome with Farquhar?

Briese also expects his readers to overlook the fact that Street did not solely rely on the public hearings to judge Wran's guilt or innocence. Professional investigators were seconded to the royal commission and conducted their own investigation of the events, including what Street said his office called the 'Wran-Humphreys-Farquhar triangle'. Street reported these investigations "have not only failed to discover any useful leads, but I am convinced to the contrary, namely that there was no such triangle." It was this investigation, as well as the formal hearings, which prompted Street's conclusion: "In short, try as I have with the unlimited resources and wide-ranging powers available to me in this Royal Commission, every avenue that has been followed in seeking to identify intervention by Mr Wran in the preparation or assistance of Mr Humphreys has ended, in so far as a path to Mr Wran is concerned, not merely inconclusively but specifically in his favour."

The farcical "new evidence" is not the only claim Briese makes about Wran in his book. More than once Briese claims that "corruption got into the magistracy under Wran". Nowhere in his book does Briese provide any evidence for this claim. The only instances of corruption he cites involve Murray Farquhar. The Street royal commission found Farquhar's claim that Wran had interfered in a committal hearing was false. The magistrates who testified at the royal commission admitted that the alleged political interference in the Humphreys case was unique. Briese also told the Senate Committee inquiry that "in the five years that I have been chairman there has not been at the Central Courts any case which has caused concern in terms of possible malpractice that I am aware of". Given this statement, and the admission by Briese that he was never asked to do favours by Wran or anyone in his government, there is no justification for him claiming that "corruption got into the magistracy under Wran". Wran not only did not seek favours from Briese but his government also passed the *Local Courts Act*, which gave magistrates independence from the public service, an outcome Briese had long sought.

Although Briese provides no evidence of Wran being involved in corrupt activities he does, inadvertently, provide evidence to the contrary. One example is his report of Farquhar's anger at the government's rejection of his request, just before his retirement in 1979, to increase his salary to the level of a District Court judge to boost his superannuation. Briese writes that he supported Farquhar in this pay demand although he fails to tell the reader that the increase would also have had substantial financial benefits for himself if he became chairman. Briese claims that it became clear to him only later that Farquhar's anger "was because Farquhar in past years had carried out 'special favours' for Wran, Murphy and Ryan". Briese provides no evidence for including Wran in that sentence. He writes that, although Wran had the influence to have the Public Service Board approve Farquhar's application, "that didn't happen". It does not occur to Briese that his own words demonstrate Wran was under no obligation to Farquhar.

Briese carries his obsession with Wran to ridiculous extremes. Delays in giving independence to magistrates becomes a sinister act. Wran had committed himself to this in a meeting with Briese and the Attorney General, Frank Walker, who shared the reservations of senior officials in his department about this move. The operation of the *Local Courts Act* was delayed by the Street royal commission, by several changes of attorneys general, by the appointment of a senior committee to work out procedures and by lobbying of the government not to reappoint some magistrates. These understandable delays are now seen by Briese as part of Wran's displeasure with him. "With hindsight" – there is plenty of hindsight in the book – " I came to recognise that I had received 'coded' warnings from Premier Wran. If I was to have support from him I would need to give attention to what he wanted from me." How does this sit with Briese's admission that Wran never asked him to "give attention" to anything? How does this sit with the fact that it was Wran who finally delivered independence for magistrates, which Briese had lobbied for?

Similarly, a rejection of an application by a magistrate for minor financial assistance to attend an international conference is explained by Briese thus: "I believe the reason for the Premier's decision was, inferentially with hindsight [that word again!], that Morgan Ryan had been committed for trial." Does Briese seriously believe that the decision on such a trivial matter, as opposed to the letter of rejection, was made personally by a premier? Nor does he explain how making a magistrate put his hand in his own pocket to help fund an otherwise tax-deductible overseas junket would constitute a rebuke to Briese.

The *Herald*'s report of Briese's book asserted that Wran "tried to have [Briese] removed from the judiciary." This is false. Wran had the opportunity to replace Briese when the *Local Courts Act*, which began in January 1985, changed the position to Chief Magistrate. Wran did not act against Briese even though the question of his reappointment came after Briese had come forward as a witness against Lionel Murphy. Terry Sheahan was appointed attorney general in December 1984 following the death of Paul Landa. One of his first tasks was to decide whether all existing magistrates were to be reappointed under the new *Local Courts Act*. There was pressure, including from Briese, not to reappoint as many as a dozen magistrates who were not considered up to the job. This was one of the reasons why senior public servants had opposed independence of the magistracy. Sheahan says Wran, who had appointed himself attorney general in the brief period between Landa's death and Sheahan's appointment, told him that he (Wran) had reappointed Briese as chief magistrate but that it was up to Sheahan to sort out the rest of the appointments. Sheahan subsequently decided not to reappoint five magistrates, an action which landed in the High Court and led to a major decision on procedural fairness.

Briese had certainly given Wran plenty of reasons not to reappoint him. As Wran told Parliament: "in order to enhance his chances for the chief stipendiary magistracy [Briese] was prepared to agree with Farquhar, at Farquhar's behest, that he was prepared to do favours". Wran was also not impressed, as Briese admits, after reading a report by the Solicitor General, Mary Gaudron, concerning allegations that a District Court judge, John Foord, had sought to influence committal proceedings involving Ryan. Gaudron had reported that, in an interview with her, Briese admitted he had canvassed with Barrie Unsworth, then Minister for Transport (and subsequently Wran's successor as premier), his suggestion that "people at the top level" should "change the leadership".

He does not deny this in the book. "If organised corruption in the judicial system was occurring under the leadership of Wran –

and I believed it was – then changing the leadership was indeed a valid option for consideration even though difficult, or at the time impossible, to achieve," Briese wrote. He produces not a single piece of evidence to justify this claim about Wran. Nor does he question whether it was appropriate for a senior public servant (as he then was) to canvas such political opinions. Independence of the magistracy is a one-way street for Briese.

Briese claims his book shows "an entire interconnected web of corrupt activity existed among a very high-level and influential group of mostly legal people. This extended to Neville Wran." Again, Briese provides no evidence for such a defamatory statement about Wran. It is necessary to restate: Briese agreed in the book that he was never asked to do anything illegal or improper by Wran or by any member of his government; nor does he provide any evidence of corrupt activity on the part of Wran. This is a disgraceful statement by a person who had held a senior judicial position, someone who is supposed to draw conclusions based solely on reliable evidence.

At no time did Briese report the existence of such a "web of corrupt activity" to anyone in authority. Briese claims in his book that he had various discussions with Barrie Unsworth (whom he consistently calls "Barry"), including one at a dinner at Parliament House, "around about August or September 1979" where he told him "some of the details of the dinner at Morgan Ryan's home". The claim was included in Briese's evidence to the Senate Committee. Barrie Unsworth took issue with Briese's claims that Briese was a secret whistle blower. On 9 October 1984 Unsworth told the NSW Legislative Council that the dinner meeting had taken place on 16 September 1980, a full year after the date Briese told the committee and around 17 months after the dinner at Ryan's house. Unsworth told the Parliament: "I must confess I am disappointed in Mr Briese. I have known him since 1977 and have a high regard for him, but he has certainly misused his association with me concerning the evidence he presented to the Senate Committee."

If such a web of corrupt activity existed Briese did nothing to bring that web undone. Briese admitted in his submission to the second Senate Committee inquiry that he had told Ryan and Murphy at the end of a long dinner party – Briese denies, unconvincingly, it was also boozy – "what my policy was going to be in connection with approaches from government or the Premier." He told the Senate Committee: "So I indicated that I was sympathetic to the Labor Party and its policies and was interested in good government. I said that if I could assist the Premier in that objective, to let the Premier know that he could come to me for my advice and I would tell him what could be done and what couldn't be done." Briese gratuitously volunteered this invitation to Ryan and Murphy – it was not in response to anything either man had said or asked. Briese had already been appointed to the top job. He was no longer actively lobbying to be Farquhar's replacement and speaking to people he believed, wrongly, might influence that decision. There was no reason or justification for offering such a pledge, unless Briese was already looking ahead to his need to be reappointed as chief magistrate once the *Local Courts Act* came into operation.

Briese was later cross-examined on this at Murphy's committal hearing. Briese said he had made the reference to the premier because "I wanted to test, to see what their reaction was." Really? Who is he trying to kid? If Briese wants us to believe he is the crusader for justice that his book portrays, why did he attend the dinner party if he had suspicions about the motives of the participants? Why did he boast of his Labor Party sympathies? More importantly, why did he not tell Murphy and Ryan that he would not tolerate any political interference in the administration of justice, whether that was by the premier or anyone else? That is what a person who was deeply committed to the independence of the magistracy would have done. That is what a person deeply committed to ensuring there was no corruption in the magistracy would have done.

The only conclusion to be drawn from Briese's book is that he is so anxious to settle a score with Wran that he has tried to turn unsubstantiated and insubstantial claims into firm proof of guilt. He has failed. He seems determined to prove Wran's complaint that Briese was prone to draw conclusions entirely unsupported by the evidence before him, a dangerous sin for any judicial figure. Those who believe Wran was wrong to express publicly his lack of confidence in Briese, or who believe Wran went 'over the top' in his comments, may now need to reconsider those views.

Journalist David Marr, in a television retrospective in 2017 of the 'Murphy affair', declared: "Clarrie Briese is the hero here." Marr sets a low bar for heroism. A magistrate who only discovers two years after the event, and only after he fears being publicly outed, that certain conversations were an attempt to influence him is no hero. A magistrate who fails to report those conversations to the head of the Department of Justice, as he was required, cannot be a hero. A former magistrate who waits until Wran is dead before making demonstrably false allegations against him cannot be admired for his courage.

5

THE GHOST TRAIN FIRE CONSPIRACY

"*Essentially the allegation is that the reason why [the investigation] didn't go any further was because of corruption further up. There are a lot of powerful people in powerful places protecting Abe [Saffron]. So, it went right to the top we are told.*" ABC-TV's 'Exposed: The Ghost Train Fire'.

"*This program in no way suggested that Neville Wran had any involvement in or knowledge of the fire at Luna Park … it did not say that Wran was involved in a cover-up of the cause of the fire.*" ABC managing director David Anderson.

"'*The top' is an ambiguous phrase but given the many references to Wran in the preceding several minutes, many viewers would interpret it as referring to the Premier. The cumulative effect of interview commentary, the storyboard graphic, the sequence summarising findings with family members and absence of rebuttal content left [us] with a strong impression the program concluded Wran was complicit.*" Rodney Tiffen and Chris Masters.

Brian Dale will never forget the horrible scene at Sydney's Luna Park on Sunday morning, 10 June 1979. He still remembers the little flags showing where the burned bodies of an adult and six children had been found following a fire the previous night in the fun fair's ghost train ride. Nor will he forget a policeman calmly describing to him the process of human flesh burning. Dale had been taken to the site by Jim Lees, who only days earlier had been appointed acting police commissioner and would later be confirmed as commissioner. Neville Wran had decided not to visit Luna Park as he did not want the site of the tragedy to become a media circus. Dale's task, as Wran's press secretary, was to report to Wran and to decide with him the government's response. Unsurprisingly, given the extent of the tragedy and despite Wran's reticence, it became a media circus.

More than 40 years later the Luna Park fire again became a media circus. This time the ringmaster was an ABC-TV program 'Exposed: The Ghost Train Fire'. The three-part program, broadcast in March 2021, cost $2 million, the most expensive single program by the ABC. Three journalists worked full-time on the program for 18 months and, according to the credits, more than 50 other staff were involved at various stages. A replica of the ghost train was built and burned to the ground for the sake of verisimilitude.

The program drew a number of conclusions: that the fire had been deliberately lit by a group of bikies; that the bikies were acting on the instructions of Sydney crime boss, Abe Saffron; that Saffron ordered the fire because he wanted to gain control of the harbourside site for commercial development purposes; that the cause of the fire had been deliberately covered up by corrupt police; that Saffron eventually gained the lease for Luna Park through a Saffron-linked corporate vehicle; and that Neville Wran was instrumental in both delivering the lease to Saffron and in the cover up of the crime.

The ABC produced scant evidence for any of these conclusions. It would later emerge that the program, with the knowledge of ABC editorial management, breached the corporation's published Editorial Policies on the need for corroboration. The program was also accused of selectively editing interviews and of ignoring evidence which contradicted its conclusions.

In examining these allegations, it is necessary to sketch the background, much of it ignored or skimmed over by the program. When the Wran government was elected in May 1976, the lease for Luna Park had expired. The lessee, Luna Park (NSW) Pty Ltd, continued to operate the park on a 'holdover' basis while negotiations continued with government instrumentalities. This company was something of an accidental lessee of an amusement park since it had originally acquired the lease with the intention of commercially developing the site, a venture rejected by the Askin government. Luna Park was closed after the fire. On 31 July 1979 the government called tenders for a new lease. The advertisements by the Department of Services stipulated the lease was strictly for an amusement park: "The lessee will be required to operate an amusement park on the site". When tenders closed on 23 November 1979, there were six tenderers. Despite the program's claims that Saffron had long desired the site and had organised the fire to gain possession, there is no evidence that Saffron was involved in any of the six tenders.

None of the parties fully met the conditions of the tender. In December 1979 – the exact day is uncertain – the Policies and Priorities Committee of Cabinet ('P & P') decided all six tenders should be rejected and authorised further negotiations with the one tenderer who apparently came closest to meeting the conditions. This was a consortium called Camingo Pty Ltd, in which the Reg Grundy entertainment organisation was to be a key investor. Around 19 December 1979 – again the exact day is unclear – the Minister for Public Works, Jack Ferguson, wrote to the Minister for Services, Bill Crabtree, advising him that 'P & P' had decided all tenders were to be rejected and negotiations should be conducted between Camingo and a committee of government officials.

The negotiations with Camingo were unsuccessful in reaching agreement on terms. On 4 February 1980 'P & P' decided to call fresh tenders and this was announced by Jack Ferguson the following day. Cabinet records show the 'P & P' decision was based on several factors, including complaints about the scarcity of information provided, unclear criteria and difficulties in accessing the site because of the fire. This decision was endorsed by the full Cabinet on 12 February. On 12 March 1980 newspaper advertisements called for fresh tenders, closing on 17 June 1980.

Seven tenders were submitted. The government established a special committee to assess the new tenders. This committee comprised six very senior public servants: the head of the Department of

Services; the head of the Department of Lands; the deputy head of the Premier's Department; the Valuer-General; the principal architect of the Department of Public Works; and the regional manager of the Planning and Environment Commission. The special committee eventually recommended that a tender lodged by Australasian Amusements Associates Pty Ltd be accepted. This consortium included the Michael Edgeley organisation, another major entertainment company, as a shareholder. The company subsequently changed its name to Harbourside Amusement Park Pty Ltd, apparently because of difficulties in gaining registration for the former name. On 27 May 1981 the government, through the Minister for Lands, Lin Gordon, granted a 30-year lease to Harbourside. The delay was caused by the need for the NSW Parliament to pass the *Luna Park Site Act* to obtain vacant possession of the site.

This was strictly a lease to operate an amusement park. Any attempt to convert the site to commercial development over the next 30 years would have been a breach of the lease. Commercial development could only be undertaken with the agreement of the lessor and, as subsequent events have shown, no government has ever been prepared to take such a controversial step. Even if a government was sufficiently brave – or so politically stupid – to decide to permit commercial development on the historic site, fresh tenders would have been called. So much for the claim that Saffron wanted the lease for commercial development of the site.

Although the program alleged that Harbourside was a Saffron-linked company, there is no evidence that Saffron was involved at the time of the granting of the lease. Five months later, in October 1981, solicitor David Baffsky was appointed as a director of Harbourside. Baffsky's firm, Simons and Baffsky, had allegedly done legal work for Saffron. In 1982 a return of directors showed that Samuel Cowper, apparently a nephew of Saffron, had been appointed as company secretary. It is these appointments which gave rise to rumours of Saffron's involvement.

In 1986 an inquiry into Harbourside was begun by the NSW Corporate Affairs Commission. The inquiry was an initiative of Neville Wran, following allegations in Parliament. On 19 November 1985 Wran wrote to the Attorney General, Terry Sheahan, requesting the Corporate Affairs Commission "examine the affairs of Harbourside with a view to establishing one way or another whether Abraham Saffron has links to Luna Park and if so, the nature and extent of the links". The letter also requested that consideration be given to making the results of the investigation available to the National Crime Authority. In a second letter to Sheahan on 25 February 1986 Wran asked for a further investigation into whether Saffron "has acquired ownership or significant interest in Harbourside or whether significant interest accrues to Saffron as a result of the present ownership, management and financial structure".

Note that Wran authorised an inquiry into the very same company which the ABC later accused him of favouring. He specifically requested the inquiry to examine whether Saffron was involved. This is very strange behaviour by a premier who, according to the ABC, had a friendship with Saffron and had intervened to ensure Saffron got the lease. Not surprisingly this fact did not fit the ABC's narrative. The viewers were left unaware that it was Wran who had instigated this inquiry.

The Corporate Affairs Commission conducted a very thorough investigation over 17 months which examined Harbourside and other companies involved in the ownership structure. Twenty-three witnesses, including Saffron, were examined on oath and another 11 witnesses were interviewed. A National Crime Authority official was included in the investigation team. The report was tabled in Parliament on 27 October 1987. The Commission concluded, at the end of this lengthy inquiry: "There is no evidence … that suggests that Abraham Gilbert Saffron has any actual or beneficial ownership in Harbourside". The inquiry did find that Saffron controlled a trading trust, Arcadia Machines, which had supplied amusement machines to the park. The Commission concluded: "There is no evidence that

Mr Saffron's dealings with Harbourside, through Arcadia, were other than normal business dealings except that the appointment of Arcadia may have been influenced by the family relationship between Coleman Goldstein [then a director of Harbourside and described as a distant relation to Saffron] and Abraham Saffron".

The Commission found that David Baffsky had ultimate control of Harbourside through various nominee companies in which he had a controlling interest. In 1988 Baffsky successfully sued *The Sydney Morning Herald* over an article claiming he had been involved with Saffron in Luna Park. *The Australian Financial Review* in 2018 apologised to him for claiming he had a questionable involvement with Saffron. Baffsky, who died in 2022, was a prominent company director and held many government-appointed positions, both federal and state. The Corporate Affairs Commission was not the only body to conclude Saffron had no ownership interest in Harbourside. The National Crime Authority subsequently also found no evidence of Saffron's ownership.

While the Corporate Affairs Commission's investigation was underway, Harbourside proposed to the Department of Lands that the lease for Luna Park be assigned to a new company, Prome Investments, a company chaired by Baffsky. Prome said it intended to spend $50 million redeveloping the site, while maintaining its use as an amusement park. The shareholding of Prome was divided among nine companies, a mixture of publicly listed, private and trustee companies. As a result, the Commission widened its investigation. The Commission reported: "The conclusion reached from an examination of the evidence available with regard to the shareholding and management of the various parties who are interested in Prome Investments together with the legal and managerial structure of Prome Investments and some of the companies that control Prome Investments is that Abraham Gilbert Saffron has no controlling interest in Prome Investments and has no significant financial interest or benefit in the proposed assignment of the lease".

Prome was therefore assigned the lease and closed the park in December 1987 ahead of a promised redevelopment which did not occur. In 1990 the Greiner Coalition government cancelled the lease. Prome was later awarded $3.5 million in compensation by an independent arbitrator, a quantum much less than it had been seeking. The park remained closed until January 1995 when it reopened with a new lessee, following a $25 million grant by taxpayers. The site has remained problematic for subsequent governments.

Despite the findings of the Corporate Affairs Commission and the National Crime Authority that Saffron had no ownership interest, the ABC journalists, with no apparent qualifications in the intricacies of corporate law and regulation, still told viewers that "the lease swung over to Abe Saffron". The program could only make such an assertion by completely ignoring the evidence. Incidentally Luna Park was no financial bonanza for Harbourside. The Corporate Affairs Commission found Harbourside did not trade at a profit in any year, notwithstanding a substantial investment in new and renovated facilities. By 1986 Harbourside owed Citicorp $13.7 million (the equivalent of $43.6 million today), a loan guaranteed by the directors.

If the ABC had a properly functioning editor-in-chief, what would that person have concluded under the ABC's so-called 'upward referral' policy? Saffron did not tender for the lease. The lease was strictly for the operation of an amusement park and commercial development was not possible under the lease. All relevant decisions on the tendering process were made by Cabinet or by a Cabinet committee, not by Wran. The corporate regulator in NSW, after a lengthy investigation, found no evidence that Saffron had an actual or beneficial ownership of the company which was awarded the lease.

The editor-in-chief would also have concluded that the recommendation to the Cabinet on the winning tender was made by a committee of very senior public servants. The program included an interview with the only surviving member of that committee, the respected former Government Architect, Andrew Andersons. He made no claim on the program that the committee members had been pressured into making their recommendation. Andersons subsequently told Troy Bramston in *The Australian*: "The tender process was totally above board. Nobody influenced the panel process – certainly I was not told by anybody to do anything. The public servants on the panel were all very experienced and professional". Andersons also complained about the professionalism of the program: "They used tendentious editing to try to prove a predetermined view".

Why then did the program make the allegation about Wran, despite overwhelming evidence that the lease did not end up with Saffron? The ABC relied solely on the report on the infamous 'Allegation No. 27', one of the allegations being examined by the Parliamentary Commission of Inquiry into High Court judge Lionel Murphy. This inquiry was established in May 1986 after other High Court judges had expressed concern about Murphy resuming duties on the court, following his acquittal in April 1986 on the charges outlined in the previous chapter. The purpose of the inquiry was to establish whether Murphy's conduct amounted to misbehaviour under section 27 of the Constitution, the only way in which a High Court judge can be removed. The inquiry was discontinued when Murphy announced in July 1986 that he was dying from cancer – he died three months later – since its purpose was now irrelevant.

Various documents before the inquiry, including Allegation No. 27, were only released in 2017, and were widely reported at the time. Allegation No. 27, to cite it in full, was that "Morgan Ryan arranged for Mr Justice Murphy to intervene on behalf of Abe Saffron in order to gain the lease for Luna Park in place of the Reg Grundy organisation which had allegedly been awarded the lease. It is said that a Saffron related organisation ultimately acquired the lease." As noted above, the Reg Grundy organisation had not been awarded the lease and there is no evidence that a Saffron-related organisation acquired the lease. The allegation is therefore not off to a good start.

Allegation No. 27 relies solely on the word of former police sergeant Paul Egge, one of the police involved in the illegal police wire taps on the phone of Morgan Ryan, discussed in the previous chapter and in the following chapter. This repeats evidence Egge gave in 1986 to the Royal Commission of Inquiry into Alleged Telephone Interceptions, headed by Justice Donald Stewart. According to the report of Allegation No. 27, Egge told the royal commission that "Abe Saffron rang Morgan Ryan and told him that he was interested in gaining the lease for Luna Park. Morgan Ryan said to Saffron that it was going to be given to the Reg Grundy Organisation. Saffron said: 'Well I want the lease'. As a result of the conversation Morgan Ryan got in contact with Mr Justice Murphy. Murphy said leave it with me. Shortly after Murphy rang Morgan Ryan back and said that he had spoken to Neville and that Neville was going to try and make some arrangements for Abe to get the lease. Then, the next day or shortly after Wran said the Government is going to review the lease to Luna Park and a decision on the lease would be made by the Government within 7 or 14 days."

There is not one reference to Luna Park in the transcripts of the illegal wire taps obtained by *The Age* newspaper. None of the other police officers involved in the wire taps substantiated Egge's claims about Wran. Sergeant Robert Treharne, according to the report on Allegation No. 27, "recalled similar but not identical conversations from the taps on Ryan's phone. He said: 'he recalled that there was 'a fair amount of discussion as to gaining control of that lease'. He said that the discussion was between 'Saffron, Morgan Ryan and [Eric] Jury – although I am unsure of Jury's participation.' [Jury was a nightclub owner]. Treharne was unable to recall the conversations relating to Luna Park with any precision and said, 'I know there were a number of conversations about it and Morgan Ryan feeling that he could swing the lease'. He was unable to recall any other person with whom Ryan spoke by telephone concerning the Luna Park matter."

Another police officer, Sergeant Michael Ogg, said "his recollection was that Ryan was trying to make representations to get the lease for a friend of his. He said that the friend's name was 'Colbron or something like that.' Although he was unable to be precise, he said that he had a 'feeling' that Ryan had made representations to Mr Justice Murphy. When asked for his recollection of any conversations he said: 'I cannot possibly actually recall the exact conversation on what he was going to do but I remember along those lines that [words missing] were going to try and get the government to agree to this company, receiving the favour and getting the lease for Luna Park'".

The document also refers to another police officer, Sergeant JB Meadley, "who spent considerable time while he was attached to the BCI [Bureau of Crime Intelligence] involved in surveillance of Ryan and who had heard tapes of Ryan's telephone conversations at the TSU [Technical Support Unit] from time to time, had no recollection of hearing any references in the Ryan conversations to Luna Park."

To summarise, the only witness to claim that Wran was involved in the lease was Sergeant Egge. The report on Allegation No. 27 states: "It should be noted that although it may appear on a reading of Egge's evidence that he actually heard some telephone conversations as they occurred, this was not the case." Nor are there any transcripts, tapes or summaries to back up Egge's claim. Despite this lack of corroboration, the ABC relied solely on the word of Egge for its claim that Wran engaged in a conspiracy with Ryan and Murphy to deliver the lease to Saffron. Asked by the interviewer whether Wran was involved, Egge replies: "He was involved – big time". We are expected to accept Egge's claims, despite him not hearing any telephone conversations and despite him not being able to produce tapes or transcripts or summaries to back up his claim.

Egge was also unable to provide any details of when this conversation supposedly occurred. The report says: "Egge was not sure of the period". Further it says: "if the conversations occurred it is probable they would have taken place in January, February, March or

April of 1980, for which period the Ryan transcript material is obviously incomplete". Egge's account of the alleged conversation does not tally with the timetable of the tender process outlined earlier. If Ryan supposedly tells Saffron the lease is going to the Grundy organisation, this means the conversation must have occurred between 17 January 1980 (when the government advised tenderers it was continuing negotiations with Camingo) and 12 March 1980 (when advertisements appeared for fresh tenders). The relevant period is even narrower. Justice Stewart found NSW police only began tapping Ryan's phone (in a second operation) on 7 February 1980, so the conversation must have occurred between 7 February 1980 and 12 March 1980. Why would Wran "the next day or shortly after" say the lease was going to be reviewed and a decision made within seven or 14 days when he had known on 4 February 1980, following the P & P meeting and before the wiretapping began, that fresh tenders were about to be called?

Egge's allegation was first made to the Stewart Royal Commission. The royal commission was scathing about the reliability of the testimony of the police involved in the illegal wiretapping who were given immunity from prosecution for testifying. The report noted: "The police witnesses' inability for the most part to identify with any precision elements of the tapes, or to give firsthand evidence about them, renders it highly unlikely that any such material would be admitted as evidence in criminal proceedings". Further the royal commissioner said: "The Commission is not satisfied that the transcript material in summary form has been prepared with sufficient care to be affirmed as wholly accurate. In addition, the Commission does not consider that many of the police concerned in the task of summary material possessed the necessary objectivity to render the summaries reliable." Incidentally Justice Stewart found that the tap on Ryan's phone in this operation was discontinued because the Bureau of Crime Intelligence considered it had produced "a lack of worthwhile intelligence." The BCI's conclusion does not support Egge's claim.

Egge's own credibility as a witness did not emerge intact from the royal commission. He had made another allegation against Lionel Murphy, known as Allegation No. 23, which was also released in 2017. This involved the alleged blackmail of a Liberal MP and former minister, Milton Morris. The report on Allegation No. 23 quotes from Volume 2 of the report of the Stewart Royal Commission, which has never been made public. "The Commission found the evidence of Egge confused and vague. He said the source of his information was transcripts of telephone conversations involving Ryan but he could not recall the background to the conversations nor the sequence of events. The Commission does not propose to detail the evidence of Egge as the Commission finds it unreliable." Despite the significant reservations by the royal commission about the reliability of the police witnesses' testimony, and of Egge's testimony in particular, the ABC treated Egge's claims as gospel, even though there are no tapes, transcripts or summaries to support his claims.

Notwithstanding the reservations of Justice Stewart about the reliability of the police summaries, there is one summary referred to in the Allegation No. 27 document that was deliberately overlooked by the program. This is a summary of a conversation between Morgan Ryan and Eric Jury: "They agree that Wran is not a crook, not game, Wran worked out a deal with Murdock (sic) for his support." This conversation attesting to Wran's honesty occurred on 6 April 1980 at a time when, according to the program, Wran was supposedly fixing the lease for Saffron. This was ignored by the ABC.

Despite providing no evidence of Wran's involvement, and despite evidence that the lease did not end up with Saffron, the program's presenter posed the question: "Why would Neville Wran get involved in this? Why would Neville Wran have taken that call from Murphy and make sure that the lease swung over to Abe Saffron?" These are good questions. At this point a properly functioning editor-in-chief would have pointed out there was no corroborating evidence that Wran did "get involved" and that all the evidence collected suggested Wran was not involved. The program makers should have been told to find rigorous corroborating evidence of Wran's involvement. Instead, the program cut to a former police prosecutor Wayne Evans, who told viewers: "There had to be something in it for Wran". Evans is the same person Clarrie Briese relies on for his "sensational evidence" which was discredited in the previous chapter. The program did not explain why it used Evans as a talking head since Evans had not been involved in investigating the Luna Park fire or in the subsequent coronial inquiry.

At this point the viewer would have been waiting for the ABC to reveal, in the words of Evans, what was "in it for Wran". Will they produce evidence of money being paid? Or evidence of a blackmail obligation? What was in it for Wran that he would jeopardise his entire political career by ensuring that the lease for a major public asset was delivered to a person of whom Wran had said in Parliament in November 1978, seven months before the fire: "It is a matter of notoriety in the community that Mr Saffron is not a person of good repute".

This is where the program descended into complete farce. The ABC produced as evidence a female consort of Saffron, Rosemary Opitz, who claimed Wran "on occasions" attended Friday night drinks at Saffron's house, in the company of others, and that the two were "pally, really pally". We are meant to draw a sinister conclusion, solely on the word of a Saffron intimate, that Wran was benefiting from a long-standing association, indeed friendship, between the state's most senior politician and the state's most prominent criminal.

Does anyone outside the ABC believe that Wran, universally acknowledged as intelligent and politically astute, would mix socially with the person widely known as "Mr Sin" in an environment where he would have been observed by others? Did not anyone inside the ABC wonder why these 'Abe-Nifty Happy Hours' had remained secret for the last 40 years in a city which floats on rumour and malicious gossip? Healthy scepticism is obviously in short supply in the ABC.

The ABC did not provide a single piece of corroboration for this claim. Nor did the program, for balance, approach former close personal staff of Wran, such as his private secretary or his press secretaries. These were the days when a premier's staff allocation was a fraction of that of today and these staffers lived in Wran's pocket from morning to night. All would have poured scorn on the claim if asked. That is not what the ABC wanted to hear.

Given Wran was unable to defend himself, the ABC should have informed viewers that Wran had told the NSW Parliament on 30 November 1977: "I do not know, I have never met, I have never eaten with and I have never been in any circumstances with a gentleman called Abe Saffron." Is it likely that Wran would have made such a declaration if it was possible that others present at these 'happy hours' could come forward and assert that Wran had misled the Parliament? The consequences of a such a misleading of Parliament would have been severe. Wran, as noted in chapter nine, forced one of his ministers to resign for misleading the Parliament.

It may have been salutary for the ABC to have noted that Wran's denial came after the then Opposition Leader, Sir Eric Willis, had claimed in Parliament that Wran had lunched with Saffron at La Causerie restaurant on 14 July 1977. Willis later altered his allegation to say that on this day Wran was lunching with the police commissioner when Saffron approached the table and engaged the police commissioner in conversation and he did not know if Saffron had spoken to Wran. Willis was further embarrassed when Wran was able to demonstrate that on the day in question, he was guest of honour at a luncheon of the Australia-America Association at the Wentworth Hotel, in the presence of several hundred people. Willis learned the hard way not to trust uncorroborated eyewitness accounts of Wran being in Saffron's company. That should have been a warning to the ABC.

Former Labor Premier Bob Carr, who understands the constant public attention the office brings, has said: "It is absolutely inconceivable that Wran would have attended on Saffron, sipping drinks in the home of Sydney's celebratory crime lord". Gary Sturgess, a former senior adviser to Liberal Premier Nick Greiner, and a political opponent of Wran, has also rubbished the allegation. "I do not accept the claim that Wran attended social functions organised by Saffron. Based on everything I know about Wran, having studied him closely for many years and helped design the tactics which repeatedly exposed his refusal to take corruption seriously, I do not believe for a moment he would have attended a social gathering with a person of Saffron's reputation," he said.

We turn now to the program's second allegation about Wran. Towards the end of the program the presenter, Caro Meldrum-Hanna, told the families of the victims, in a segment that good taste should have excluded, their findings about the cause of death of their loved ones. The fire, according to the ABC, had been lit by three bikies; the bikies had been acting on the instructions of Abe Saffron; and the cover up of this crime "went right to the top". The presenter's exact words were: "Essentially the allegation is that the reason why [the investigation] didn't go any further was because of corruption further up. There are a lot of powerful people in powerful places protecting Abe. So, it went right to the top we are told." In the context of the program this statement – "went right to the top" – can only mean that the ABC was now accusing Neville Wran of also being involved in covering up a mass murder.

In three episodes the program produced no evidence at all that Wran was involved in a cover up. This false statement was allowed to go to air by those supervising the program. ABC management quickly distanced themselves from this claim. Managing director David Anderson told a Senate Estimates hearing on 26 May 2021: "This program in no way suggested that Neville Wran had any involvement in or knowledge of the fire at Luna Park". Further, "it did not say that Wran was involved in a cover-up of the cause of the fire".

Anderson can only make this claim by ignoring the words of the presenter cited above. He did not explain how this statement went to air, and remains in the program, if the ABC does not believe it.

Was there a conspiracy to cover up the cause of the fire? The first episode of the program dissected the police investigation and discredited the initial police finding that the cause was an electrical fault. That conclusion, however, was not new. It had already been effectively dismissed by the coronial inquiry in September 1979. The magistrate conducting the inquiry, Kevin Anderson, described an electrical fault as "most unlikely" although he added "the possibility of such a cause cannot be completely excluded". He made an open finding: "how the fire was ignited the evidence adduced does not enable me to say". Anderson found "the most probable cause of the fire was ignition of flammable litter by a cigarette or match carelessly or recklessly discarded by a person riding a train".

The National Crime Authority, with far greater investigative expertise and resources than the ABC, concluded that "it cannot say whether the fire was deliberately lit or not" but found no evidence to suggest it was arson. The NCA also found that the initial police investigation was "grossly inadequate" but that there "is no evidence that the inadequacy of the police investigation was due to dishonesty or corruption". The NCA also found no evidence that organised crime was involved. The involvement of the NCA in investigating the fire, incidentally, was an initiative of the Wran government. As noted in chapter two, the NSW government and the Federal government collaborated in requiring the NCA to investigate, as described in the title of the report, "certain matters arising out of certain fires which took place in Sydney in the period 1979 to 1982." This was Commonwealth Reference No. 1 and NSW Reference No. 3. So much for the cover up going "right to the top".

To reach the conclusion that bikies lit the fire the program selectively relied on the words of the only witness who claimed to have overheard the bikies talking about the fire. This witness, whose claims are not new, said he heard one bikie say: "I spread the kerosene out and I lit it with a match". The same witness also said he then heard another bikie say: "You shouldn't have done that", while a third bikie said, "Come on, let's split". The comment that "you shouldn't have done that" is an odd statement by a member of a gang of bikies who had been commissioned to start the fire. If the bikies had been so commissioned, would they have needed one of their number to say they needed to "split"? If this witness is to be believed – and his evidence is uncorroborated – this suggests the fire was probably a mindless act of arson, of the sort seen every bushfire season. The program relies completely on the first bikie's alleged statement and ignores completely the second and the third, even though the alleged comments came from the same witness.

Even if we make the heroic assumption that the program is correct in fingering the bikies as the culprits, what evidence was produced to link the bikies to Saffron? The only direct evidence was an interview with a former bikie, who did not claim to have been one of those involved, who was not named, would not be filmed and whose voice appears to have been deliberately distorted. At no point in the interview did this person directly accuse Saffron. When asked if Saffron was behind the fire, he replied: "Yeah, pretty close to the mark". Further asked: "Do you reckon he got away with it? Abe Saffron?" he replied: "Well he ran the show". Questioned further the reply was: "Everyone slung each other a quid and the world was their oyster and they could do what they liked". This is not 'evidence' that would be considered useful in a committal hearing.

The only other 'evidence' produced is circumstantial. Saffron was investigated by police, and as noted above by the National Crime Authority, for a series of arson fires around Kings Cross and Oxford Street. Saffron was never charged. These fires, however, were professionally lit and nobody lost their lives. If Saffron was the mastermind behind these fires presumably the motive was an insurance payout. He had no such motive at Luna Park since he was not the lessee. The *modus operandi* of a professional arsonist is to light fires in the dead of night when a building is unoccupied. Why would Saffron have not used the same professional arsonist at Luna Park to ensure there was no loss of life? Why engage three bikies who, judging from their alleged comments, were rank amateurs as arsonists?

The ABC was not the first media outlet to claim that Saffron was behind the ghost train fire. *The Sydney Morning Herald* on 26 May 2007 had made this claim, based on the uncorroborated word of a niece of Saffron, Anne Buckingham. She was dissatisfied with the amount left to her in Saffron's will and was preparing to challenge it. The challenge should have been a red light to the *Herald*. A person who believes her uncle is a mass murderer but, nevertheless, puts her hand out for a greater share of his ill-gotten gains should not be considered a trustworthy source. Buckingham subsequently retracted her claims but the *Herald* apparently has proof she made the accusation. Buckingham's claims were also disputed by Saffron's son, Alan, who was not normally a defender of his father's reputation. Alan Saffron, now dead, was another dissatisfied with his share of his father's will. He was reported in the same paper on 27 May 2007 as saying: "It was a straight-out accident. There was no suggestion that anyone had anything to do with the fire".

For the ABC to tell the victims' families there was a cover up, the program must first have established without doubt that there was a crime and therefore a criminal or criminals on whose behalf those involved in the conspiracy were protecting. Without a crime there can be no cover up. The ABC did not establish that a crime of organised arson occurred that night at Luna Park. The uncorroborated evidence of arson it produced points in the direction of a senseless act by one person. No convincing evidence was produced to undermine the conclusion of the National Crime Authority that there was no evidence the fire was started deliberately and that it could find no evidence of dishonesty or corruption in the police investigation.

Neville Wran was not the only victim of the program. The families of the victims were cruelly misled by the ABC. They were fed a story that had little substantiation and lacked credibility. The ABC falsely led the families to believe they now knew the truth about the deaths of their loved ones.

The ABC was extremely disappointed with the reception of the program. The rest of the mainstream media largely ignored it. A broadcast that a widely respected and electorally popular NSW premier had a close and corrupt relationship with a leading crime figure and had been involved in the cover up of a horrible crime is, in news terms, the equivalent of a bomb exploding in a crowded venue. Normally such revelations merit page one treatment in newspapers and are lead items on commercial television news bulletins. Instead, there was scepticism about the program in other media, a quality lacking inside the ABC. Despite heavy promotion by the ABC, the only major follow up was a negative one in *The Australian,* on 24 April 2021, almost a month later. A long article by Troy Bramston highlighted flaws in the program.

The 'Wran haters', of course, lauded the program. Richard Ackland was typical. Although educated in the laws of evidence he wrote in his online legal newsletter that the program found "there was strong evidence that [the fire] was down to bikies engaged by Saffron". Ackland also claimed Wran "would be passionately involved in knowing details about valuable property deals and future developments on the foreshore of the harbour". He overlooked the fact that the new lease for Luna Park was to continue to operate an amusement park and commercial development of the site was not permitted.

The program may have failed to excite the rest of the media but it cannot be said the program, after broadcast, was ignored inside the ABC. When the many flaws of the program were brought to the attention of ABC Chair, Ita Buttrose, she commissioned an external review by a veteran investigative journalist, Chris Masters, and political scientist, Dr Rodney Tiffen. Their report, while positive about aspects of the program, was critical of the program's conclusions about Wran. The reviewers found "there is no evidence of Wran interfering with [the bureaucratic committee's] decision-making" over the new lease. On the claim that Wran was "pally" with Saffron the reviewers found "no solid evidence was given to corroborate her most serious claims and no contrary views were presented." On the claim that the cover up of the police investigation went "right to the top" was not a reference to Wran, they found the comment, and other material presented, "left the reviewers with a strong impression the program concluded Wran was complicit".

The program was also critically dissected by the ABC's own *Media Watch* program which supported the criticisms by the external reviewers about the program's allegations about Wran. The presenter, Paul Barry, was scathing about ABC staff's dismissal of the review's findings in a statement by the head of ABC News and Current Affairs, Gaven Morris. "Frankly, we are dumbfounded by that response. To argue that the program did not point the finger at Wran – and that those eminent reviewers had got it wrong – is in our view indefensible. The ABC really needs to do better. In some respects, it was a great program; in other respects, it went too far," Barry concluded.

ABC executives must have been aware before it was broadcast that the program was in breach of the ABC's Editorial Policies (relating to 'accuracy' and 'fair and honest dealing') and its Editorial Guidance Notes. These stress that "one of the central challenges for any journalist or content maker is how far they need to cross reference, investigate and confirm through multiple sources". Obligations of accuracy and obtaining multiple sources are not cancelled if a person is dead and unable to sue. The obligation is even more important when a person is unable to defend himself or herself. The external reviewers were not permitted to assess the program against the Editorial Policies but no reader of their report is left in any doubt they considered the policies had been breached.

Senior executives were clearly embarrassed about the program's lack of corroboration for the allegations about Wran when questioned at the Senate Estimates hearing on 26 May 2021. Craig McMurtrie, then the ABC editorial director, told senators, in effect, that the editorial guidelines do not apply if a person is simply collateral damage in a program. McMurtrie said: "The matter concerning Mr Wran was not the focus of the documentary. Normally, in these sorts of situations where they were going to explore a particular allegation or line of inquiry, that would certainly require them to speak to other sources." This was nonsense. There were two specific allegations of criminality against Wran, as well as a claim that he was friendly with Saffron, so it was absurd for McMurtrie to state Wran was not a focus of the documentary. McMurtrie, who was the ABC executive in charge of the corporation's Editorial Policies, must have known there is no such carve out in these policies.

ABC editorial management's failures on this program, and the dismissal of the reviewer's criticisms, had significant consequences internally. The ABC Board also commissioned an external review of the internal complaints-handling procedures – after a complaint about the program had been dismissed – and this led to the establishment of an internal ombudsman to consider future complaints. To the dismay of some the board decided the ombudsman would report to the board, not to the managing director. The dismissal of the reviewers' criticisms of the program was also reportedly a factor in the appointment of a new head of News and Current Affairs.

Judgment of the program by the journalistic establishment came later in 2021. The program did not make the short list for the Walkley Awards, the Australian media's premier awards for journalism. Nor did the program win an award in that year's Kennedy Awards for crime journalism. The program was also entered in the awards of the Australian Academy of Cinema and Television Arts (AACTA) but won only for its photography. That is an extremely poor return for the ABC for a program which cost $2 million at a time when the ABC was complaining about funding shortfalls. Unsurprisingly ABC management let it be known internally that it would not commission any further programs in the 'Exposed' true crime series.

This was not the end of the ramifications of the program. On 10 April 2021, shortly after the final episode was broadcast, the NSW Coroner, Teresa O'Sullivan, announced she had received an application for a fresh inquest into the fire from a person "with sufficient standing" under the *Coroners Act*. The coroner said she had formally asked NSW Police to review "all evidence concerning the cause and origin of the fire and the circumstances surrounding the deaths as a result of the fire". She said she would consider whether a further inquest would be held when she had received a report from the police. In July 2021 the NSW government also announced a $1 million reward for information about the fire to assist the police investigation. Three years later the reward is unclaimed.

Following the coroner's request, the then police commissioner Mick Fuller announced the matter would be investigated by a special Strike Force Sedgeman. This would be drawn from the Homicide Squad's Unsolved Homicide Team under the supervision of the Homicide Squad's Commander, Detective Superintendent Danny Doherty. This was to be the second major investigation of the fire by police, not counting the original investigation in 1979. On 13 October 1985 *The Sydney Morning Herald* reported that the NSW Police Internal Security Unit, a special section of Internal Affairs, had launched a fresh investigation following allegations of a cover-up of the cause of the fire. The article relied on the same witness, later to feature in the ABC documentary, who claimed the fire had been started by a group of bikies. The article noted this was now the third version given by this witness who had originally given a statement to the police who investigated the fire in 1979. The witness said he had then changed his original story, admitting he had been trying to impress his companions. This 1985 investigation found no evidence of a cover up.

The original police investigation of the Luna Park fire was criticised as hasty and inadequate by the National Crime Authority. No such criticism could be made of the thoroughness of the lengthy investigation by Strike Force Sedgman. This is despite its work being hindered for several months because of the ABC's refusal to hand over material which the police requested. The strike force included two of the force's most experienced homicide detectives. The report was delivered to the coroner on 11 January 2023. Sixteen months later, at the time of writing, the coroner had still not decided whether she would hold a new inquest. The wheels of justice grind slowly at the Coroner's Court.

According to senior police sources, the strike force found no evidence to dispute the findings of the previous inquiries into the fire by the police, and the National Crime Authority, or to dispute the findings of the original coronial inquiry in 1979. The report apparently notes that the ABC refused to hand over material, including the full tape of the witness who claimed to have overheard the conversation of the bikies. The ABC placed considerable reliance on this witness. Both the ABC and the coroner refused to answer questions about whether and why the ABC withheld material from the NSW Police.

6

THE RUSSIAN TANK AND THE NETWORK OF INFLUENCE

"Just before I left for overseas I got in touch with N, you see, the trump. I said to him, You owe us one favour. You're always f***n' howling about this fellow, but I said, but please appoint him to this f***n' job and get him off my back, that big Jegorow… I just got a phone call from his … er, you know, the other trump. And he said, By the way, he said, er, Nif said to tell you that he's given that big bastard the appointment …(They both laugh) … as permanent deputy chairman or someone of the Ethnics Commission." Police transcript of an illegally recorded telephone conversation between Morgan Ryan and an official of the Department of Immigration, 31 March 1979.

"Again it should be noted that Ryan appears, from his later discussions with others (in relation to the information he received from Justice Murphy) that he has a propensity to embellish". Report of the Parliamentary Commission of Inquiry into the behaviour of Justice Murphy, 'Allegation No. 18, Appointment of Bill Jegorow'.

Morgan Ryan was a small-town boy who became, for a time, the best-known solicitor in NSW and possibly in Australia. His paternal grandfather, after whom he was named, had opened a small store in Gundagai in 1882. By the time of his death in 1904, the store had grown into the town's largest business. On his death a local paper noted "his success in life was due to his perseverance, steady habits and business uprightedness" and described him as "a sound, sensible and upright Christian." When the young Morgan was born in 1920, the family was established as one of the most respected in the Gundagai district, prominent in community affairs and the Catholic Church. The apple was to fall a long way from the tree.

Morgan Ryan's early ambition was to be a jockey and he retained a lifelong interest in horse racing and gambling. He later told a newspaper that he was part of a group who won sixty thousand pounds on Dream King in the 1961 Australian Cup at Flemington. The newspaper took Ryan's account of his good fortune at face value. Digging reveals that Dream King, suspiciously, won at odds of 10 to 1 after being unplaced in its previous 10 starts. Ryan apparently managed to place bets at 33 to 1, before the odds shortened. Ryan's share of the winnings enabled him to build a house at Neutral Bay on Sydney Harbour, which in 2019 was listed for sale for $33 million by his widow Dorothy.

After war service Ryan studied to become a solicitor and qualified, through the Solicitors' Admission Board, in 1948. In 1950, with a partner Ron Brock, he founded a law firm, Morgan Ryan and Brock. Among the barristers the law firm briefed were Lionel Murphy and, later, Neville Wran. They were not alone. A list of barristers briefed by the firm is an honour roll of the Sydney Bar. In 1984 Wran was forced to defend himself in Parliament from Opposition claims that he was a "known associate" of Ryan. Wran said that to claim Ryan, the person who had nicknamed him 'Nifty', was a friend of his was to put the relationship at too high a level. Wran listed in Parliament 30 federal and state judges, many of them distinguished, who had been briefed as barristers by Ryan's firm. "Is anyone willing to say that any one of those reputable, honourable judges is in some way tainted because he was briefed by the firm of Morgan Ryan and Brock?", he challenged.

One of Lionel Murphy's early legal successes was to gain the reinstatement of Ray Gietzelt, later to become a prominent national union official, in a factional brawl within the NSW branch of the Miscellaneous Workers' Union. The solicitor who briefed Murphy was Morgan Ryan and the two men became friends. Unfortunately for Murphy, Ryan's client list would come to extend well beyond the union movement to include people who, in the words of historian Frank Bongiorno, "tended to figure whenever a royal commission or muckraking journalist was reporting on the seamier side of Sydney". These included crime boss Abe Saffron, who in 1973 was represented by Morgan Ryan and Brock at the Moffitt royal commission into allegations of organised crime in clubs.

Beginning in the late 1960s, NSW police mounted an increasingly sophisticated operation involving the illegal interception of telephone conversations of alleged criminal targets. The operation was only discontinued in January 1984 after a transmitter used by police was discovered by a Telecom technician who informed federal authorities. This was not a rogue police operation as widely believed. The phone tapping began at the direction of the then police commissioner, Norman Allen. A royal commission in 1986 found: "The existence of the system was known to and either expressly or tacitly approved by each succeeding commissioner prior to the present Commissioner [John Avery]". The illegal phone tapping was widely known among the senior ranks of the NSW police. The royal commission also discovered: "Officers of the Victorian Police knew of the system and were prepared to use it. Even members of the AFP [Australian Federal Police] were prepared to use the system when the AFP's limited powers did not permit a particular interception to be made".

Over 200 interceptions were conducted in the 15 years of operation. One of the interceptions involved the home phone of Morgan Ryan. This involved three separate operations. The first, from 18 March 1979 until late April 1979, was code-named 'Mad Dog'. This seems to have been instigated after Ryan was mentioned on an intercept of an arrested drug dealer. The second operation, code-named 'Rabid', began on 7 February 1980 and was terminated on 10 May 1980 because the Bureau of Crime Intelligence (BCI) considered it delivered "a lack of worthwhile intelligence". The third operation, from January to March 1981, was instigated at the request of the AFP even though the AFP had the ability to seek legal authorisation of its own intercepts.

The existence of the taping remained secret outside the police force until 25 November 1983 when Marian Wilkinson revealed in the *National Times* the bugging of a person "reputed to be a 'Mr Fix-it' for organised crime in Australia". The story, under the heading "Big Shots Bugged", alleged the tapes revealed possible crimes but did not name participants or publish transcripts. It was an open secret in Sydney that the 'Mr Fix-it' was Ryan and that Justice Lionel Murphy, then on the High Court, was one of those caught on the tapes. The NSW Police Commissioner Cec Abbott ordered an investigation by the head of the BCI, Superintendent RC Shepherd. This was a bizarre choice since the BCI was a key player in the illegal taping, as Abbott must have known. The royal commission found that Shepherd had reported to Abbott on 9 December 1983 that "the only telephone intercepts (with) which this Department is involved are those where a combined operation is taking place with the Australian Federal Police and the warrant for such intercepts are taken out by the Australian Federal Police." The royal commission concluded: "This statement was blatantly untrue, both to the knowledge of Shepherd and Abbott."

On 2 February 1984 *The Age* newspaper in Melbourne began publishing a series of articles, with a tag line 'A Network of Influence', based on an edited version of 524 pages of photocopied transcripts and summaries. The newspaper later confirmed these were given to it by crime journalist Bob Bottom, who had also provided the material for the *National Times* story. Even though *The Age* did not name the participants in the transcripts, the identities were soon revealed in various parliaments. Most attention was given to conversations between "the solicitor", Morgan Ryan, and "the judge", Justice Lionel Murphy.

We noted in the Wran biography: "Wran himself was mentioned in conversations on the tapes but there is no evidence of impropriety. In fact, one reference was flattering to Wran: a police summary said that, in a conversation Ryan had with a business acquaintance, 'they agree Wran is not a crook'". The full reference is: "They agree that Wran is not a crook, not game. Wran worked out a deal with Murdock (sic) for his support."

The Wran biography further noted that Ryan "invoked the Wran name regularly in the taped conversations, but it seems that his influence with him did not match his boasts about it to other people". This is obvious in the only questionable incident in which Wran can be considered to figure. According to *The Age*, the transcripts showed that in March 1979 "the judge promised to help secure a highly paid public service job for a man connected with the solicitor". The actual transcript, however, showed only that the judge agreed to inquire if the man was being appointed. In fact, as later revealed, this person was not appointed to the position until 19 months later, in October 1980. Documentation released in 2017, and not previously reported, confirms the appointment was a sideways transfer, on existing salary, and neither Murphy nor Ryan had any role or influence in the appointment.

This allegation was one of a number made against Murphy when the Federal Parliament established in May 1986 the Parliamentary Commission of Inquiry into Murphy's conduct. The commission was established after other High Court judges objected to Murphy returning to the bench following his acquittal on charges that he had sought to pervert the course of justice. The allegation, number 18, stated: "It is alleged that Justice Murphy in or about March 1979, and while a Justice of the High Court of Australia, agreed with Morgan Ryan that he, the Judge, would speak to the Premier of New South Wales, the Honourable Neville Wran, for the purpose of procuring the appointment of Wadim Jegorow to the position of Deputy Chairman of the Ethnic Affairs Commission of New South Wales. Further the Judge subsequently spoke to the Premier for that purpose and later informed Ryan that the Premier had told him that Jegorow would be appointed to the position."

This allegation arose from a transcript of a taped conversation on 20 March 1979 in which Ryan urges Murphy to "ring Nift" and to "please get onto him for the Jegorow. They're driving me mad." He further advises Murphy that "Jegorow is suited for the job, mad and all as he is." It finishes with a plea: "Will you ring him, please, and talk to him about it, please", to which Murphy replied: "Okay". Eleven days later, on 31 March 1979, the transcripts record Murphy telling Ryan that he had talked to "Neville" and he was appointing Jegorow as Deputy Chairman. Murphy is further recorded as telling Ryan: "He'll give it to him. But I think your fellow might have been wanting to make it some long tenure or something. Don't know what it is. He said he wasn't doing that …" to which Ryan replied: "Righto".

In a later conversation Ryan told Jegorow: "You're getting that appointment… don't push this ten year business … just take the appointment and then we'll make it ten years okay? … All I know was that he just said to tell me that you are getting that appointment as Deputy Chairman, but not to push the ten year part of it, because, er, we can talk about that later …" Jegorow is pathetically grateful in his recorded response: "Oh Morgan, you're a beauty. Look, when am I going to shout you a big fat dinner?"

Ryan, who had what the parliamentary commission staff describe as "a propensity to embellish", later reports to an official of the Department of Immigration: "Just before I left for overseas I got in touch with N, you see, the trump. I said to him, You owe us one favour. You're always f****n' howling about this fellow, but I said, but please appoint him to this f****n' job and get him off my back, that big Jegorow …I just got a phone call from his …er, you know, the other trump. And he said, By the way, he said, er, Nif said to tell you that he's given that big bastard the appointment …(They both laugh) …as permanent deputy chairman or someone (sic) of the Ethnics Commission (sic)." There is no evidence from the transcripts that Ryan "got in touch with N", who is presumably Wran. Ryan would not have been harassing Murphy if he had the ability to ring Wran himself.

Wadim Jegorow, widely known as Bill, was born to Russian parents in Vilnius (then part of Poland) and migrated to Australia in 1951 as a 16-year-old from a displaced persons camp. He graduated in law from Sydney University and joined the NSW Public Service in the 1950s as a parole officer. He left the public service and practiced for a few years as a barrister before re-joining in 1971 as a senior legal officer in the Forestry Commission. *The Sydney Morning Herald* noted in his obituary on 4 May 2006: "He was a big man and his manner was so relentless that he was also called, occasionally and with less affection, the 'Russian tank'". Wran's staff regarded him as an office pest, constantly turning up without appointment and loitering in the hope of tugging Wran's sleeve.

Jegorow was an early member of what became known, cynically but not entirely unfairly, as the "professional ethnic industry". Ethnic community leaders jostled each other for political preferment and, in turn, were courted by the political parties seeking the electoral support they believed the various ethnic leaders could deliver. Jegorow, who had been an unsuccessful Labor candidate at a NSW election in the 1960s, was an alderman on Ashfield Council and active in the work of the Inner Western Suburbs Migrant Group. This group, along with others, morphed into the Ethnic Communities Council of NSW, which Jegorow chaired. The council was launched by both Prime Minister Gough Whitlam and Opposition Leader Malcom Fraser in July 1975. Jegorow was later appointed to the Australian Ethnic Affairs Commission by Prime Minister Fraser.

In 1977 the new Wran government established the Ethnic Affairs Commission of NSW. Jegorow was appointed a part-time member of the commission and its part-time deputy chairman. There was only one full-time commissioner, the chairman Dr Paolo Totaro, an Italian-born businessman and arts administrator. Documentation prepared for the Parliamentary Commission of Inquiry, which was only made public in 2017, shows Jegorow took his honorary responsibilities seriously. He was apparently spending so much time on ethnic affairs work, to the neglect of his responsibilities in the Forestry Commission, that he was being threatened with public service disciplinary action. Jegorow wrote to the Premier on 12 March 1979 advising Wran of the difficulties he was facing. He concluded his letter with a request: "I therefore seek your assistance in resolving the present situation by enabling me to work on a full-time basis in the area of ethnic affairs." The letter makes no reference to seeking a full-time position of deputy chairman of the Ethnic Affairs Commission.

Jegorow's letter to Wran appears to have prompted him to approach Morgan Ryan seeking to make use of his supposed influence. The phone conversations recorded in the transcripts occurred two weeks after the letter. Jegorow might not have specifically mentioned in his letter the full-time job "in the area of ethnic affairs" he was seeking but he appears to have been lobbying Ryan to have his part-time position as deputy chairman turned into a full-time one. Morgan Ryan was not the only person whom 'the Russian tank' lobbied. Wran told Parliament, on 23 May 1984, that Jegorow "has more contacts than anyone I know. I would not know whether anyone rang me to ask me to give Bill Jegorow a lift up the ladder but I do know that he probably rang about 5000 people to try to get one, including members of the Opposition."

Jegorow seems to have approached Ryan because he apparently believed Ryan's boasts to others that he had influence with Wran. Ryan's motive in taking up Jegorow's cause with Murphy – there is no evidence he spoke to Wran – appears to have been venal. The transcripts suggest Ryan believed Jegorow may have been useful to him in immigration matters, the issue that caused Ryan's troubles with the law in the 'Murphy affair'. If this was the reason, Ryan had an extremely poor understanding of the role of what was a state government advisory body. The commission had no role or influence in immigration matters which are a federal government responsibility.

It is not known if Jegorow got the chance to shout Ryan a "big fat dinner" but, if so, it was for nothing. Jegorow soon learned that he was wrong in his belief that Ryan had influence with Wran. Despite Murphy apparently telling Ryan in March 1979 that "he'll give it to him", Wran took no action. Six months later, in September 1979, and with Jegorow facing a renewed threat of public service disciplinary action, the secretary of the Premier's Department, Gerry Gleeson, intervened. In a memo, he presented Wran with three options. These were: make Jegorow a full-time member (or deputy chairman) of the Ethnic Affairs Commission; appoint him to Wran's personal staff; or appoint him to the Premier's Department. Gleeson said he did not favour either of the first two options. Appointing Jegorow as a full-time deputy chairman "would make the position of the Chairman [Dr Totaro] quite difficult" while placing him on Wran's personal staff "would create jealousies within the ethnic affairs area and with the Ethnic Affairs Commission." Gleeson advised he favoured the third option because "it distances Mr Jegorow from the Premier and puts him under the control of the Secretary."

Wran accepted Gleeson's advice. With the approval of the Public Service Board, Jegorow was appointed under section 75 of the *Public Service Act* in a temporary capacity as Consultant (Ethnic Communities) in the Premier's Department. He assumed these duties on 22 October 1979. This appointment does not appear to have attracted a higher salary. The parliamentary commission's staff reported that "the material contained on the files suggests that the appointment of Jegorow to that (and other) positions was made on the basis of recommendations emanating from State Government Departments and based on valid and appropriate staffing considerations." Ironically, given Jegorow had apparently wanted to become a full-time deputy chairman of the Ethnic Affairs Commission, Gleeson decided Jegorow's new position in the Premier's Department meant it was no longer appropriate for him to be on the commission. Jegorow was forced to resign as deputy chairman and from the commission. He was replaced as part-time deputy chairman by Dr George Peponis, a medical practitioner and captain of the Canterbury-Bankstown rugby league team.

One year later, on 13 October 1980, Jegorow was finally appointed, on his existing public service salary, as a full-time deputy chairman of the Ethnic Affairs Commission. This appointment was prompted by Peponis resigning from the commission in July 1980 because of his rugby league and professional commitments. Peponis advised Wran by letter that he regretted that these commitments – the Canterbury-Bankstown Bulldogs won the rugby league premiership later that year – were causing him to miss commission meetings and he felt this was unfair on others. He resigned as deputy chairman and from the commission. The parliamentary commission staff noted: "There is no suggestion that Dr Peponis who was the part-time Deputy Chairman of the Ethnic Affairs Commission was forced from that position to make way for Jegorow."

A further irony in this story is that Jegorow now resisted his appointment as full-time deputy chairman. No reason is given but it is possible he believed this would be a downgrading in status. A memo to the premier from a senior officer of the Premier's Department suggests the department considered he was not providing value for money. Peter Rath, Assistant Secretary of the Community Relations Division, "recommended for the Premier's consideration that Mr Jegorow be appointed as Deputy Chairman of the Ethnic Affairs Commission for a period of two years on his current salary …". Mr Rath advised the Premier: "It is known that Mr Jegorow does not wish to transfer to the Ethnic Affairs Commission. However, it is considered that his contribution does not justify him occupying the present position." The desire by senior departmental officials to ensure 'the Russian tank' was no longer their responsibility appears to have outweighed their previous concern that appointing Jegorow to this position would "make the position of the chairman quite difficult". Wran accepted the recommendation and on 13 October 1980, nineteen months after *The Age* transcript conversations, Jegorow was appointed to the full-time position of deputy chairman of the Ethnic Affairs Commission. This was a position he no longer desired; was a sideways transfer on his existing salary; was not an elevation to a "highly paid public service job"; and Morgan Ryan and Lionel Murphy played no role.

Not surprisingly, the parliamentary commission staff concluded: "In view of the circumstances it is recommended that no further inquiries be made in this matter." This judgment was repeated later by Justice Donald Stewart, who was appointed to examine *The Age* transcripts, and who found no criminal offence had been committed. Ian Temby QC, the Federal Director of Public Prosecutions, had already reached a similar conclusion, even though the belief at that stage was that Jegorow had been appointed to a highly paid public service job. Temby advised the Federal Government on 28 February 1984: "There is nothing unusual about people in high places suggesting or urging that given individuals should be appointed to particular Government positions. It would of course be a matter of great concern if that was done in order to secure some favour, or for any sort of consideration. One can imagine circumstances in which the taking of steps to secure such an appointment would be by reason of accompanying circumstances be criminal in nature. There is nothing in material I have seen to suggest any such accompanying circumstances. I cannot think that any further investigation of the matter is likely to be at all fruitful."

The confusion over Jegorow's appointment began with *The Age*. At the time the newspaper received and published the transcripts, in February 1984, Jegorow was a full-time deputy chairman of the Ethnic Affairs Commission. Reading the conversations between Ryan, Murphy and Jegorow, which took place almost five years earlier, in March 1979, *Age* journalists obviously assumed Jegorow's current position was the "highly paid public service job" arranged by Ryan. This was an understandable assumption for *The Age* to make but is a lesson that the transcript conversations should not be taken at face value. Two and two made five in this case.

In the Wran biography we wrote: "At worst, Wran had done Morgan Ryan a favour on one occasion – if Ryan's version of events on the tape can be believed – by appointing Bill Jegorow as Deputy Chairman of the Ethnic Affairs Commission." This was written in 1986, well before the documentation of the parliamentary commission became available in 2017. We were right to add the qualification: if Ryan's version "can be believed." It is now apparent that not even our tentative conclusion can be justified. Despite the recorded comments by Murphy and Ryan, Wran did not appoint Jegorow to this position in March 1979 and the job he was appointed to six months later was not the position which Jegorow had sought. In the biography we also noted: "Clearly, Ryan was not loath to take credit, whether or not it was due." The parliamentary commission staff reached a similar conclusion: "Again it should be noted that Ryan appears, from his later discussions with others (in relation to the information he received from Justice Murphy) that he has a propensity to embellish". A "propensity to embellish" is a generous phrase; Ryan had a propensity to lie. If there was a 'network of influence', as *The Age* believed, the network did not include Wran.

Jegorow became another victim of *The Age* transcripts. After they were published, he was sidelined while this allegation and others were investigated by the Royal Commission of Inquiry Into Alleged Telephone Interceptions, headed by Justice Donald Stewart. The *Herald* noted in Jegorow's obituary: "Justice Stewart found that there was no criminal offence but Wran's successor, Barrie Unsworth, did not reappoint Jegorow, who was replaced by Irene Moss." Jegorow left the public service in 1987. He paid a high price for believing Morgan Ryan's boasts that he had influence with Neville Wran.

The publication by *The Age* of the transcripts and summaries has become known as 'the Age tapes' but this is a misnomer. *The Age* had possession of only three cassettes of recordings. These were also the only tapes in Bottom's possession. The royal commission found these cassettes were "not in any sense 'original' since they had been copied from reel-to-reel tapes." The correct name should be '*The Age* transcripts' since it was the 524 pages of photocopied material on which *The Age* relied. Even this name is not strictly accurate since some documents were summaries of taped conversations. Justice Stewart was later scathing about the accuracy of the summaries. In most instances *The Age* was unable to verify the transcripts against the actual recordings. If it had it would have spared the Murphy family from at least one embarrassing error. One transcript confused two speakers and reported the judge, when asked by the solicitor if he'd had a good time on holidays, replied: "If you can call getting tired and drunk and f…ng everything a good time." The question had been asked by the judge and it was the solicitor who boasted of his drunkenness and sexual exploits. *The Age* eventually corrected this mistake but it took two weeks to do so.

There has never been an explanation from the newspaper, or from Bottom, of why he possessed 524 pages of transcripts and summaries but so few tapes. A claim has since been made, and frequently repeated, that the tapes were destroyed by the relevant police because Wran had threatened to jail the offenders. This claim makes no sense since Wran made this comment after *The Age* had published. This cannot therefore be an explanation for why *The Age* and Bottom had so few tapes.

Justice Stewart found the destruction of the evidence began as soon as *The Age* published the transcripts, and this was obviously before Wran's comment. The destruction appears to have been prompted by Abbott's decision to hold an investigation, this time a more serious one than that prompted by the *National Times*' story. Abbott announced a special task force drawn mainly from the Internal Affairs Branch of NSW Police. Justice Stewart reports a meeting of BCI and Technical Survey Unit (TSU) staff, addressed by Superintendent Shepherd and his second-in-command, Inspector RP Morrison. The staff were informed that "an investigation would take place and Morrison was of the view that the AFP might execute a search warrant on the offices of the BCI and the TSU." Instructions were given to the TSU staff to "get rid of all the gear here." They were also instructed to "locate and destroy all transcripts they held." A systematic destruction of all evidence began, including farcical attempts to burn material at a public barbeque spot and obtaining a boat and dumping equipment in the ocean somewhere off North Head.

Wran was certainly outraged and did say that those responsible for the taping ought to be jailed. His comments were not the reason police undertook the systematic destruction of all evidence but they did lead to a meeting being called of all former and present members of the TSU. This was held, according to the royal commission, at the Western Suburbs Soccer Club in March or April 1984. Justice Stewart records: "Shepherd addressed the meeting and suggested that the officers involved in such activity should deny any involvement when interviewed by the investigators of the Special Task Force. This approach was agreed to by all present." Stewart records similar meetings of BCI members.

Wran's comment about jailing was an empty threat as Wran, the lawyer, knew. This must also have been known by the police. The recordings were illegal because they were in breach of the *Telecommunications (Interception) Act*, which was federal law, not state law. Any move to charge the relevant police would have to be instigated by the Federal Attorney General or Director of Public Prosecutions. The Attorney at the time was Senator Gareth Evans, a prominent supporter of Murphy, and Evans took no such action, nor threatened such action.

The confusion over Wran's comments arose because the NSW government was in the process of amending the NSW *Listening Devices Act* before *The Age* published the transcripts and summaries. The government had announced its intention to amend the Act in July 1983, four months before the existence of the taping became known in November 1983 with the *National Times*' article. On the face of it, the *Listening Devices Act* seems to be relevant. The legislation makes it an offence to be in possession of a transcript or other records of a private conversation illegally recorded on a listening device. These provisions, however, must be 'read down' (to use legalese) to give effect to relevant federal legislation. Accordingly, the NSW law applies to listening devices other than telephone interception. The *Listening Devices Act* did not apply, and could not apply, to the illegal police telephone recordings. This had been confirmed by the High Court in *Miller v Miller* in 1978. The court ruled the NSW Act was invalid under section 109 of the Constitution as far as it purported to deal with the use of devices to listen to private conversations on a telephone. Section 109 provides that when Commonwealth and State law conflict then Commonwealth law prevails.

This truth did not prevent claims by Bottom that he was forced to seek publication of the transcripts at that time because of the threatened changes to the NSW Act. Nor did it prevent claims that Bottom was forced to take the material to Victoria because he was threatened with punitive legislation in NSW. We made this error in the Wran biography: "Bottom took the material outside the jurisdiction of NSW law." The material was in breach of federal law so it did not matter whether Bottom was temporarily residing in Melbourne or had stayed in Sydney. Bottom has since claimed that the amendments to the NSW Act were specifically aimed at him and that the police commissioner, personally, intended to arrest him. This is nonsense as was explained in chapter one.

It is unlikely that the NSW police involved in the telephone tapping were similarly confused. An operation of this magnitude, with official blessing, could not have been initiated and maintained without legal advice. The police would certainly have known they were breaching federal law, not state law, and were under no threat of fines or jailing by the NSW government. Similarly, these police must have known that the tapes and transcripts would, certainly, be inadmissible in any subsequent court proceedings against any individuals caught on the tapes or mentioned in transcripts or summaries. This raises the question, which has never been satisfactorily answered, of why NSW police embarked on this operation and did not instead seek the co-operation of the Federal Police thereby gaining proper authorisation under the federal legislation.

Wran's fury was not simply because his good friend Lionel Murphy was one of those caught by the illegal taping. Wran was a committed civil libertarian and was genuinely outraged that NSW police – and not just a rogue few – regarded themselves as being above the law. He was also offended that many people who were critical of his failure to 'clean up the cops' saw nothing wrong with this example of mass illegality by NSW police. Wran regarded this as hypocrisy and was critical of the NSW Council for Civil Liberties at a dinner in April 1984. He described the council's resolution, which condemned the taping but called for an inquiry into the contents, as "insipid." Wran's address was widely leaked and described as "a tirade", a description which would have been disputed by his staff and Labor MPs who had often witnessed Wran in full cry.

An eternal dilemma in a free society is how to balance respect for peoples' privacy with the need for effective law enforcement. This is why legislation such as the *Telecommunications (Interception and Access) Act*, as the federal legislation is now called, and the *Surveillance Devices Act*, which is now the relevant NSW legislation, include processes and safeguards to achieve this balance. These checks and balances have been rigorously investigated and debated by the relevant parliaments. The actions of NSW police in this instance cannot be described as effective law enforcement given that no charges were ever laid, and could never have been laid, based on the illegally recorded material. This is despite the Federal and NSW governments agreeing to a joint police task force, under the supervision of Ian Temby QC, to investigate whether charges could be brought for breaches of federal and state laws.

Wran also criticised *The Age* because the material could not be authenticated. He was entitled to be suspicious of its authenticity given he knew the transcripts told a false story of his role in the Jegorow appointment. Verification would have been a better word for Wran to have used. There seemed little doubt that the transcripts and summaries were genuine and had originated from within the NSW Police Force. This was later confirmed by the royal commission which concluded "that the material is the product of illegal telephone interceptions carried out by officers of the NSW Police in New South Wales". It was beyond the ability of *The Age*, however, to verify that the transcripts and summaries were a true and accurate transcription of the tapes, given the absence of most of the recordings. Even if the documents were faithfully transcribed, the Jegorow material showed that Ryan was a liar and any reliance on his claims was problematic.

Justice Stewart was only able to examine the material after the Federal government had given the police officers immunity from prosecution so they would be able to testify before his royal commission. He reported on 30 April 1986 and concluded: "The Commission is not satisfied that the transcript material in summary form has been prepared with sufficient care to be affirmed as wholly accurate. In addition, the Commission does not consider that many of the police concerned in the task of summary material possessed the necessary objectivity to render the summaries reliable." Justice Stewart also reported: "The police witnesses' inability for the most part to identify with any precision elements of the tapes, or to give firsthand evidence about them, renders it highly unlikely that any such material would be admitted as evidence in criminal proceedings." Ian Temby QC had already advised the Federal government, after reviewing the 524 pages provided to him by *The Age*, that "even if the material is authentic, and the identity of the speakers can be established, it does not follow that what has been said by any individual is true. It is not unusual for men to brag, to claim greater power than they have, even to tell simple untruths."

Temby's healthy scepticism was not shared by the editor of *The Age*, Creighton Burns, who was awarded in 1984 the Graham Perkin Award for 'Journalist of the Year' for his decision to publish the transcripts and summaries. These certainly provided good fodder for the media and titillation for readers but the publication by *The Age* achieved nothing for law enforcement. No prosecutions were attempted or achieved resulting from publication of the material.

Nothing in the 524 pages implicated Murphy in the following court cases and inquiries alleging he sought to interfere in court proceedings against Ryan. Nor is there a single reference to Luna Park in the material provided to *The Age*, even though later allegations against Wran over the lease of the amusement park are claimed to have been based on the illegal wire taps. The Jegorow incident shows that the transcripts must be treated with extreme caution in making judgments about evidence of criminal activity.

Wran, in a television interview after he announced his retirement as premier, acknowledged he had made a mistake with *The Age* transcripts. "I was so concerned about the rights and liberties of other people that I forgot about myself. If I had the time over again, I would have taken the transcripts and had them tabled in Parliament and to heck with the consequences because any fair reading of those transcripts will indicate to the public that neither myself nor any member of my government was answerable for anything at all", Wran said.

Historian Frank Bongiorno, assessing *The Age* transcripts in his book *The Eighties: The Decade That Transformed Australia*, concluded the material "while of a knockabout variety, was fairly innocuous and even without context seemed a long way from indicating corruption on the part of either interlocutor." In the Wran biography we noted: "On the night before publication, *The Sydney Morning Herald* baulked and decided not to use what was already a more sanitised version of the story than *The Age*. The *SMH*'s concerns were the difficulty of verifying the material and the credibility of its source, Bob Bottom, following the Cross Commission" (which is discussed in chapter nine). The decision was taken by the editor Chris Anderson and was supported by the editor-in-chief Vic Carroll and Fairfax's chief editorial executive Max Suich. An objective assessment of the significance of *The Age* transcripts, 40 years later, suggests that the award of 'Journalist of the Year' in 1984 should have gone instead to Chris Anderson.

7

THE MYSTERIOUS FORTY MILLION DOLLARS

"Are we to believe that this man, after he left parliament essentially at retirement age, made so much money between the age of 60 and 70 that he accumulated a property portfolio and other assets worth $40 million?" Andrew Rule.

"Neville Wran, when he got out of politics, had a pension and he had a house, and that was it." Former Liberal Prime Minister, Malcolm Turnbull.

"He expressed [to me] his amazement at the sheer wealth awash around Sydney and the underserving ease with which insiders appeared to acquire it." Wran, after leaving politics, according to Graham Freudenberg.

One Christmas Neville Wran and Graham Freudenberg were both alone. Wran's wife, Jill, was on an overseas holiday. Wran had accepted Christmas dinner with one of his sisters, Dorothy, who had 'married well' as the old saying goes. Wran phoned Freudenberg, his speechwriter, and invited him to accompany Wran to dinner. During the car trip to Roseville, on Sydney's north shore, Wran apologised to Freudenberg, explaining that during the evening he needed to take aside "Dottie", as he called his sister, because he had to borrow $10,000 from her.

Freudenberg relayed the conversation to me a few days later. We found it amusing since we were both familiar with the rumours already surrounding Wran. In typical Sydney fashion, there were whispers about Wran's supposed financial corruption and alleged Swiss bank accounts. His staff knew differently: Wran was always short of money. One of his assistant private secretaries had the task of organising payment of his bills. Often Wran's pen would hover over a cheque to settle a utility bill before he pushed it aside with a comment that it could wait another week or two. Wran's staff and colleagues also knew he was tight with his money. Brian Dale said: "Neville knew the value of a quid." Jack Ferguson joked to another Labor MP, Rodney Cavalier: "He takes every penny a prisoner."

Andrew Rule has claimed, correctly, that Wran became premier without a great deal of money behind him. Rule is wrong, however, in his explanation for Wran's lack of financial security. He told listeners to his podcast: "Neville Wran is no dill. He's a good young lawyer who, by and large, worked for the small end of town, for unions, and working people, against the big end of town. Neville Wran did not go off and work for big tobacco or big automotive . . . You know you could be a successful lawyer and win a lot of cases but it's not going to make you into a millionaire, working for battlers and for unions. It should not make you into a millionaire if you are honest. And the reality is that as a barrister, albeit a pretty good one, Neville Wran in the late 50s and early 60s, would not have been making a fortune".

If Rule had read our biography of Wran, he would have known Wran had been a remarkably successful barrister and had been "making a fortune". Leading industrial barristers in Sydney in the 1950s and 1960s earned big money. The struggle against communism was being played out inside Australian trade unions. Elections in key unions often ended in the courts with industrial barristers representing the various factions which were challenging or defending control of the union. Money was no object. Wran was a protégé of Jack Sweeney QC, considered the doyen of industrial barristers. He 'took silk' in 1968, only 11 years after being admitted to the Bar, an unusually brief apprenticeship in those days. The post-nominal QC meant a significant rise in his daily fee. Wran was frequently retained by several union-leaning law firms, including W.C. Taylor and Scott and J.R. McClelland and Company (later McClelland, Wallace and Landa), as well as regular briefs from other firms. He represented both left-wing and right-wing unions, a feat which eluded many other industrial lawyers. A profile of Wran by Gavin Souter in *The Sydney Morning Herald* noted that after the departures of John Kerr (to the Bench) and Lionel Murphy (to the Senate), "Wran came to be regarded in the late 1960s as probably the best fighting industrial counsel in Phillip Street."

Wran was a prodigious worker, arriving early and leaving late, and weekends were not sacred. Michael Kirby, later a High Court judge, occasionally appeared as Wran's junior. Kirby, himself a renowned workaholic, described Wran as "remorselessly diligent." We noted in the biography: "Wran's practice was a high volume one and he had a reputation for hanging on to briefs. The custom is for barristers who are 'jammed' with work to pass on briefs, generally to more junior lawyers. Wran did this as well but he did it less than many of his peers." I recall lunching with Wran at a city restaurant on a Friday in the late 1970s. Wran noted a table of barristers settling in for what was obviously going to be a long lunch. "In my day on Friday afternoon I would still be chasing a third brief", Wran told me.

Wran's practice was not confined to trade union matters, workers compensation, and common law. He represented Jorn Utzon in his battles with the Askin government over the Sydney Opera House and successfully represented Martin Sharp in his obscenity trial. His only payment from Sharp was the original cartoon which had attracted the attention of NSW police. Ironically, in the light of subsequent ABC controversies, Wran successfully defended ABC *Four Corners* when it was sued over a program, although this was not a defamation action. A newspaper profile in 1991, after he left politics, reported Wran having told friends that as a barrister, he "took it home in trucks". Brian Dale has written: "As a successful barrister in 1973 Wran had been making big money – in the $150,000 – $200,000 range", which is equivalent to $1.7 million to $2.4 million in today's dollars. He swapped that for $23,000 a year plus allowances as Leader of the Opposition. Unsurprisingly, Dale revealed that

Wran intended only one shot at becoming premier. If unsuccessful in 1976 he intended to head back to the Sydney Bar.

Wran may have made big money as a barrister but his divorce in 1975 from his first wife, Marcia, set him back considerably. As a politician hoping to become premier, and with a critical election just a year away, Wran was not in a position to risk a messy divorce. It is not correct, as he told one colleague, that he left the marriage with little more than his wardrobe. The sale of the family home enabled Wran to purchase a terrace in Woollahra and Marcia to purchase an apartment at Darling Point. When he married Jill Hickson, a few months after he became premier, he was still indebted to Marcia. He told Jill that if anything happened to him, she must remember he still owed Marcia $55,000. Even though Jill was on a reasonable salary until 1981, as a senior Qantas executive, money was now much tighter. Hence the pen hovering over the cheque book when it came to settling bills and the need to borrow money from his sister.

Although the couple later purchased a larger house in Woollahra (for $600,000), Malcolm Turnbull is correct in saying that when Wran left politics, "he had a pension and he had a house, and that was it." The house was not mortgage-free. An opportunity to purchase a smaller house next door, for a desired expansion, had been passed up because the couple could not afford it. Only later, after Wran had left politics, could they buy the house when it again came on the market.

Wran's parliamentary superannuation was not miserly. It was reported that he qualified for an indexed yearly payment of $60,000 for life or, if he converted it to a lump sum, he would receive a one-off payment of $360,000 and a yearly indexed pension of $24,000. Wran apparently took the lump sum option of $360,000 which is the equivalent of $1,176,000 today. The $24,000 pension was indexed to increases in parliamentary salaries with the index applied to the $60,000 amount, not the $24,000.

Wran's lack of financial security during his political career was observed by others. As noted in chapter one Phillip Adams has written of Kerry Packer feeling sorry for Wran and his lack of money. Admittedly a billionaire's conception of a lack of money differs from that of most but it corroborates the verdict of Wran's staff and of Malcolm Turnbull. In 1989, after he had left politics, Wran was asked in an interview why he had got involved in a particular commercial venture. He bluntly replied: "money." He added: "I really need to make some money because I had 15 years in politics where my financial position just went downwards all the time. So, I'm in the throes of endeavouring to restore my fortunes."

Wran was always a lucky politician. He won the Labor leadership on a countback of primary votes after the ballot with Pat Hills had tied and with one of Hills' certain voters unable to vote because of a byelection. He won the 1976 election by only one seat. If just 60 votes in the electorates of Hurstville and Gosford had been cast differently, he would have been heading back to the Bar. Wran's friend, and later enemy, Jim McClelland said of him: "In politics it's better to be lucky than smart and he's both." Wran's luck continued after he retired from Parliament. He had initially intended to go back to the law and then flirted with the idea of joining an old legal friend, Peter Valkenburg, who had entered the world of merchant banking, then in its infancy in Australia. Wran had previously appointed Valkenburg as NSW Agent General in London. When Wran mentioned this tentative plan to a young friend, Malcolm Turnbull, he was dissuaded. This was to be another lucky break for Wran.

Turnbull had left journalism, where he had occasionally earned Wran's displeasure with some of his reporting, to become a barrister and was then appointed legal counsel to media mogul Kerry Packer. He later set up a law firm with another old friend and Packer adviser, Bruce McWilliam. Cheekily, Turnbull persuaded Wran to go into business with him, instead of Valkenburg. Turnbull said later, on Wran's death: "I asked Neville: why would you go into business with someone as old as you?" Wran began working as a consultant to the legal firm, Turnbull McWilliam, but that was not the business

Turnbull had in mind. Despite the legal fame which the Spycatcher case had brought Turnbull, he had bolder ambitions. Working for Packer had grounded Turnbull in the world of corporate finance. One of the major tasks of the newly minted Turnbull McWilliam had been to manage the sale of Packer's Nine Network to the controversial Perth entrepreneur Alan Bond for $1.05 billion, a mixture of cash ($800 million), options ($50 million) and preference shares ($200 million). This turned out to be a bargain for Packer. He was able to buy back the network four years later for less than half the sum for which he had sold it.

Turnbull refuses to make the claim himself but there is no doubt that it was Turnbull, later to enter federal politics and become Liberal prime minister (2015-2018), who made Wran a multi-millionaire. Nick Whitlam's contribution, over a shorter period, should also not be forgotten. If Andrew Rule wants an explanation for how Wran could accumulate "a property portfolio and other assets worth $40 million", he need look no further than Malcom Turnbull and Nick Whitlam for an explanation. Wran's 10-year business partnership with Turnbull gave Wran wealth and a financial security he had not had since his divorce in 1975.

The Turnbull-Wran business partnership had an inauspicious beginning. In early 1987 both invested in a contract cleaning start up, Allcorp, along with two experienced cleaning operators, James Cook and John Laws (not the broadcaster). Turnbull and Wran used their extensive contact books to snare contracts prompting criticism from business rivals and attracting media scrutiny. Within 12 months the business had around 40 customers and a turnover of $4 million. Both men were to learn that profit margins in the cleaning industry are notoriously thin, if profits are achieved at all. There are no barriers to entry to the industry and there are always competitors willing to ignore award rates and conditions. Turnbull's biographer, Paddy Manning, reports the business made small losses in its first two years, despite quickly achieving a high turnover. It turned a profit in 1990 but a negligible one considering the turnover. Although the business outlook appeared encouraging, with the Greiner Coalition government promising the outsourcing of government office cleaning work to the private sector, Allcorp descended into internal recriminations and lawsuits.

Turnbull's real ambition was to establish an investment banking business with Wran. To cover their lack of experience in banking, Wran suggested they bring Nick Whitlam into the venture. Wran had appointed Whitlam as chief executive of the State Bank of NSW, then government owned, after a 20-year career overseas in investment banking. In his memoir Turnbull records: "In short order, we'd set up Whitlam Turnbull & Co. Nick and I each had 40 per cent of the partnership and Neville had 20 per cent. Kerry Packer, flush with cash from the sale of the Nine Network, agreed to contribute $25 million in cash, as did Larry Adler, whose company FAI insurance was a buccaneering deal maker and stock-market darling." None of the three working partners put any of their own capital into the business. All drew salaries – reportedly $300,000 a year for Turnbull and Whitlam – but Turnbull insists these were not large by industry standards. Their main rewards were fully franked dividends from the business. In Wran's case his dividends were paid into a private company, Vakivi Pty Ltd, of which he owned 66 per cent and Jill Wran owned 34 per cent.

Whitlam Turnbull opened for business on 1 July 1987. It was not a propitious time to launch with the stock market bull run soon ending. Paradoxically it was the stock market crash in October 1987, less than four months later, that was to be the making of the firm. Fortunately for the new venture the $50 million founding capital was still mainly in cash. Both investors wanted their money back. Adler had already become a nuisance for the partners because of his hands-on style and the crash caused FAI's market capitalisation to collapse. This could have been fatal for the new venture but the partners refunded the $50 million and persuaded British & Commonwealth Holdings PLC (B&C) to invest $10 million in preference shares. B&C would later go into liquidation and the partners were able to purchase its interests from the liquidator at a 40 per cent discount.

The second fortunate outcome of the crash for the firm was the delivery of 27-year-old Warwick Fairfax, a scion of the Sydney dynasty which had founded *The Sydney Morning Herald* in 1831. Whitlam told Manning that Warwick Fairfax was "the deal that set us up". Turnbull told me in an interview: "We all made a lot of money out of Warwick Fairfax". Fairfax had made an ill-timed $2 billion takeover bid for the Fairfax company, which then included *The Age* (Melbourne) and *The Australian Financial Review*, a range of other newspapers and magazines, including suburban and regional newspapers, as well as radio and television interests. The bid was in jeopardy after the stock market meltdown. Adroit footwork by Turnbull and Whitlam had secured the rights to dispose of the many assets which Fairfax needed to sell to get his debt down to a more manageable level. The sales included Fairfax's stakes in Australian Associated Press (AAP) and Australian Newsprint Mills, Macquarie Radio network and the Fairfax magazine division. Manning reported, on information from Whitlam, that Whitlam Turnbull's total fees from the Fairfax transactions in its first year of operation was $7.6 million and its total fee income that year was $10 million.

The firm was reconstituted in February 1990 as Turnbull & Partners Ltd (TPL) after Whitlam's departure, with Turnbull holding 70% and Wran 30%. TPL also benefited from Turnbull winning the right to represent the Fairfax junk-bond holders, who were the most vulnerable creditors when Fairfax went into administration after Warwick Fairfax's bid collapsed. The junk-bond holders were crucial to the reconstitution of the Fairfax company. Turnbull was able to drive a hard bargain with the prospective new owners, benefiting both the bondholders and TPL. Manning reported that TPL's fee from the junk-bond holders was $6 million. This amount appears to include the $2.8 million fee to TPL as adviser to Ord Minnett, the underwriter of the float of the new company. Both Turnbull and Wran reinvested some of the proceeds in Fairfax shares when the company was floated. At one point Turnbull was the largest individual shareholder in the new company. "Neville did very well for himself, including from his shares in the later floating of the company," Turnbull told me. He estimates that Wran made a capital gain of between $2 million and $3 million when he sold his shares.

A second windfall for Wran came when TPL made a $500,000 investment in 1995 in a fledgling internet service provider (ISP) called OzEmail, started by tech entrepreneur Sean Howard. Turnbull later wrote that "of all the Turnbull and Partner's deals and projects in the '90s, and there were many, the biggest and best was undoubtedly OzEmail." Howard had started *Australian Personal Computer* magazine, eventually purchased by Kerry Packer. Howard had approached Turnbull's friend, Trevor Kennedy, seeking investors for OzEmail. Kennedy, as well as investing himself, pointed Howard to Turnbull.

OzEmail was not a passive investment and Turnbull and Howard had to work hard to grow the business, including raising additional capital from sceptical overseas investors. By 1998 OzEmail was the largest ISP in Australia. Facing the need for additional capital to consolidate, and with growing competition from Telstra's Bigpond, OzEmail began fielding takeover offers. In late 1998 Turnbull, Howard and Kennedy negotiated the sale of the company to a US telco, WorldCom. TPL's initial investment of $500,000 was worth $60 million on the sale, a multiple of around 120 in just over three years. Profiles of Malcolm Turnbull over the years have noted the importance of OzEmail in building Turnbull's personal wealth. Few have realised this was a TPL investment and that Wran was also a beneficiary. Wran's share of this windfall was more than $18 million before tax.

Warwick Fairfax and OzEmail may have been the standout successes of Whitlam Turnbull & Co and TPL but they were only two of many. Turnbull has admitted they were lucky to have established their business at a time of churn in media ownership in Australia. In this period, as Turnbull wrote, "the ownership of almost all the major media assets in Australia changed hands – apart from Murdoch's News Corporation – and our firm was at the centre of most of these deals." This included the sale of Bond Media back to Kerry Packer for which TPL earned a reported $3 million fee. Turnbull also negotiated the sale of the Ten television network to Canwest Global, a Canadian company. In an interview with me, Turnbull claimed Whitlam Turnbull and, later, TPL "was the most profitable M&A [mergers and acquisitions] business of its kind from the late-1980s to the mid-1990s".

In 1995 TPL was also engaged by the Federal Labor government to advise on the restructuring of the government's unprofitable shipping line, ANL Ltd, and its possible sale to P&O. Federal Transport Minister, Laurie Brereton, defended in Parliament the payment of $574,000 to TPL for the firm's work in restructuring the company and asset sales. "If through that process they help us turn around a loss-maker with $115 million of operating losses – and they do that all for half a million dollars – I say that is very good value indeed," Brereton said. ANL's stevedoring arm was sold to Patrick Corporation and the shipping line was eventually purchased by a French company after the Howard Federal Coalition Government was elected.

When Malcolm Turnbull speaks of the financial success of TPL he uses phrases such as "very, very successful". The emphasis does not seem an exaggeration. Although advisory work fluctuated from year to year, in line with M&A activity, some years were bumper ones. In one year alone in the 1990s, TPL made a gross profit of $20 million. Nick Whitlam, who left the business after he and Turnbull fell out over contrasting management styles, has said of the three years of operation of Whitlam Turnbull & Co: "we had enormous success". Whitlam described Turnbull as a "transaction driven" investment banker, rather than one who is "relationship driven". Wran did not follow Whitlam out the door following the bust up between Whitlam and Turnbull. Whitlam later wrote that Wran's decision to back Turnbull was because "he was always closer to Malcolm than me". That may be true but Wran, still needing "to make some money", took a bet on Turnbull's superior abilities as a 'rainmaker'. Wran also said of Turnbull: "The fact that he is a controversial character makes him more appealing to me rather than less. I am not interested in bland characters."

Wran and Turnbull had a successful financial partnership for 10 years. They had complementary styles. Brian Dale told a journalist in 1991: "Neville opens doors and Malcolm kicks them down." Turnbull, despite bringing in most of the business, valued Wran's role and guidance. "I never felt I was carrying him", Turnbull told me. TPL was not just an investment bank, relying on advisory fees and success fees from negotiating deals. Turnbull is proud that the firm also invested in many of the transactions in which it was involved. "TPL was essentially a private equity/venture capital business with its own balance sheet", is how he described it to me. Turnbull used this as a selling point to clients: they would never recommend a deal in which the partners were not also prepared to invest. As well as the OzEmail investment, TPL also invested in gold mines in Ghana and Siberia, a zinc mine in China and a forestry business in the Solomon Islands. None of these investments turned out to be another OzEmail but Turnbull says the firm did not take a bath on any of its investments. Some of those who invested in the Ghana venture, including two who did so on Wran's advice, would disagree. The forestry business, Axiom Forestry Resources, delivered a healthy capital gain for TPL, although the firm's forestry practices came back to haunt Turnbull in his later political career.

Wran's business partnership with Turnbull ended in August 1997 when the firm was sold to Goldman Sachs. This was more a case of Goldman Sachs buying Turnbull and his advisory team, rather than being a normal business acquisition. The sale price enabled TPL to be shuttered. The firm's remaining investments were allocated between Wran and Turnbull. Wran, about to turn 71, was never going to be part of the human capital transfer to Goldman Sachs, although he had an advisory role for a couple of years. Turnbull quickly became a partner in Goldman Sachs and made another fortune from the firm's IPO in 2000. He retired from the firm at the end of 2001 and set his sights on replicating his business success in federal politics.

While Wran remained active in investment banking for some years afterwards, linking with another investment banker, Albert Wong, this does not seem to have been as financially rewarding, or as emotionally satisfying, for Wran as the previous decade had been. Wran remained involved in the investments he inherited from TPL, none of which rivalled the deals he did with Turnbull. He chaired an Australian-listed company, PharmaNet Online, which established joint ventures with several state-owned enterprises in China. This was an early blockchain-type e-commerce business which sought to establish online trading of pharmaceutical products for hospitals and health centres. The venture was reliant on software being developed by a US firm which was not forthcoming and it became a victim of the bursting of the tech bubble. Wran had seen the writing on the wall and had bailed out. He also had minor investments and directorships in other tech companies, including Powerlan, ESR (a speech recognition venture) and Ester Online Trading (an online share broker service). Turnbull, Howard, Kennedy and Wran also established a tech investment company, FTR Holdings, hoping to replicate the success of the OzEmail investment. None of these investments, including FTR Holdings, survived the 'tech wreck'.

Turnbull recalls most of Wran's subsequent roles were advisory ones although these began to wind down. An investment banker confided to me in the early 2000s that Wran had been responsible for his firm being unable to close a lucrative deal. He claimed all that was needed was for Wran to fly to London and "shake a few hands." Wran, by now in his mid-70s, could not be persuaded. Turnbull doubts Wran substantially further built his wealth in this period. "Neville and Jill chose to invest a large part of their income in what you could call lifestyle assets, such as the place at Palm Beach, which is fair enough. Neville wasn't an especially active investor, although he was involved in a lot of activities. He was unlikely to be putting a large amount of his money at risk. He was a very cautious man", Turnbull told me.

The decade following the dissolution of TPL was not a happy time for Wran, either professionally or personally. Friends say Wran missed the interest and excitement that had come from Turnbull's deal making. His commercial ventures were small beer compared to the TPL days. On the personal front this was a very unhappy time. Close friends were dismayed by the distress caused by his family circumstances at a time of life when parents usually earn emotional dividends. He separated from Jill on two occasions although they later reconciled. Wran died on 20 April 2014, after nearly two years residence at Lulworth House in Elizabeth Bay in Sydney, a nursing home for the well-heeled. Wran had been admitted to Lulworth with Lewy body dementia, a particularly aggressive and unpleasant brain disease. His mental and physical deterioration was fortunately witnessed only by his loved ones and nursing staff.

Death may have been a relief for Wran but it set off a demeaning squabble among family members over his estate. Some beneficiaries of his will appeared to have had an unrealistic expectation of the amount of money available for distribution. These expectations were not assisted by the repeated publication in the media of Wran having left an estate worth $40 million. Wran's executors were puzzled by the published figure. The first media reference to his notional estate appears to have been an article on 15 August 2014 in *The Daily Telegraph* by Annette Sharp, which referred to "his $30 million estate". This figure was soon replaced by $40 million in other articles. Louise Hall in *The Sydney Morning Herald* reported "a fortune estimated to be worth up to $40 million largely made up of an impressive property portfolio." The $40 million figure was also used by law firms in their public Client Notes, which seized on the family squabble to advise clients of the need to ensure that estates are carefully planned and distributed after death (and, of course, to advertise their expertise).

Untangling the value of Wran's actual estate is not easy. Most of Wran's wealth was tied up in property which he owned, as joint tenants, with Jill and which by law meant title transferred to her on his death. The three properties – their house in Woollahra (which had been expanded to include the house next door), a holiday home at Palm Beach and a farm in the Yarramalong Valley – were valued at less than $17 million around the time he made his last will in December 2011. A unit in Woolloomooloo, valued at around $2 million, had been purchased for his two youngest children. Wran's parliamentary superannuation pension by law also reverted to Jill, discounted by 25%. Under a shareholder agreement with Jill, Wran's remaining share of Vakivi also reverted to Jill on his death. This is understood to have been around $1 million.

In 2011, the year before Wran was admitted to Lulworth, it was estimated that the net assets of Vakivi amounted to around $16 million. If this figure is correct, Wran's share (66%) was around $10 million and Jill's was around $6 million. If it is correct that Wran's share of Vakivi's net assets on his death was only around $1 million, this suggests that Wran must have distributed or transferred some assets prior to his death. Wran's notional estate, which included his share of the assets now transferred to Jill, seems to have been around $25 million.

In his will Wran left $500,000 to his son Glenn and $250,000 to a god daughter. His two youngest children with Jill, Harriet and Hugo, were left all his public company share investments, to be held in trust. Wran also made provision for the ongoing medical care of his sister Dorothy, who was then residing at Lulworth House with dementia. (She died before Wran.) Jill was bequeathed all his personal items, including paintings and antiques. The balance of his estate was left to his daughter Kim, a long-time resident of California. It was a distribution of assets guaranteed to lead to family disputation.

The actual amount available for distribution to beneficiaries is believed to have been less than $3 million. This amount shrank during the family dispute, as legal and accounting fees piled up. The dispute reached the Supreme Court in July 2015, initiated by a challenge by Wran's son Glenn, on the grounds that fair provision had not been made for him in his father's will. Glenn's adopted status was not at issue since under NSW law legally adopted children have full rights. The court was told the actual estate was now valued at less than $1.6 million. The relevant parties agreed to private mediation by a former President of the NSW Court of Appeal, Keith Mason. The mediation costs further eroded the estate but it was successful and the claims of all family members were resolved. The outcome seems to have involved some dipping into the notional estate. The *Succession Act (NSW) 2006* permits claims against the notional estate if the deceased estate is insufficient to meet the needs of eligible claimants.

When Wran went into business, after leaving politics, he told Graham Freudenberg he was amazed "at the sheer wealth awash around Sydney and the undeserving ease with which insiders appeared to acquire it." Malcolm Turnbull would no doubt object to the phrase "undeserving ease". He worked hard and took risks but Turnbull made Wran one of those "insiders". Even though the size of Wran's estate was exaggerated after his death, he nevertheless died a wealthy man. Politics did not make Wran wealthy. Wran's wealth can be attributed to his good fortune in deciding to go into business with Malcolm Turnbull.

8

Media Mates

"The others [media proprietors] weren't for us but they were never totally against us. If we win, we should try and defuse their hatred of us. It may be a vain attempt but we'll try it." Neville Wran, after the election in May 1976, according to Brian Dale.

"Despite some gossip, neither during nor since Wran's years as premier has any evidence emerged that he received bribes or sought other forms of personal enrichment. That's not to say he was unaware of the patronage potential of government decisions – for political advantage, though, rather than personal gain. In particular, Wran treated media proprietors ... as targets of inducements intended to attract support in return." Rodney Tiffen.

The NSW election on 1 May 1976 took 10 days of vote counting for a victor to emerge. Wran retreated to a friend's holiday house on the South Coast to wait out the agonisingly slow counting of votes in the electorates of Gosford, Hurstville, Blue Mountains and Monaro. These electorates would eventually give Wran a one-seat parliamentary majority and make him premier. While waiting on the results Wran and his press secretary Brian Dale discussed the media's role in the election. None of the major media groups gave Labor editorial support in their newspapers and some were hostile. We noted in the Wran biography: "Wran was convinced it was not possible to remain in office without the support of at least one of the three major media groups which dominated publishing and television in Sydney."

Wran, like most Labor leaders, had a deep distrust of John Fairfax and Sons, which published five newspapers in Sydney and held one of Sydney's three television licences. The editorial policies of Fairfax's flagship, *The Sydney Morning Herald*, in those days were solidly conservative. Only twice had it failed to support the non-Labor parties at the federal level and only on one occasion had it directly advocated a vote for Labor. It had never supported Labor in NSW elections. Wran had been particularly wounded by a rare, and unhinged, page-one editorial in the *Herald* on the day of the 1976 election, which also attacked Wran personally. Wran told Dale, as they waited on the election count: "The others weren't for us but they were never totally against us. If we win, we should try and defuse their hatred of us. It may be a vain attempt but we'll try it."

Wran's ambition to defuse the hatred of "the others" did not seem propitious. Rupert Murdoch's News Ltd published *The Daily Telegraph,* the tabloid competitor to the *Herald, The Daily Mirror*, an afternoon newspaper and competitor to Fairfax's *The Sun,* and *The Sunday Telegraph* (which absorbed *The Sunday Mirror*), a competitor to Fairfax's *Sun-Herald*. Murdoch's papers, including the national paper *The Australian*, had supported Labor at the federal election in 1972 but had turned viciously against Labor in 1975.

The third major media group, Consolidated Press Holdings, controlled by Kerry Packer, no longer published a daily newspaper but owned influential suburban newspapers and magazines and held Sydney's third television licence. Kerry Packer's father, Sir Frank Packer, had been a long-standing opponent of Labor, but his son, who assumed control after Sir Frank's death in 1974, was regarded primarily as a businessman.

This is the context in which several controversial Wran government decisions involving Sydney's media proprietors must be analysed. Rodney Tiffen has written that "Wran treated media proprietors ... as targets of inducements intended to attract support in return." Wran would not have disputed this was a deliberate strategy. This tactic was a realistic response to the media landscape he faced, as his comment to Brian Dale demonstrates. This also proved to be a successful strategy for Wran and News Ltd newspapers and the Packer magazines and television station provided a supportive media environment for Wran from 1978 onwards. In the Wran biography we provided examples where Wran was able to rely on both.

Tiffen, after clearing Wran of allegations of personal corruption, has also suggested these decisions are examples of what nowadays is regarded by some as 'political corruption', although Tiffen does not use this term. He has cited the decision to grant the licence to run the gambling game, Lotto, to a consortium including the companies of Murdoch and Packer as "the most important example" of Wran being "happy to use the government's prerogatives to advance Labor's interests and that he wouldn't be inhibited by procedural niceties." Tiffen also cites two other examples, both of which were also mentioned in the Wran biography. We also extensively reported in that biography on the political controversy within the Labor Government and the Labor Party over the Lotto decision.

The game of lotto is now well-known in Australia through nationwide games such as OzLotto and Powerball. In the late 1970s, outside Victoria, it was unfamiliar. TattsLotto had been introduced in Victoria in 1972 and had proved a handy revenue-earner for that state. NSW also had a lotto-style game, Soccer Pools, which had been introduced in 1975. The Coalition government had given the licence to a private company, Australian Soccer Pools Ltd, which was 30% owned by Murdoch's News Ltd. Although the winning numbers in Soccer Pools were based on the results of UK soccer matches, most players treated it as a game of chance by selecting random numbers, rather than as a game of skill. Soccer Pools was a relatively minor source of revenue for the NSW government and a portion of its receipts was hypothecated to the development of community sport and recreation facilities in NSW. Labor had opposed the granting of the licence to a private company but Wran, although leader at the time, was careful in his comments not to criticise private company involvement.

Wran's economic advisers, David Hill and Nigel Stokes, had considered the lotto game as a means of raising revenue in Wran's first term. They had advised Wran that, in revenue terms, this was likely to be more beneficial and less problematic than legalising casinos. It was doubtful it would be as successful as in Victoria because of the wider range of gambling outlets in NSW but was still thought likely to boost overall lottery revenues. Lotto-style games, prior to the full computerisation of such gambling, were a vastly more difficult game to administer than lotteries, which are essentially giant raffles with draws only held when fully subscribed. Lotto draws are held at a fixed time each week and a critical mass of subscriptions is needed every week to generate and boost the attractiveness of the prizes. Even the purchasing of tickets was more complicated than lotteries. Tickets had to be manually filled in by the player and comprised an original and a carbon copy. The original had to be delivered to a processing centre and optically scanned so that immediately after the draw a computer could determine the winners in each prize division. The player retained the carbon copy.

Wran's advisers were not oblivious to the political benefits which might accrue to the government from the lotto licence going to a company in which Murdoch was involved. They believed for lotto to be a success it had to be run by an experienced outside organisation, as was Soccer Pools. The key issue for them was which option would deliver the most revenue to the NSW budget. The history of lotto launches overseas was also a factor: they were either great successes or poor performers. Most recently the launch of a lotto game in Massachusetts had failed after 13 weeks. Wran's advisers had no doubt for the game to succeed it had to be run by an experienced outside organisation. The same conclusion had been reached by senior NSW Treasury officials who had overall responsibility for the Lotteries Office. Treasury head Norm Oakes forcefully expressed this view at a Caucus committee meeting to which he had been invited by Treasurer Jack Renshaw because of opposition from Labor MPs. There was strong support in the Labor Caucus and in the Labor Party for the Lotteries Office to run the game. The Lotteries Office was very experienced in running lotteries but lotto was a vastly different game. We noted in the Wran biography: "The NSW Lotteries Office was considered too moribund and too lacking in entrepreneurial flair to successfully run the game."

There were only two organisations considered sufficiently experienced to be able to successfully operate lotto. One was Australian Soccer Pools Ltd which, as well as News Ltd, included the Vernon organisation, owned by Robert Sangster. Vernon was experienced in running lotto-style games overseas, as well as Soccer Pools in NSW, and already had a proven system with newsagents to pay the large number of smaller prizes on the day after the draw. The other was the Tattersalls organisation in Victoria, the operators of TattsLotto in that state. Tattersalls may have been more palatable to the Labor Party, given the absence of Murdoch, but did not satisfy the party's demands that the Lotteries Office be the operator. Tattersalls in the 1970s was also an unusual organisation. The owners were the families, mostly Victorian, fortunate enough to be beneficiaries of the estate of the state's early gambling entrepreneur, George Adams. That was not a corporate structure which would appeal to the Labor Party or, for that matter, the voters of NSW. Tattersalls has since evolved into a public company, the Tatts Group Ltd, but it took years for successive Victorian governments to unravel the peculiarities of the Tattersalls legacy.

Wran's advisers had no doubt that the Murdoch/Sangster option would deliver the greatest turnover for lotto and therefore the greatest revenue boost to the NSW budget. They also believed it had the best chance of being a success. In the Wran biography we described Wran's preference for a Sangster/Murdoch consortium on political grounds, and Wran's advisers' preference on financial grounds, as a "happy coincidence of financial and political considerations." It was a coincidence which most in the Labor Party failed to appreciate and this led to the first torrid year of Wran's premiership. Eventually, through clever work by Wran and the ALP president John Ducker, the Labor Party opposition was successfully blunted. On 24 July 1979 Wran announced a joint licence to operate lotto would be granted to the Director of State Lotteries and Lotto Management Services (LMS), the consortium formed by News Ltd and Vernon. The inclusion of the Lotteries Office came as a surprise and prompted Wran to assert: "Lotto will be government run." That claim was something of a stretch. The division of responsibilities between the two organisations left the Lotteries Office responsible mainly for selling tickets but the union was satisfied. Brian Dale said Wran gained satisfaction when the Director of State Lotteries told him, after familiarising himself with the vast operation in which he now had responsibility, that the Lotteries Office could not have done it on its own.

There was a further surprise in Wran's announcement. There was now a third shareholder in LMS: Kerry Packer's Publishing and Broadcasting Ltd (PBL) which controlled the Channel 9 television station. We noted in the Wran biography that the Labor Council of NSW, through a wholly owned subsidiary company, 2KY Broadcasters, had a substantial shareholding in PBL. John Ducker, who was also secretary of the Labor Council, was a director of PBL. Ducker denied any knowledge of, or connection with, PBL's emergence as a shareholder of LMS. Kerry Packer would have been an obvious choice as a partner by Murdoch and Sangster as it gave them what they lacked: a television station. Packer's Channel 9 was the leading station and its involvement 'locked in' the network, and its stable of stars, for the promotion of the game, particularly the weekly televised lotto draw. Buying time for these promotional activities on a television network would otherwise have been expensive. Just as importantly, locking in Packer locked Channel 9 out of rival consortia.

It was later revealed that a clumsy attempt was made by a business intermediary to also bring Fairfax into the LMS consortium. The overture was predictably declined. *The Sydney Morning Herald*, despite 150 years of support for private enterprise over state enterprise, had editorialised in favour of the lotto licence going to the Lotteries Office. The inconsistency was pointed out inside the *Herald* and an economics writer, Alan Mitchell, was requested to examine the controversy. In a detailed feature, published just before the decision was announced, Mitchell concluded that in terms of the government's objective of maximising short-term financial returns "private enterprise looks the best bet."

According to Rodney Tiffen in *Inside Story* the lotto decision was "the most important example" of Wran not being "inhibited by procedural niceties" in the use of government prerogatives. He claimed the licence decision had been "made without calling tenders." This was wrong as was outlined in the Wran biography. Tenders for the game were called and the tenders were assessed by an independent committee of prominent businessmen and a senior lawyer. The committee described the LMS tender as "outstanding". This is not surprising given the marketing firepower which Packer's television station and Murdoch's newspapers could bring to the promotion of the game. Equally crucial was Vernon's proven history, in Australia and overseas, in successfully operating lotto-style games. *Inside Story* later added a footnote to the original story that "a tender was indeed called for the Lotto franchise." The reference to the Lotto contract remains in the story, however, as "the most important example" of Wran being prepared to use government prerogatives and not being inhibited by procedural niceties. Neither *Inside Story*, nor Tiffen, explain how awarding the contract to an organisation recommended by an independent tender assessment committee is contrary to "procedural niceties." This makes a nonsense of its retention in the article.

Tiffen concedes there was a strong argument that the involvement of media companies in the promotion of the game would ensure more revenue would flow to state coffers. He qualifies this by saying: "it's also true that the franchise gave those companies a reliable, government-guaranteed source of income." This reveals a lack of understanding of the economics of the lotto game compared to lotteries. There is no 'government guarantee' for the operators of Lotto. The operators earn their revenue according to a fixed and sliding percentage of turnover. If they are successful in building turnover, so their revenue grows; if turnover falls short, so does their revenue. The challenge for the operator was to quickly achieve a critical mass of turnover, and continue to grow turnover, which was necessary to generate attractive prizes on a weekly basis. The only guarantee operates in favour of the state which is ensured a minimum of 31% of turnover without putting any capital at risk.

LMS succeeded in boosting overall lotteries/lotto turnover in NSW even though, as expected, the new game cannibalised turnover for traditional lotteries. In 1978-79, the last full year before the introduction of Lotto, lotteries turnover in NSW was $108.3 million. In 1979-80, the year in which Lotto began (in November 1979), the combined lotto/lotteries turnover in NSW was $181.4 million, an increase of 67%. This increase was despite Lotto operating for only two thirds of the financial year. By 1985-86, the last full year before Wran retired from Parliament, combined lotto/lotteries turnover had grown to $395.4 million. Lotteries share of that turnover had fallen from $108.3 million in 1978-79 to $73.4 million in 1985-86 while Lotto's share in 1985-86 was $322 million. The NSW government's take from Lotto had grown to $110 million a year by 1985-86. Introduction of the game also gave a welcome boost to the revenues and foot traffic of newsagents throughout NSW. Wran's advisers, not without reason, regard the Lotto decision as a major achievement.

The game was also a success for LMS but was hardly the financial bonanza that Tiffen and others suggest. Those who made this claim did not understand the breakdown of Lotto revenues. Sixty per cent of the subscription pool went on prize money and 31% went as duty to the government. This was the same breakdown as TattsLotto in Victoria. The remaining nine per cent, however, did not line the pockets of the LMS partners. From this remaining nine percent the operators had to fund the promotion and operation of the game, including the normal organisational expenses, and the commission paid to newsagents and to the Lotteries Office. The operator was also required to guarantee minimum levels of prizes and to supplement the prize pool, if necessary, to ensure this. Only a smaller percentage, on a sliding scale which reduced as turnover increased, went to the operator as commission. Even experienced journalists, such as the *Herald's* Evan Whitton, made this elementary mistake of assuming that nine per cent of the subscription pool went to the operator's bottom line.

LMS's commission was set at 7% for the first $100 million of annual net turnover, 6% for the second $100 million and 5% thereafter. LMS had originally sought a flat 7% of net turnover. This was considered reasonable by Treasury and by Wran's advisers since it provided an incentive for LMS to build turnover. This was not acceptable to Labor MPs, however, most of whom had little understanding of the finances of the game. Wran sent Hill and Stokes to deliver the blunt message to LMS that it was '7,6,5 or nothing'. This led to a brutal confrontation with the LMS team but they eventually accepted the revised commission scale.

The licence granted to LMS was only for seven years, something also overlooked by Wran's critics. In 1986, when the licence was about to expire, the Minister for Finance, Bob Debus, commissioned a review. This was prompted by plans to take the game fully online. Following the review Debus recommended to Cabinet that the licensing arrangements be extended for two years, until January 1989, by which time it was estimated the computerisation of the game would be complete. Debus also recommended that when the extended licence expired full control of Lotto be transferred to the Lotteries Office. He also recommended the commission to LMS be reduced to 5% for the first $300 million of turnover and 4% thereafter. The justification for reducing the commission, according to Debus, was that LMS would have a lesser role in processing entries with the switch to an online game. The recommendations were adopted by Cabinet and announced by Debus in March 1986. This was four months before Wran resigned from Parliament.

Debus was from the ALP's Left faction and had originally opposed the lotto licence going to a private company. He told me that it was the then Director of Lotteries, Pamela Grant, who had been appointed in 1982, who had convinced him that the computerisation of the game meant the Lotteries Office could now run it alone. Computerisation meant entries could be processed at point-of-sale terminals in newsagencies. This conclusion was supported by the review and was not opposed by the Cabinet, including by Wran. The Greiner government, elected in March 1988, did not reverse the decision although it was forced to extend the contract for a further six months to complete the online transition. At the end of 1989, 10 years after Lotto was introduced, control of the game reverted exclusively to the Lotteries Office, except for marketing and promotion which was put to private tender.

In 1989, the year the licence expired, Lotto contributed $117 million to the government coffers bringing the total take to the government over the 10 years to more than $800 million. LMS's net profit in the financial year 1988 was $1.76 million, which was split three ways. This profit appears to have been impacted by the reduction in the commission paid to LMS. In 1986, to choose an earlier year, the net profit for LMS was $3.5 million, again split three ways, while the government received $110 million in duty. Rodney Tiffen wrote: "The state-licensed monopoly became extremely lucrative both for the government and the companies running it." Extremely lucrative for the NSW government, certainly, but the sliding scale of commission, and subsequent reduction in the commission, gave LMS only modest profits from the game. Debus does not recall any resistance from LMS to the decision to end the contract. No doubt the meagre profits were a factor. Lotto was hardly a financial bonanza for Murdoch, Packer and Sangster.

The decision by the Wran government to introduce Lotto and to grant the start-up licence to an experienced private operator involving media companies was certainly in the best interests of the government. To be regarded as 'political corruption', however, the decision must be a breach of established procedures and manifestly against the interests of the people of NSW. Contrary to the assertion by Tiffen, the decision did not involve a breach of "procedural niceties". It is also difficult for critics to convincingly argue the decision was not in the best interests of NSW taxpayers given the substantial revenue boost to the state budget. Wran would have been amused when in 2010 another Labor government sold NSW Lotteries, lock-stock-and-barrel, to the Tatts Group (which was now a public company) for just over $1 billion. The sale came with a 40-year licence to Tatts to conduct all public lotteries in NSW except Keno, although the government continues to receive the 31% duty on ticket sales. Unlike the long-running brawl Wran had fought within the Labor Party over the introduction of Lotto, there was hardly a peep from the party over the total privatisation of NSW Lotteries. In 2021 the NSW Treasury announced it had also commissioned a scoping study into the possible sale of the annual revenue streams from the lotteries and lotto duties. This sale did not proceed.

A friend returned to Sydney in the early 1980s after residing overseas for several years. Living back in the city which floats on malicious gossip, he found plenty of people wanting to tell him that Wran had been paid $1 million by Rupert Murdoch to gain the Lotto license. Others said it was $2 million and the payer of the bribe was Kerry Packer. The gossips never asked themselves: why would Murdoch or Packer need to pay a bribe? The brawl over Lotto was a fight over public enterprise versus private enterprise. If Wran had lost that fight, the licence would not have gone to any private company. Once Wran had won that fight it was always most likely that LMS would emerge the victor, given the expertise of Vernon and the resources which the media companies could bring to the marketing and promotion of the game. Neither Packer nor Murdoch needed a bribe to convince Wran that it was in his government's best interests for the licence to go to their company. What motive would Wran have had for wanting payment to ensure the running of the game went to the company likely to be of greatest political benefit to the government? An organisation such as Tattersalls could not deliver to Wran the political benefits likely to come, and which did come, from Murdoch and Packer.

The second example Tiffen gave of Wran treating media proprietors as "targets of inducement" was to "give [Kerry Packer] access to the Sydney Cricket Ground and helped finance the construction of light towers that enabled play to take place in front of prime-time TV audiences." The government's generosity extended even further than Tiffen reports. The SCG Trust and the government footed the bill for the entire $1.3 million cost of construction of the light towers. Packer paid nothing. Wran's intervention wasn't simply a case of handing a benefit to a media proprietor. It was a direct and deliberate entry by Wran into the 'cricket civil war' of 1977-79 and one which was decisive in ending the war. His intervention certainly benefited Packer's rebel World Series Cricket (WSC) but not even the small band of cricket traditionalists in NSW would have expected Wran (or any other Labor premier) to enter the war on the side of the cricket establishment. It also seems unlikely that Wran's Liberal successors, Nick Greiner and John Fahey, would have sided with the cricket establishment in similar circumstances.

Nor did Wran ignore "procedural niceties" as Tiffen claimed. His intervention was by way of legislation, which was debated and passed by the NSW Parliament, including ultimate approval by the then Opposition-dominated Legislative Council. A mythology has developed that the Wran government had 'stacked' the SCG Trust to ensure it reversed its refusal to permit WSC access to the ground. Andrew Webster, in his 2021 book on the Sydney Cricket Ground, wrote: "Within 24 hours of the SCG Trust rejecting [Packer's] bid to use the ground, the government of Labor Premier Neville Wran performed a stunning about face; dissolving the Trust … The revamped SCG Trust cleared the path for Packer to use the famous ground as he'd wanted all along." Rodney Tiffen wrote: "Immediately [after the trust's rejection in July 1977] the Wran government intervened, over-ruling the Trust, and compulsorily retiring most of its members." Both accounts are wrong and reveal a failure to check the chronology of events. The Wran government did not have the power, by fiat, to overrule the trust. Nor did it have the power, arbitrarily, to sack or stack the trust. Any change to the trust required legislation and such legislation could not be achieved "immediately" or "within 24 hours", particularly with an Opposition-dominated Legislative Council.

The "about face" of which Webster wrote was performed by the SCG Trust and was engineered by the trust chairman, Pat Hills, an influential Wran government minister. On 25 July 1977 the trust wrote to Packer and informed him that no WSC games would be permitted on the SCG. Hills later revealed to Parliament that he had not supported the decision. There were four MPs on the trust: Hills, Treasurer Jack Renshaw, former Liberal Premier Tom Lewis and Country Party Federal MP, Frank O'Keefe. Renshaw had missed the relevant meeting. Lewis and O'Keefe had supported the rejection of WSC. Hills, who had earlier and unsuccessfully sought to bring the warring parties together, was helped in persuading the trust to reverse its decision by Packer promising additional revenue for the trust. Hills eventually achieved the "about face" but it took much longer than 24 hours. On 30 September 1977 Hills announced the trust had reversed its decision.

This was not the end of the matter. The NSW Cricket Association (NSWCA) took legal action against both the trust and WSC. After the case concluded, but before the court's decision, the Minister for Sport, Ken Booth, introduced the *Sydney Cricket and Sports Ground Bill 1977*. There seems little doubt the government was anticipating an adverse decision by the court. A court case in 1903-04, also involving the trust and the NSWCA, had created a precedent which was to the detriment of the trust. It is likely that Crown Law officers believed the case would be lost by the trust. That proved to be the case. Before debate began on the Bill, Justice Helsham, Chief Judge in Equity, found the trustees were obliged to permit the NSWCA to use the SCG on whatever days it wished during the cricket season. This effectively blocked the ambitions of WSC. The government's

Bill removed the relevant provision which Helsham found made the trust subject to the dictates of the NSWCA.

The Bill also reconstituted the SCG Trust, although this did not occur until the following year. Previously appointments to the trust, always much prized, were virtually life-time appointments with the lucky trustees appointed until 70 years of age. Booth, who had signalled a year earlier his intention to reform the trust's anachronistic governance, introduced four-year terms for trustees, with a right to reappointment. He also gave SCG members the ability to elect two trustees. The reform of the trust has been described as the Wran government 'stacking' the trust. This is a claim that cannot be sustained. The new government-appointed trustees were drawn from a broader range of sporting, community and business interests than had previously been the case. The number of former or serving politicians was reduced from four to two: Pat Hills and the Labor Council's Peter McMahon, who was also an MLC which was then a part-time role. New trustees were drawn from the sports of rugby union, rugby league (two), soccer and athletics while cricket maintained its two representatives. Apart from Hills the only other trustee reappointed was the respected former test cricketer, Arthur Morris, and he was joined by a member of the NSWCA. The new term limit of four years meant that future governments would also be able to make their own appointments, rather than having to wait until a trustee died or reached 70 years of age. One person's democratic reform is another person's 'stack'.

The opposition to WSC did not cease despite the *Sydney Cricket and Sports Ground Bill*. The Opposition parties in the Legislative Council in November deferred consideration of the Bill until February 1978, thereby denying WSC access to the SCG for the 1977-78 cricket season. As a result, the Liberal and Country parties got a taste of what it was like to anger a media proprietor. Packer 'let slip the dogs of war'. Two savagely critical articles about the Upper House appeared in *The Bulletin*, at the very time the Opposition was seeking conservative support to oppose the government's proposed democratic reform of that chamber. Popular writer Ron Saw, after observing the council in action, was savage in his observations, describing MLCs as "living fossils", "stuffed codfish" and "decrepit free-loaders and time-servers." Not even Labor MLCs, who had opposed the Bill's deferment, were spared Saw's onslaught. "Two of them, sharing a fat, comfortable, red arm-rest, are so sluggish their heads nodding so close together, that they're either kissing each other, God forbid, or asleep", he wrote. The Opposition was particularly wounded by the author of the other article, the conservative columnist David McNicoll, who did not hide the fact that he had been motivated (or instructed) to comment by the Opposition's decision to defer the SCG Bill. "This had the effect of preventing World Series Cricketers using the ground this season; it deprived the Sydney Cricket Ground of $260,000 in revenue … and, further, it deprived 18,000 members of the SCG seeing the best cricket of the season on their own ground," McNicoll wrote.

In the new year the Opposition declared its innings closed and the Bill passed the Legislative Council without amendment. The SCG Trust, at last, was able to make its own decisions concerning the use of the SCG. On 1 May 1978 Pat Hills announced that six light towers would be installed at a cost of $1.3 million, two-thirds funded by the trust and one-third by the government. The lights were a world-first for major cricket grounds. This was one of the last decisions by the old trust. In July 1978 Booth announced the new trustees. Unsurprisingly Pat Hills was reappointed as chairman.

The Wran government's intervention was a critical step in ending the cricket war. Obtaining access to the SCG, at a time when WSC was locked out of all other traditional cricket grounds, was a breakthrough for Packer. This meant, according to Daniel Brettig, that "Packer was able to stage matches in the establishment heartland – a welcome change of surroundings after the WSC troupe had endured the less attractive scenery of the Sydney Showgrounds." Just as important was the installation of lights at the SCG since this enabled the WSC innovation of international day/night cricket. More than

50,000 turned up to WSC's first day-night cricket match at the SCG on Tuesday 28 November 1978. Ground authorities were forced to throw open the gates to avoid a crowd stampede and Pat Hills gave permission for non-members to sit in empty seats in the Members' Stand. Arunabha Sengupta has described the match as "a tipping point in the evolution of cricket. A shift of cricket's centre of gravity. Cricket would never be the same again." Adrian McGregor in *The National Times* said of the match that Packer had "enticed sports fans out of the pubs … transforming the subtleties of traditional cricket into the spectacle that is night-time cricket." Andrew Webster subsequently wrote: "This was the night, really, that changed cricket forever. The night Kerry Packer won the war." Shortly after a truce was reached between WSC and Cricket Australia, as it is now known. One year later, almost to the day, the first official day-night international cricket match was played at the SCG.

The actions of the Wran government, by legislation and not by fiat, certainly benefited Kerry Packer but procedural niceties were not ignored. It is difficult to argue that Packer was the sole beneficiary. The long-term beneficiaries of the resolution of the cricket war and the accompanying day/night cricket include the SCG Trust, the official cricket authorities, the current television rights holder (a company unrelated to the former Packer organisation) and cricket fans, most importantly. Cricket fans are not the only ones to have benefited. The lights broadened the ground's appeal for other sports and non-sporting events. As surely as night follows day, a forgivable cliché in telling this story, lights would eventually have been installed at the SCG, as they have now been in all other comparable cricket grounds. Payment would also have been at the expense, in some form, of the NSW taxpayer. Even Sir Donald Bradman, an influential warrior on behalf of the cricket establishment – who had furiously lobbied his old teammate and trustee, Arthur Morris, to oppose WSC's access to the SCG – eventually laid down his arms. In 1998 he wrote: "Despite my deep feeling for the traditional game, and my conviction that a vast majority of players and public still regard test cricket as the supreme contest, we must accept that we live in a new era. I am satisfied that one-day cricket, especially day/night cricket, is here to stay." Bradman was writing before the arrival of T20 cricket and the Big Bash League, another beneficiary of the SCG lights.

The third example by Tiffen, also mentioned in the Wran biography, involved a Packer-controlled company, which operated the ski resorts at Smiggin Holes and Perisher Valley. *The Sun-Herald* reported on 29 July 1979: "Without calling for competitive tenders the Wran government renegotiated all the key leases in the two valleys until the year 2025". These ski resorts were an accidental side business for the Packer family. In 1973 Sir Frank Packer had purchased Murray Publishing, a magazine and comic business, which also held leases at Perisher Valley. Sir Frank had little interest in the snow but his son Kerry saw possibilities. After his father died in 1974, Kerry Packer acquired assets at Smiggin Holes and began building Perisher-Smiggin Holes into modern resorts. Because of the different times of acquisition, the leases had different expiry dates. Packer was keen to consolidate the leasehold and gain the lease security necessary for planned redevelopments.

Paul Landa had been appointed Minister for Planning and Environment in August 1976, after Wran admitted he had made a mistake in May in initially splitting the planning and environment portfolios. Landa was disappointed to find that responsibility for the National Parks and Wildlife Service (NPWS) remained in the lands portfolio, under Bill Crabtree, and he lobbied Wran to correct this anomaly. Wran did act after the 1978 election but neglected to tell Crabtree, who only found out he had lost the NPWS when he turned up at Government House for the swearing-in of the ministry. Among the NPWS files Landa found on his desk was the file dealing with Packer's leases. The leases had already been renewed. It is unlikely that Crabtree would have done so without Wran's blessing or instruction. A former NPWS official, who is familiar with the leases, says there was nothing unusual about the lease renewals and that the terms of the new leases were standard. The rent was based on a percentage of gross turnover, typical of most national park leases. The more successful the business, the greater the return to the NPWS.

This would not be the only occasion when the Packer ski leases were renegotiated, or a renegotiation was contemplated, without a call for tenders. However, it seems to be the only occasion that is remembered 40 years later. *The Australian Financial Review* reported on 24 November 1997 that the Greiner government in the early 1990s "was prepared, without calling tenders, to grant Packer's company the head lease to control the Perisher Range ski resorts." This was to be accompanied by a substantial expansion of the resorts, by around 3,500 beds, and an $80 million upgrade of the existing resort and ski lifts. According to the newspaper this proposal fell over after opposition from conservation groups and other resorts.

This newspaper account does not tell the full story. In 1990 the Greiner government passed legislation to allow it to give control of the Perisher-Smiggin Holes' head lease to a single lessee. The government intended to put the lease to tender. The decision to tender the lease was prompted by recent criticism by the newly established Independent Commission Against Corruption (ICAC) of a lack of tendering or auctioning of Crown land. This followed ICAC's inquiry into North Coast land development. The proposed tender fell through when it was realised that Packer held the lease over the Perisher car park, which was critical to the proposed expansion and upgrading of the ski resorts. The government was therefore forced to negotiate directly with Packer. The negotiations lapsed, not because of the opposition from conservation groups, but because Packer came to the view that the proposal was uneconomic.

The failure of these plans prompted Packer to consider selling the resorts as part of a general liquidation of assets. He was persuaded to retain the resorts by his son, James, who took management control. This was a repeat of the previous family transition when Kerry

Packer persuaded his father to give him responsibility for the ski field business. In 1995 James Packer achieved a merger of the Packer interests and Transfield's Blue Cow and Guthega assets to form Perisher Blue. Murray Publishing, the Packer company, owned 73% of the merged company and Transfield, owned by the Belgiorno-Nettis and Saltieri families, owned the rest. According to the *Financial Review*, the merger, although profitable, was not a great success and promised savings from the consolidation were not achieved. James Packer gave up day-to-day management in 1996 when he was appointed to run the parent company, Publishing and Broadcasting Ltd.

In May 2009 James Packer, after what was described by a newspaper as "several years of wrangling", reached agreement with the then NSW Labor government for a 40-year lease, expiring in 2048, and an option for a further 20 years. The agreement amalgamated 10 separate leases into one head lease. The agreement also involved Perisher Blue giving up its lease over the Perisher car park which was earmarked for a future village. The government trumpeted Perisher Blue's commitment to a capital investment over the period of the lease of around $112 million.

The renegotiation of the lease did not involve a public calling of tenders and was reported by *The Sydney Morning Herald* under the heading: "Secret deal to expand Perisher." Despite the headline the newspaper did not make an issue of the fact that the lease had been extended for 40 years without public tenders being called. Only a few other news outlets reported the outcome of the lease renegotiation and none made any issue of the lack of tenders. Nor were media eyebrows raised, six years later, when James Packer negotiated the sale of Perisher Blue to Vail Resorts, the largest US resort operator, for $177 million. The Wran government's renegotiation of the Packer leases is cited as an example of "using government prerogatives" to assist a media mogul. Strangely no similar judgment has been made of the Rees government's renegotiation, even though the ultimate beneficiary in this case was an American company.

The administration of NPWS leases has now been codified in the *Office of Environment and Heritage NSW National Parks and Wildlife Service Property Leasing Guidelines 2015*. These guidelines provide that most new leasing opportunities will be offered through an "open market process" and this would also generally be required upon the expiry of leases. On lease renewals the guidelines state that a competitive selection process is "the default position" but they do provide circumstances where a direct negotiation with an existing lessee may be justified where the "current lessee has demonstrated a positive track record." The guidelines provide a non-exhaustive list of circumstances where direct negotiations of new leases, and renewal of leases, may be justified.

If these guidelines had been in place in 1978 the renewal of the Packer leases without an open market process would not necessarily have been in breach. Whether the people of NSW would have been better off if the renewal of the Packer leases had gone to the open market process can never be known. It can be said confidently, however, that the renewal did not substantially enrich the Packer family. Owning and operating a ski resort in a country with Australia's mild winter climate and small population will always be problematic.

The three examples cited by Tiffen of Wran using "the government's prerogatives to advance Labor's interests", and not being "inhibited by procedural niceties", shrink to one and even that remaining example is arguable. Procedural niceties were certainly observed in the other examples. All three events were undoubtedly part of the Wran strategy of defusing the previous hostility towards Labor by media proprietors. For these decisions to be regarded as political corruption, however, the critics must do more than simply express their distaste for a government dealing with Rupert Murdoch and Kerry Packer. Even the respected historian Frank Bongiorno has written that "the Wran government's award of the contract for Lotto in 1979 to a consortium that included both Kerry Packer and Rupert Murdoch seemed typical of how Labor political business was done in New South Wales."

Both Murdoch and Packer were pursuing legitimate business interests. They achieved government support for lawful purposes according to normal standards of process. Wran acted, most certainly, to advance the re-election prospects of his government. Most decisions by elected governments in a democracy are similarly motivated. Wran is not the only political leader, before or since, to have evaluated government actions in terms of favourable media coverage and the potential gain or loss of votes. Wran's critics need to demonstrate the decisions were a breach of established procedures and to have been manifestly contrary to the interests of the people of the state. None has done so.

9

BUCKETS OF TROUBLE

"I hope Neville knows what he's doing. There's a lot of temptation in that portfolio." Deputy Premier Jack Ferguson on Rex Jackson's appointment as Minister for Corrective Services.

"Wran handled the Jackson issue with uncharacteristic clumsiness. He had to be dragged reluctantly into taking any action and consequently the initiative always lay with his political opponents or the Press." Wran biography 1986.

Rex Jackson was an unlucky gambler but he won one life-changing lottery. He was the last person elected to the first Wran ministry after the 1976 election victory, winning a draw from the hat. Three candidates tied for the final position but under the arcane Labor Caucus rules only two names went into the hat – Rex Jackson and George Paciullo. Wran wanted Paciullo, who had established a high profile in opposition, and was dismayed when Jackson won the draw. Jackson had been the only Left faction MP not to vote for Wran in the leadership ballot three years earlier. Many of Jackson's colleagues, including Wran, believed he had promised his vote to Pat Hills in return for a frontbench position if Hills won the ballot. By then Jackson had been in Parliament for 20 years without being regarded as a candidate for a ministry. Jackson's lottery win may have been lucky for him but certainly not for Wran. Jackson's later involvement in a corrupt prisoner early-release scheme, which would eventually see him jailed, has undoubtedly and unfairly coloured perceptions of the Wran government.

In his early years in Parliament, Jackson had aligned himself with his electoral neighbour, Rex Connor, and Labor colleagues referred to them as Rex Senior and Rex Junior. Jackson retained the nickname 'Junior' when Rex Connor departed for the Federal Parliament. After 1973, he acquired a new nickname, 'Buckets', from Labor colleague Mike Cleary, a prolific bestower of sobriquets. The new nickname reflected the smears and accusations with which Jackson regularly bucketed opponents in Parliament.

To the surprise of most, Jackson initially proved a successful and effective minister. "Jackson was placed out of harm's way in Youth and Community Services where he astonished everyone by performing well", wrote Rodney Cavalier later. Jackson was orphaned in his teens and, although not placed as a state ward, he had been separated from his siblings. As minister he had genuine empathy for those for whom he was responsible and succeeded in increasing the departmental budget by 23 per cent over three years, including increasing pocket money for state wards. This was achieved despite budgets being tightly controlled to fulfil Wran's pledge of "no increases in state taxes and charges".

Jackson was so successful and popular in the portfolio that in 1981, when Wran needed to get stories of prisons and escaped prisoners off the front pages of the newspapers, he appointed him as Minister for Corrective Services. This portfolio had been a graveyard for politicians, including Jackson's predecessor, Bill Haigh, who failed to be re-elected to Cabinet after the 1981 election. Jackson quickly dispelled any notion that the Wran government was 'soft on prisons'. He made clear his sympathies were with prison officers and once told Parliament that a critical report by the Ombudsman had been "filed in the wastepaper basket." Jackson's pugnacious nature and prize fighter features helped add to the notion that prison reform now had a much lesser priority for the government.

Not everyone agreed with Wran's appointment of Jackson to this portfolio. On the afternoon of the ministerial ballot in October 1981 a small group of Labor MPs gathered in the office of Deputy Premier Jack Ferguson. The conversation turned to the ministerial portfolios announced by Wran. Commenting on Jackson's new portfolio, Ferguson told the group: "I hope Neville knows what he's doing.

There's a lot of temptation in that portfolio." Jackson's gambling was well known to Ferguson, who is rumoured to have lent Jackson money on occasions to get him out of a spot. The generosity went both ways. Ferguson later told Parliament: "When I was a young backbencher struggling to put five children through school, Rex was always there when I needed money to tide me over." Jackson's gambling was also known to Wran. In 1973 a securities company had filed a bankruptcy petition against Jackson over a debt of $12,000 which was ultimately paid. After the 1976 election Wran had toyed with appointing Jackson as Minister for Sport – the portfolio he had earmarked for the unlucky Paciullo – but Brian Dale reminded him that the portfolio included responsibility for the TAB.

Ferguson's foreboding, however, is surprising since few people would have thought at that time that the prisons portfolio was an avenue for corruption. Although there had always been allegations about prison officers supplying contraband to prisoners for money there had never been allegations of ministerial involvement. Suspicions were therefore not aroused when, in April 1982, Jackson initiated a scheme to use his ministerial power to grant the early release of certain prisoners on licence. His public rationale that NSW had a much higher prison population than other states – 33 per cent more per capita than Victoria – seemed plausible. Jackson and his departmental head argued the scheme was not only about prison overcrowding. Justice John Nagle, in the 1978 report of the royal commission on prisons established by the previous government, had advocated a reduction in the use of prisons as a method of punishment. Nagle also recommended imprisonment, other than for very serious crimes, should be a matter of last resort and then for as short a period as possible. This was an argument for reforms in sentencing, however, a matter for the judiciary. It was not an argument for a system of ministerial release on licence.

It would later be revealed that by the time of the introduction of the early-release scheme Jackson's gambling addiction had become chronic. Despite a big win of $150,000 in December 1981 on a long shot at Randwick, by February 1982 Jackson was forced to take out a loan of $15,000 from a finance company, agreeing to repay $22,842 over five years. Over six months in 1982-83 he lost $136,000 to just one bookmaker. In this period his ANZ bank account, into which his parliamentary salary was paid, was overdrawn by around $60,000.

In March 1983 Jackson announced that the early-release scheme was so successful he was extending it from first offenders serving up to one year to prisoners serving up to three years. The scheme had already been criticised by the judiciary and prison officers on the grounds that it usurped the function of the courts to set non-parole periods. A pertinent warning, ignored by the government, was given in 1982 by Justice Michael Kirby, no enemy of the Wran government: "Executive decisions lack the most vital elements of judicial ones: openness and public accountability. They smack of decisions made behind closed doors".

Once again, as in the Bill Allen affair, there was an intervention by the Federal Police who came across conversations about the early-release scheme on an authorised wiretap in a drug trafficking investigation. The phone taps suggested money may have been paid to NSW officials, including a government minister, to secure the early release of prisoners. Prime Minister Bob Hawke later told Federal Parliament that, following a briefing, he had authorised the relevant Federal minister, Mick Young, to contact the relevant minister in NSW and "ensure so far as it is within the Commonwealth capacity to do so, that all necessary steps were taken to fully investigate the matters in issue."

On 16 May 1983 Young briefed Acting Premier Jack Ferguson – Wran had stepped aside as premier on 10 May when the Street royal commission was called – after phoning him at home the night before to arrange an urgent meeting. At the meeting Young informed Ferguson, and the head of the Premier's Department, Gerry Gleeson, that the telephone surveillance had also revealed the possible involvement of Rex Jackson. On the same day the Commissioner of the Federal Police, Ronald Grey, handed two folders of transcripts and tapes to the NSW Police Commissioner, Cec Abbott.

Later the same day, Ferguson and Gleeson met with Abbott. In a file note dated 16 May, Gleeson records that Grey had requested Abbott not to take any action that would compromise or jeopardise investigation of the 'target' of the narcotics investigation. The target was not Jackson. Grey told Abbott, in writing: "The drug investigation being conducted by the Australian Federal Police is an important one, and your cooperation in avoiding any action which may jeopardise that investigation would be appreciated." Gleeson further noted that Abbott, in the light of this request, had decided not to investigate the allegations at that stage and would review his decision "in one month or earlier if warranted."

Grey's request was later confirmed in the Federal Parliament. The then Special Minister of State, Kim Beazley, said on 4 October 1983 that Grey "made it clear [to Abbott] both orally and in writing that the Commissioner was concerned that any investigation of the prisoners in question did not jeopardise its ongoing narcotics investigation, which was a major one." Until now it has never been revealed that the Federal Police investigation was at the behest of the Royal Commission into Drug Trafficking, headed by Justice Donald Stewart.

Grey's request that no action be taken to jeopardise the narcotics investigation left Ferguson with a dilemma. Ferguson later told Parliament that "not telling [Jackson] was perhaps the hardest decision I have had to make in my political life because Rex Jackson is a man I regard as a real friend and comrade."

At around this time alarm bells also rang inside Government House. Since decisions on the early release of prisoners involve exercise of the prerogative of mercy, the Governor must approve them. In the official history of NSW Governors, Evan Williams wrote in the chapter on Sir James Rowland: "It seemed to His Excellency that an unusually large number of early release applications were coming forward. At one Executive Council meeting Rowland raised his concerns with Pat Hills, a senior Wran minister and former rival for the leadership. 'If you're worried' said Hills, 'I'll take the minutes back and talk to Gerry Gleeson'. Gleeson, the permanent head of the Premiers' Department wasted no time in alerting Wran." Williams' account seems to be incorrect in one respect. The chronology of developments in the early release scheme suggests this occurred in the period when Wran was on the sidelines so Gleeson is likely to have briefed Ferguson. This is confirmed by a file note by Gleeson on 6 June in which he undertakes, after discussion with Justice Slattery, the Chairman of the Parole Board, to "maintain liaison with Mr Wills [Official Secretary to the Governor] concerning the numbers and kinds of cases being submitted." The note further records: "In a review of today's group [of applications before the Governor] there were two prisoners sentenced to life that were being released after only serving 5 years. There was also a case of a prisoner sentenced to 3 years and 10 months being released after 6 months."

Fred Smidt, Ferguson's long-time staffer, has written that Ferguson had contacted Government House after Mick Young's briefing, to request a halt to approval of early-release applications. Gleeson's file note of 6 June appears to confirm that applications had already been frozen. The scheme was formally suspended on 21 June at a meeting of the Policies and Priorities Committee of Cabinet (P & P), chaired by Ferguson. The committee decided "in respect of the release of prisoners on licence, that there should be a review of the current system because of public concern and that the Attorney General and the Minister should have further consultations with and obtain the written advice from the Chief Justice and the Chief Judge of the District Court with a view to having further proposals before Cabinet within the next month." Crucially, it was further decided "that in the interim the release of prisoners under licence should be restricted to require the serving of the full non-parole period but allowing remissions to be granted on this non-parole."

On the same day Ferguson issued a media statement announcing these decisions. The final paragraph stated: "Mr Ferguson also said that the current conditions for the release of prisoners under licence were being reviewed and that during the period of this review release on licence would only be recommended for prisoners who have served their full non-parole period less any remissions earned during this period." The Attorney General, Paul Landa, subsequently reported back, after discussions with the Chief Justice and the Chief Judge of the District Court. "Their Honours indicated satisfaction with the Government's announcement on 21st June that limits were to be imposed on the operation of the scheme pending completion of a review of current conditions providing for the early release of prisoners under licence," Landa wrote.

By 21 June, when P & P formally suspended the scheme, Grey's desire to keep a lid on matters was in tatters. On 12 June the new Opposition Leader, Nick Greiner, alleged that prisoners could buy their release by paying sums between $2,500 and $15,000. On the same day the *Sun-Herald* had carried an article to this effect, which appears to have been supplied in advance by Greiner. This claim was denied by Jackson who argued this was impossible under the way the scheme was administered. The next day, 13 June, Ferguson announced a police task force to investigate the material and requested an interim report by 20 June. On 16 June Abbott advised Gleeson that the Federal Police Commissioner had advised that, in view of the NSW police investigation now underway, he had lifted the previous request not to jeopardise investigation of the target of the federal investigation. It seems unlikely that Grey had any option, now the allegations were public.

Wran resumed duties on 28 July 1983, following his exoneration by Chief Justice Sir Laurence Street, and wasted little time in terminating the scheme. He did not bother waiting for the result of the review. Nor did he consult Jackson. The termination simply confirmed what had already occurred in practice as applications had not been approved by the Governor since at least 21 June and probably not since 6 June or even earlier.

We noted in the Wran biography that the police investigation was not the NSW Police Force's finest hour. We also concluded: "Wran handled the Jackson issue with uncharacteristic clumsiness. He had to be dragged reluctantly into taking any action and consequently the initiative always lay with his political opponents or the Press." Both judgments now seem unfair. Documents not available to us at the time show the investigation was obviously hampered by the reluctance of those involved to incriminate themselves and by Abbott's reluctance, at the request of Grey, not to reveal the existence of the phone taps. The head of the task force, Chief Inspector Jim Loombes, was highly regarded as an investigator within the police force. Frustration with progress is obvious in Abbott's reporting back to Gleeson. On 9 August Abbott advised Gleeson that the prisoners identified on the tapes had been interviewed but had, unsurprisingly, "not given any information." On 6 September Abbott advised the investigation "was running into a brick wall" and that he would soon have to decide whether to interview Jackson. Gleeson told Abbott that Wran supported this course of action. Jackson was interviewed on 12 September and Abbott later reported the police investigators had specifically refrained from informing Jackson of the Federal Police material.

Wran led a trade mission to Japan and Hong Kong for one week from 1 October. While he was overseas the Federal Opposition Leader, Andrew Peacock, alleged in Federal Parliament on 4 October that NSW government officials and a minister had accepted bribes for the early release of prisoners. This was the first time "a minister" had been publicly implicated although within the government it was known that the tapes implicated Jackson. Ferguson, again acting premier, immediately recalled Abbott from London where he was attending a conference. Ferguson announced that he had requested from Abbott a written report regarding the early-release scheme. Jackson vehemently denied Peacock's claims.

On 10 October, following Wran's return from overseas on 8 October, Abbott submitted the task force's report. Wran subsequently informed Parliament of the task force's conclusion: "As a result of our extensive inquiries into all matters that were raised in this investigation of allegations of corruption in the release of prisoners under the 'early release scheme' it can be indicated that no evidence of a criminal nature was forthcoming that would justify criminal proceedings being instituted against any person. In this regard, and of the matters that are unresolved, this inquiry from our point of view is complete." Wran also advised Parliament that Abbott had told him he was satisfied that the task force had conducted a "most thorough investigation" and that Abbott agreed that there was no need for further investigation. Wran was criticised by the Opposition for not releasing the task force report. Abbott had advised Wran, by letter on 10 October, and revealed here for the first time, that "to release the report and thus publicly identify the drug syndicate members would compromise a very important drug informant area and in my opinion any breach in this regard would be a most irresponsible decision."

Despite the task force's conclusion, it was becoming increasingly difficult for Wran to publicly defend Jackson. David Hill, then heading the State Rail Authority, was given information from an impeccable source integrally involved in the Stewart royal commission. The source told Hill that Wran was being imprudent in asserting Jackson's innocence as the commission held detailed incriminating evidence. Hill arranged to visit Wran at his home on 8 October, the day Wran returned from overseas. Sitting in the kitchen Hill informed Wran of what he had been told. Wran reacted angrily and told Hill he was sick of people asserting Jackson's guilt but refusing to provide solid evidence to back this up. Hill was confident of his source's truthfulness but did not have the information himself.

Commissioner Grey may have been concerned not to jeopardise the Federal Police investigation but that concern does not seem to have been shared by his officers down the line. On 26 October Marian Wilkinson, of the *National Times*, submitted a series of specific questions, based on the Federal Police wiretaps, about the early release in April 1983 of three prisoners from Broken Hill Correctional Centre. These prisoners had been interviewed by the task force. Journalist Evan Whitton later wrote that the questions were based on material from the Federal Police wiretaps and had been given to the *National Times* by crime journalist Bob Bottom. Jackson refused to answer the questions and threatened legal action against the newspaper. Wran's staff became aware of the questions and established that the newspaper was going ahead with publication. Shortly after 5pm Wran called Jackson to his office and demanded his resignation.

Wran used as justification for his demand Jackson's apparent misleading of the Parliament, a Westminster principle honoured in NSW, before and since, more in the breach than the observance. Graham Freudenberg had urged Wran to dismiss Jackson on these grounds. The misleading related to discrepancies between an answer Jackson gave in an interview with a newspaper and an answer he had given in the Parliament. Jackson complied and submitted his letter of resignation admitting to an "unwitting" misleading of Parliament. Wran's department prepared for his signature a letter to Jackson accepting the resignation. The draft letter contained a final paragraph: "I thank you for the loyal and dedicated service you have given to the Government since it assumed office." Wran crossed out the paragraph and sent the letter back for retyping. He was not in a forgiving mood. What had promised to be a brave social experiment – one that could have brought credit to his government – had ended in a mass of criticism, allegations and innuendo which now threatened to envelop it. The controversy had also pushed Wran's complete exoneration by the Street royal commission from the public mind.

Although the impending *National Times*' article was the catalyst for Jackson's resignation, political considerations had overtaken Wran's previous concerns about not jeopardising the Federal Police investigation and the lack of solid evidence against Jackson. Wran knew the long-running affair was causing the government to bleed electoral support. Four by-elections had been held on the previous Saturday. Although Labor retained the safe seats there had been substantial swings against the government. Labor MPs in marginal seats were dismayed at what they saw as the government's paralysis on this issue. Michael Egan, who had won the very marginal seat of Cronulla in the 1978 'Wranslide', told me of his relief at the news of Jackson's resignation and that night he had congratulated Wran at a function in his electorate.

Wran had for months resisted urgings to refer the early-release allegations to a judicial inquiry. Journalist Dennis Shanahan has noted that Wran acted more quickly to allow a public investigation into himself than he did for Jackson. Wran insisted the matter was being investigated by NSW Police which was the appropriate investigative body. As late as 10 October Abbott advised Wran that "because of the extremely sensitive nature of the international drug operation and the likely disclosures I believe that a Royal Commission or a Judicial Inquiry, on this occasion, is not warranted." Wran's reluctance was not surprising given Abbott's advice that this could jeopardise the federal investigation. Wran had also just endured a royal commission himself, one in which he resented having been involved, and this may also have been a factor. This attitude changed when two more corruption allegations emerged. The first was a claim by Bob Bottom that the tapes had also revealed that a magistrate, Susanne (Sue) Schreiner, had been influenced to dismiss criminal charges against a crime figure. The second was a claim by the National Party's Federal Leader, Ian Sinclair, that he had been told by a businessman and a "leading Sydney bookmaker" that criminal charges against Sinclair could be dismissed by payment of a bribe. Sinclair did not name the pair but knew that others would fill in the dots and conclude that the bookmaker was Bill Waterhouse, widely known to have been a friend of Wran since university.

Sinclair was a political gambler and had rolled the dice that Wran would not be prepared to investigate Waterhouse. His gambling on this occasion proved to be on a par with Jackson's. Wran called together his staff and the Attorney General, Paul Landa, and later announced the establishment of a Special Commission of Inquiry to investigate both allegations. Enabling legislation was quickly rushed through Parliament. The special commission of inquiry was called a 'star chamber' by critics, including by some who had previously demanded a 'judicial inquiry' into the Jackson allegations. It was effectively a royal commission although one with the ability to consider hearsay evidence in private.

Both allegations were found to be baseless. Bottom's solicitor admitted to the inquiry that his client's allegation was without foundation while the Special Commissioner, Justice Ronald Cross, thoroughly discredited Sinclair's claims. Sinclair had already run up the white flag before the inquiry began when he was critical that "remarks made in a political speech" were now to be investigated by a judge. Sinclair's complaint was an admission that his allegation was simply political smearing and should never have been taken seriously.

Cross described Bottom's allegations as "incredible and absurd" and Bottom's behaviour as "impetuousness bordering on irresponsibility". Bottom's humiliation was to have significant consequences for himself and for NSW. The magistrate he had falsely accused was highly regarded by political activists previously supportive of Bottom's work in exposing corruption. The blow to Bottom's credibility was a factor in *The Sydney Morning Herald* declining to publish the transcripts of the illegal NSW police wire taps, which had been supplied by Bottom, and which set in train legal proceedings against High Court judge Lionel Murphy. Hence the transcripts have become known, misleadingly, as the 'Age tapes' since that newspaper in Melbourne had no qualms about relying on Bottom. This was discussed in chapter six.

Having established these special commissions of inquiry Wran had little option but to also establish a similar inquiry to investigate the Jackson allegations, despite Abbott's advice that a judicial inquiry was "unwarranted". This inquiry was headed by Justice John Slattery and required the Federal Attorney General, Senator Gareth Evans, to approve the inquiry having access to the Federal Police transcripts. Evans, already dealing with Grey's sensitivity about the wire taps and the fallout from *The Age* transcripts, put strict conditions on access to the material. He tabled the conditions in the Senate on 15 June 1984. At the conclusion of the inquiry, on 31 July 1984, Slattery recommended five people, including Jackson, be charged with conspiracy.

Jackson was now out of Cabinet but remained in Parliament, as he was entitled to, and was still in the Labor Caucus. Despite his resignation from Cabinet and the allegations of corruption Jackson had not been challenged for preselection and was comfortably re-elected at the March 1984 election. The principle of the presumption of innocence still held sway in NSW in those days. The treatment of Jackson in this period contrasts with that of another NSW Labor MP, Steven Chaytor, 20 years later. In December 2006 Chaytor was immediately suspended from the Labor Party after an alleged domestic violence incident. He was expelled and deselected by Labor in January 2007 after initially being found guilty. His conviction was overturned by the District Court in July 2007 when it was established Chaytor had been attempting to prevent his then partner from committing suicide. Justice came too late for Chaytor; by then he was out of the NSW Parliament.

Journalist Fia Cumming wrote recently: "Even then, while Neville Wran cut Jackson lose at that point [October 1983] he was allowed to remain in Parliament for another three years". It is not clear who Cumming believes is responsible for Jackson being "allowed" to remain in Parliament. The voters in his electorate re-elected him in March 1984 and he was not charged with an offence until August 1984. It was open to the Opposition to move a motion for Jackson to be expelled from the Parliament but this did not happen. The power of expulsion is very much a last resort option which is why it has been used so rarely. The Opposition certainly revelled in the government's political embarrassment but, to its credit, recognised that Jackson was entitled to have the matter of his guilt or innocence determined by the courts. As matters turned out, as outlined below, Jackson was forced to resign from Parliament before the court decision.

With a trial approaching Jackson made an application to have his legal fees paid by the government. The application was put to Cabinet in November 1984 by Attorney General, Paul Landa. It was one of the last ministerial actions by Landa who died suddenly only weeks later. Guidelines adopted in February 1981 permitted ministers to apply in certain circumstances for payment of legal fees in respect of civil and criminal proceedings brought against them. Cabinet approved the application which was consistent with the guidelines. Pat Hills led the arguments in support but he was not alone. No minister voiced opposition. Jackson's fees before the Special Commission of Inquiry had been met by the taxpayers, as was the practice in such inquiries. Wran and others swept up in the Street royal commission were similarly indemnified for the cost of their legal representation. This remains the practice today.

The government's decision was not announced and only became public in March 1985. The revelation caused a public outcry. Terry Sheahan, by then attorney general, recalls being mauled on radio in an interview with Mike Carlton. Sheahan valiantly justified the decision on the grounds that the charges related to Jackson's ministerial duties and that Jackson was entitled to the presumption of innocence. Although Wran, in response to the outcry promised to review the decision, sympathy inside the Cabinet remained solidly with Jackson. Sheahan wrote in 2006 that many who knew Jackson best could not accept that he had committed the offences of which he was charged. Ken Booth, one of the most popular and respected Wran ministers, was never convinced of Jackson's guilt.

Once again Jackson made a losing bet. In a radio interview he threatened that if the government changed its mind about paying his legal fees, he would reveal the whole truth of the early-release scheme. Rodney Cavalier, a member of the Cabinet which made the decision, recalled: "The problem for Rex was telling morning radio that the government had to pay his bills or he'd tell the whole truth. Neville could not permit that to stand. I recall a Cabinet meeting, one item on the agenda, and fees withdrawn. All over before 11am." Wran's press secretary, David Hurley, had the difficult task of defending the government's backflip. He made the mistake of telling one journalist on background: "We will have to eat a turd sandwich on this one and say it was yummy." The journalist honoured the off-the-record obligation but regaled the conversation to colleagues and soon the quote appeared in print.

In June 1986 Jackson announced he intended to resign from the Labor Party but would remain in Parliament. He said he intended to run at the next election, due in 1988, as an independent. In August 1986 he bowed to the inevitable and resigned his seat, saying he needed his superannuation to pay his rapidly mounting legal bills. Jackson was now a problem for Barrie Unsworth, who had been elected premier following Wran's retirement in July 1986. Jackson later announced that he would stand in the by-election created by his own resignation from Parliament. Jackson did stand as an independent candidate in the by-election in January 1987 but gained only 6 per cent of the vote. Despite a swing of around 8 per cent against Labor, it retained the seat.

In September 1987 Jackson was found guilty after a long and complicated series of trials. Justice Adrian Roden sentenced him to a seven-and-a-half-year term, with a non-parole period of three years and three months. Jackson appealed the severity of the sentence and the Crown cross appealed. The Court of Criminal Appeal, by a two to one majority, increased the sentence to 10 years with a five-year non-parole period. The man who had argued that imprisonment should be a last resort received a sentence longer than many men found guilty of rape.

Jackson was forced to pay for his legal representation during his committal hearing but his money ran out during the long series of trials. He then applied for legal aid from the Legal Services Commission (now called Legal Aid NSW). Tom Kelly was acting chief executive of the commission and had delegated authority to approve such applications. He recused himself from the decision since he had, as a solicitor, previously acted against Jackson in defamation proceedings. He also thought it important, given the application was of such public interest, that it be determined by the full commission. The commission comprised eight part-time representatives drawn mainly from outside government and was chaired by a Supreme Court judge. The commission applied the policies applicable to all criminal trials and accepted that Jackson did not have the means to continue to pay for his lawyers. The commission unanimously granted legal aid for the duration of his trial. By then Jackson, as well as exhausting his superannuation, only narrowly escaped losing his house in settlement of a debt to the ANZ Bank of around $120,000.

If this grant of legal aid had not been made the consequences may have been even more controversial than the initial Cabinet decision to pay Jackson's legal fees. The trial judge would have either forced Jackson to represent himself or would have stayed the trial, possibly permanently. If the trial had been stayed, Jackson's criminality may never have been determined. If he was forced to represent himself, and had been convicted, Jackson may well have succeeded in having the conviction quashed by the High Court for unfairness. This is what the High Court did five years later in *Dietrich v The Queen*. This ground-breaking authority established the principle that courts should grant an adjournment in matters where an indigent accused is unrepresented through no fault of his own and if proceeding would result in an unfair trial.

In 2021 legal gossip writer, Richard Ackland, wrote that "granting legal aid to the crooked Prisons Minister (later imprisoned)" was one of the matters that left "a nasty taste in the mouth" about the Wran government. Ackland is wrong. The government did not grant legal aid to Jackson and paid only $37,000 in fees – another account says $59,000 – the amount which Jackson had incurred by the time the decision was reversed. The subsequent grant of legal aid was made by the independent Legal Services Commission. No fair-minded person can help but contemplate the consequences for Jackson if he had been found not guilty by the jury, given his parliamentary career had effectively been terminated and his superannuation exhausted.

The issue of the legal responsibility of any minister prosecuted over matters related to the administration of his or her portfolio is one with which governments continue to grapple. In 2021 it was revealed that taxpayers would pay for a $650,000 settlement of a workplace dispute brought by a mature female staffer who began a consensual affair with her boss, a Federal Liberal minister. The revelation, although criticised in some quarters, did not create a public outcry.

In NSW this matter is now codified in a Premier's Circular, *Guidelines for the Provision of Ex-Gratia Legal Assistance for Ministers, Public Officials and Crown Employees*. This establishes that a minister may apply for assistance "where the relevant legal proceedings or inquiry arises out of or is related to the performance of a Minister's public duties". The duty on an applicant is to "establish that his or her involvement in the proceedings or inquiry relates to his or her official duties and that he or she has a substantial and direct interest in the proceedings."

The guidelines are silent about whether legal assistance automatically follows if an applicant meets both tests. The circular nominates the attorney general as the person to make the ultimate decision in the case of a ministerial application. In practice it is likely that the attorney general would seek Cabinet approval of his or her decision. A decision to reject such an application, if the minister meets both tests, would be tantamount to the attorney general or the Cabinet making a judgment about the guilt or otherwise of the minister, a matter surely for the courts to decide.

Under these guidelines Jackson would obviously have been entitled to apply for legal assistance. There could be no argument that the proceedings related to his official duties and that he had a substantial and direct interest in the proceedings. A Cabinet today would be faced with the same dilemma that the Wran Cabinet faced in November 1984. It is strange that Ackland, who is legally educated, would suggest that resolution of this dilemma by other than a rejection of the application would leave "a nasty taste in the mouth".

The Wran government certainly made mistakes over the early-release scheme, beginning with permitting the scheme to operate without rigorous and transparent oversight. It was, however, quick to suspend and then terminate the scheme once it became aware of the possibility of it being a vehicle for corruption. The government can also be criticised for being tardy in investigating Jackson's involvement, although it was handicapped by a slow-moving NSW Police investigation. The NSW Police, in turn, were hampered by the commitment given to the Federal Police. In hindsight it can be argued that the government should have been quicker in having the matter investigated by an independent body, although this would have meant going against the advice of the police commissioner. The Jackson affair is certainly justification for the establishment of a body such as the Independent Commission Against Corruption (ICAC) with greater investigative powers than those available to the police. It should be noted, however, that throughout the special commission of inquiry, and the subsequent trials, there was no suggestion or evidence of corruption on the part of any other member of the Wran Government.

Jackson was released from prison in November 1989, under a Coalition government, having served only three years and three months, coincidentally the amount of the non-parole period initially imposed. His release was based on good behaviour. No-one appears to have noted the irony of him gaining an early release from prison. Jackson was welcomed with supportive banners when he returned to live in the same modest house in his former electorate. He was later elected chair of the Helensburgh precinct committee of the local council. He made a living selling hot dogs and ice cream out of a mobile canteen at Stanwell Tops, inevitably attracting attention from the media.

Wran would meet Jackson once more, in 2006 at the funeral in St Mary's Cathedral of former Wran minister, Kevin Stewart. Jackson managed to be seated in an area reserved for Labor royalty, including Wran and former prime minister Paul Keating. Jackson leaned over and tapped Wran on the shoulder. Wran was obviously startled to find Jackson in such company but quickly recovered his poise and the two chatted amiably. Jackson died in December 2011. His obituaries were unforgiving. David Marr in *The Sydney Morning Herald* was savage: "He had neither brains nor political convictions. Somewhere in there was a soft heart but his colleagues knew him as the toughest bully in Parliament – and a hopeless gambler."

Jackson, having served his sentence, should not be forever framed by his crime. Nevertheless, his actions left an indelible stain on the reputation of the Wran government. Jackson's former Labor colleagues were more charitable than the obituarists. Kevin Stewart invited Jackson to lunches he occasionally arranged with former Right faction ministers, even though Jackson had not been a member of the faction. Stewart told his colleagues this was important to assist Jackson's rehabilitation. Terry Sheahan admitted to trepidation when he again met Jackson at one of these lunches. Sheahan, as attorney general, had been the minister to formally terminate payment of his legal fees and had twice refused 'no Bill' applications by Jackson's lawyers to discontinue Jackson's trials. He told me: "I tentatively offered Rex my hand and greeted him. 'Good day mate' was the reply".

10

Riddled with Corruption

"The Wran government was riddled with corruption." Journalist Bernard Keane.

"The NSW Premier, Neville Wran, whose administration later became a byword for graft, ..." Journalist Richard Cooke.

"Every time some allegation is completely disposed of, another allegation is fabricated." Neville Wran.

Very few politicians in NSW, if they become ministers, finish their political careers without experiencing at least one false allegation of corruption against them. These days parliamentarians have a handy vehicle for immediately discrediting such allegations. The late Michael Egan, Treasurer in the Carr Labor government, demonstrated a side benefit of the establishment of ICAC, even though Egan had initially opposed it. Egan feared it would usurp the role of the police and the courts. Confronted by a newspaper claim that he had been complicit in the sale of a government building for less than the market price, Egan immediately referred the claim to ICAC which took little time in dismissing it.

The Wran ministry was not immune from rumour mongering. Frank Walker experienced a clumsy attempt to saddle him with a false Swiss bank account, which was thwarted by good staff work. Bill Crabtree, who held the police portfolio for around 18 months, was cleared of an allegation of receiving bribes and never personally recovered from the traumatic experience. Even Ron Mulock, acknowledged on both sides of parliament as one of the most decent men to have served, revealed in his memoir that he had been forced to successfully clear his name after a politically motivated allegation during the Woodward Royal Commission into Drug Trafficking.

Paul Landa, after he died, was accused in October 1987, in a short-lived magazine *The Eye*, of receiving a bribe on the uncorroborated word of an unnamed former staffer. The magazine claimed the former staffer had been present when a brown paper bag containing $60,000 in cash was handed to Landa. The magazine did not ask the former staffer how he or she could be so precise about the amount if it was in a brown paper bag. NSW police interviewed Landa's former staffers and all denied witnessing such a transaction or being aware of such a transaction. One staff member told the investigators: "Even if you believe Landa was corrupt, no-one has ever suggested he was stupid. Only a stupid person would accept a bribe in the presence of another person, particularly a staff member. The claim is nonsense." The police investigation found no evidence to support the allegation.

In the 10-year Wran administration, Rex Jackson was the only ministerial resignation resulting from a scandal. By contrast the Coalition government which succeeded the Labor government 'lost' nine ministers (including a premier) and MPs after various scandals. Admittedly none of these transgressions was as serious as Jackson's, although one of the Liberal MPs also ended up in jail. Nevertheless, despite this contrasting penalty count, it is the Wran government which has become a "byword for graft" according to one journalist, Richard Cooke, and "riddled with corruption" according to another, Bernard Keane. Both were still in short pants when the Wran government was elected so neither is relying on original work in making such claims.

Serious corruption allegations have been made against two Wran ministers after their deaths. In both cases the normal journalistic rule requiring multiple sources for an allegation were jettisoned. Wran's complaint that "every time some allegation is completely disposed of, another allegation is fabricated" also applies to two of his closest ministerial supporters: Eric Bedford, who died in 2006; and Paul Landa, who died in office in 1984. In both cases the allegations have been conveyed by an investigative journalist, Kate McClymont.

Eric Bedford has been a favourite target of McClymont. In her 2014 book (with Linton Besser) on a later Labor identity Eddie Obeid, *He Who Must Be Obeid*, she makes several corruption allegations against Bedford but provides no credible evidence. The most fanciful claim is that Bedford, as Minister for Planning and Environment (from 1980 to 1984), had solicited bribes by asking developers to admire his wife's paintings, hanging on his office wall, and commissioning similar paintings from his wife for a nominated sum.

The authors' source is a "former Bedford staffer" whom they don't identify. Since these alleged offences occurred over 40 years ago there is no justification for this person remaining anonymous. There can be no fear of retribution; no role for ICAC; and, with Bedford dead, no chance of a defamation action. The book was later withdrawn and remaining copies pulped because of a reckless defamation of a living person. The publisher announced it would only be reissued after being thoroughly fact-checked. The publisher was provided with statements by two former Bedford staffers, and by the former head of Bedford's department, all identified by name, confirming that Jo Bedford's naïve art had never been displayed in her husband's office.

In the pulped edition of the book, the authors wrote:

> Other Bedford staff members have since confirmed that the minister was indeed on the take. But instead of cash in a brown paper bag, Bedford had come up with an ingenious method for corrupt payments. The staffer said that developers were advised that when they went to lobby Bedford about a rezoning they had to 'admire' the artwork hanging on the office wall, which had been painted by his wife. If Bedford intended to assist, the supplicant was told that for a certain amount of money Bedford's wife would be happy to bend her brush on a similar artistic endeavour for the developer.

In the reissued edition, this was changed:

> One Bedford staffer recalled that the minister had come up with an ingenious method for corrupt payments. The staffer said that developers were advised that when they went to lobby Bedford about a rezoning they had to 'admire' the artwork hanging on his office wall, which the minister suggested had been painted by his wife. If Bedford intended to assist, the supplicant was told that for a certain amount of money Bedford's wife would be happy to bend her brush for a similar artistic endeavour for the developer. In fact, Mrs Bedford had nothing to do with the minister's artworks, which were on loan from the Art Gallery of New South Wales.

The changes tell us much about how the publisher now views the original allegation. First, the book belatedly concedes that this allegation was made by just "one Bedford staffer" (singular), not "other Bedford staff members" (plural). Contrary to standard journalistic practice, however, no effort was made to corroborate the anonymous allegation. Second, the book has been subtly changed from "which had been painted by his wife" to "which the minister suggested had been painted by his wife." This change is an admission by the authors that they no longer believe their source's claim that Mrs Bedford's art was displayed in the office. If the source got this crucial element wrong, why would the authors and publisher continue to believe the rest of the story? We are meant to believe that Sydney developers were so stupid that they gazed at heritage-value paintings owned by the Art Gallery of NSW and thought these were the "artistic endeavour" of Jo Bedford.

This allegation about Bedford is patently nonsense. The authors should never have reported this implausible story without corroboration and should never have persisted with it once staff members had debunked it. The revised paragraph, particularly with the important caveat of the final sentence, shows the publisher no longer believes it is true. If this was fact-checked, and found wanting, it should not have been republished.

McClymont's other allegation against Bedford concerns a proposed residential development in Perisher Valley pushed by Nick Scali and Eddie Obeid. The authors state the development required a rezoning. In fact, the development would have required an alteration to the park's plan of management, which was opposed by the National Parks and Wildlife Service (NPWS). The book is also in error in stating the opposition by the NPWS was because it exceeded the park's accommodation limit under the plan. The developers were seeking a strata title subdivision, so that individual lots could be sold, which was permitted at Thredbo but not at Perisher.

The odd thing about this episode is that, by the end of McClymont's account, she has demonstrated Bedford's behaviour was exemplary. She records that on four occasions Bedford had contacted the relevant NPWS regional director, presumably after persistent lobbying by Scali and Obeid. On each occasion, according to McClymont, the official resisted it as being inconsistent with the plan of management. It is apparent from McClymont's account that Bedford took the matter no further. We know this because she reports that in 1988 Scali and Obeid were still lobbying Bob Carr, who had succeeded Bedford in 1984 as the relevant minister. Bedford also had the power, under section 73B of the *National Parks and Wildlife Act 1974*, to propose an amendment to the plan of management and to require the director to make it. He did not do so.

Bedford behaved as one would expect an honest minister to behave when under political pressure. He sought departmental advice on several occasions; he did not lean on his departmental officials to alter their advice; and declined to exercise his lawful authority to overrule the department. Far from being evidence of corruption, McClymont's account confirms Bedford behaved honourably. Her prose is convincing to everyone but herself.

Despite providing no credible evidence of Bedford's alleged corruption in the book on Obeid, McClymont has continued to blacken his name. In her later book (with Vanda Carson), *Dead Man Walking: The Murky World of Michael McGurk and Ron Medich*, she repeats another astonishing allegation. She claims that Bedford had employed the head of the Australian mafia on his staff. "During the 1980s ... Eric Bedford and one of his staffers, Francesco Labbozzetta, had come to the attention of police. Labbozzetta was described as 'Il Capo' of the Australian mafia in the South Australian Parliament," she wrote.

'Franco' Labbozzetta was employed in Bedford's electoral office as a liaison officer among ethnic constituents. Bedford's electorates of Fairfield, and later Cabramatta, were ethnically diverse communities. Labbozzetta's job was to try to resolve problems brought to the electoral office by Bedford's constituents, particularly those among the migrant community. Richard Smyth, who was Director of Planning when Bedford was the minister, told me in 2020: "Labbozzetta often came to the department with development problems in the minister's electorate seeking to get a solution. Like all staff from the minister's office, he was requested to work through me or one of my deputies in the first instance. The problems came from across the community. Sometimes we could help him, sometimes we could not. I have no recollection of any pressure from him. He tended to accept our responses and go."

McClymont offers no credible evidence for alleging that Labbozzetta was an Australian mafia don. Her proof is the claim that Labbozzetta had been named in the South Australian Parliament but she declines to state whether this naming was by someone in authority, such as the police minister or the attorney-general or the result of a parliamentary inquiry into organised crime. It was none of these but McClymont neglects to inform the readers of the source and the circumstances. Labbozzetta was described as 'Il Capo' by a Liberal backbencher, Peter Lewis, in a question on notice clearly intended as a political smear. The questioning occurred during a period of what can only be described as 'corruption hysteria' in South Australia in the late 1980s. Much of this was directed at the Attorney

General, Chris Sumner, a person of impeccable integrity, who was subsequently found innocent of all allegations.

A flavour of the hysteria can be gleaned from the text of Lewis' question on notice. Lewis asked the minister representing the Attorney General in the House of Assembly: "Since January 1980 has the Attorney-General visited Plati or any other part of the Calabrian region of Italy and, if so, (a) on how many occasions; (b) what was the purpose of each visit; (c) was a Mr Francesco Labbozzetta, also known as Il Capo, involved in any way in the arrangement of any part of the itinerary of one or more of such visits and, if so, how? (d) where was the Attorney-General accommodated and if he did not stay at a recognised hotel, who paid or met the cost of that accommodation; and (e) who paid or met the cost of his transport?"

The minister subsequently responded: "1.The only visit which the Attorney-General has made to Calabria was in November 1974. From April to November 1974 he was studying Italian at the University for Foreigners at Perugia in Umbria. In November, he made a tourist visit of ten days or so to the south of Italy, namely the regions of Campania, Calabria and Sicily. He travelled by train. In Calabria, he spent one night in Cosenza and then travelled by train to Catanzaro, and then on to Taormina in Sicily. He met his own travel and accommodation expenses. The Attorney-General has not visited Plati. The answer to (c) is 'No'". (Hansard, House of Assembly, 14 November 1989, p.1988). This visit to Italy was made before Sumner entered the South Australian Parliament.

Since all the other claims inferred by Lewis in his question on notice are demonstrably wrong no credence should be given to his claim that Labbozzetta was the head of the Australian mafia. Peter Lewis, who died in 2017, had a colourful and erratic parliamentary career. In 2002, having left the Liberal Party and then sitting as an independent, he reneged on a deal with the Liberals to form government. He instead accepted an offer of the speakership from the Labor Party enabling it to take office. Lewis was forced to resign as

Speaker in 2005 ahead of a likely successful no confidence motion, after making unsubstantiated allegations against a serving member of parliament. Labor's then deputy premier, Kevin Foley, described Lewis' behaviour as "shameful" and "reckless".

There is no evidence that McClymont bothered to check the Hansard and, if she did, no evidence that she bothered to investigate the credibility of the person who named Labozzetta. If she did so, she should in fairness have identified Lewis as the relevant person. If she did not, she is guilty of careless journalism. Chris Sumner advised me that Lewis subsequently apologised to him for the question and told him it had been handed to him by a senior Liberal in the Parliament (whom Lewis named) who didn't want to put his own name to it. McClymont's evidence turns out to be anonymous political smearing.

McClymont's desire to tar Labbozzetta as a mafia don reaches even more ridiculous levels. In the book on Obeid, McClymont wrote about a business partnership involving Labbozzetta's wife. "Whether the name of their company Capolab was a play on Labbozzetta's rumoured position as Il Capo is not known," she wrote. A simple check would have confirmed it is unlikely the head of the mafia would have deliberately drawn attention to himself in this way. According to Labbozzetta's daughter, Michela, Capolab was a venture involving two families, the Capobiancos and the Labbozzettas: hence Capo-lab.

This brings us to McClymont's claim that Bedford and Labbozzetta had come to the attention of NSW police. She wrote in the book on McGurk: "In December 1987 [Labbozzetta] was interviewed by New South Wales police. Among the many questions they asked him was, 'Would you care to tell us if you had any suspicions or knowledge of Mr Bedford receiving large amounts of money for development approvals or rezoning applications?' 'No, no suspicions at all,' replied Labbozzetta breezily. He also denied he had received money or benefits on Bedford's behalf."

In the McGurk book McClymont supplies no information about the circumstances which caused Labbozzetta to come to the attention of police. In the earlier book on Obeid, however, she says Labbozzetta's "business card, as Bedford's ethnic affairs advisor, was found among the papers of Bruno Brizzi, who had been arrested in the early 1980s over a $6 million marijuana crop near Bourke". Nobody can be expected to perform due diligence on a person before handing over a business card, so this is hardly evidence of criminality. It is reason enough, however, for police to interview Labbozzetta. Since the police took no further action, the correct conclusion should be that the police found no evidence that Labbozzetta, or Bedford, had been involved in criminal activities.

* * * * *

Eric Bedford is not the only dead Wran government minister who is traduced in the Obeid book. McClymont also alleges corruption on the part of Bedford's immediate predecessor as planning and environment minister, Paul Landa, who died suddenly in 1984 when he was attorney general. Before examining this allegation, it is necessary to provide some background, which is not given in her book.

In May 1978 Landa announced an inquiry into a contentious mining proposal at Diamond Hill, near Kurrajong, at the base of the Blue Mountains. The inquiry was to be conducted by the head of the State Pollution Control Commission (SPCC), Eric Coffey. The inquiry followed refusal by the then Colo Shire Council of a development application to mine for basalt by a newly formed company, Kurrajong Aggregates. The council had unanimously recommended to the NSW Planning and Environment Commission, the relevant determining authority, that the application be refused. Despite the name it was basalt, not diamonds, which was considered likely to exist below the surface of Diamond Hill. Basalt was valuable as the aggregate for road surfacing. The associated breccia – more plentiful, with plenty of substitutes, and therefore less valuable – was still useful as road fill. There had been several mining proposals for the area, beginning in 1968 with an application by Farley and Lewers, a quarrying and cement company, but all had been rejected.

Landa's decision to hold an inquiry seemed sensible, given the continuing controversy over Diamond Hill and the fact that a previous SPCC inquiry into the extractive industries made no reference to a resource in this area. McClymont and Besser tell a different story, however. They claim Landa extracted a bribe of $50,000 in exchange for "setting up an inquiry that would allow the mine to proceed." It is necessary to stress those quoted words since this assertion is important in determining the truth or otherwise of the allegation. According to the book, Landa chose the wrong man to conduct the inquiry. Coffey found against the proposal. The authors claim the minister "had no wriggle room – the money paid to Landa was for nothing." The authors further claim, solely on the word of one of those who claimed he paid the bribe, that he demanded Landa repay the money and that Landa had handed back the cash.

The authors rely solely on claims by two people from Kurrajong Aggregates, Karim Kisrwani, who claims he paid the bribe, and Dr Peter Solomon, a Liberal Party activist. Oddly, the authors withheld pertinent information about both men which would allow readers to assess the credibility of those making the allegations. Kisrwani (who died after the book was published) is described as a "once close friend" of Eddie Obeid. Like Obeid, Kisrwani was prominent in the Australian Lebanese community but on the Liberal side of politics. He also had a colourful business reputation.

In 2003 he figured in a 'cash-for-visas' controversy with claims in the Federal Parliament that he had used his close relationship with the then Liberal Immigration Minister, Philip Ruddock, to obtain visas for people in return for payment and political donations. Labor's Julia Gillard also claimed in Parliament that a controversial Filipino businessman, Dante Tan, paid Kisrwani $220,000 to help persuade Ruddock to overturn a departmental decision to refuse Tan a visa. Gillard, who said Tan was "responsible for the single biggest corporate fraud that there has ever been in the Philippines", claimed Kisrwani raised the issue with Ruddock's office only a month after Kisrwani contributed $10,000 to Ruddock's re-election. The minister reversed the decision but has strongly denied any connection between his decision and the donation. There has never been any suggestion that Ruddock, known for his integrity, acted improperly or dishonestly.

The controversy led to a Senate Inquiry into Ministerial Discretion in Migration Matters. The report lists several allegations about Kisrwani who, despite not being a registered migration agent, had a remarkably high success rate in supporting candidates for ministerial intervention. The committee reported "of the cases where a decision had actually been made by the minister before 29 August 2003 close to half had received ministerial intervention." According to the committee, this success rate was much higher than other individuals and community groups, including Amnesty International. The committee further noted its attempts to investigate whether there was any connection between Kisrwani's success and his political donations had been hampered by a denial of access to relevant files and by Kisrwani's refusal to appear before the committee.

Solomon does not make a specific allegation against Landa but is quoted as saying "the whole issue was full of corruption". While the authors note Solomon was preselected as the Liberal candidate for the federal seat of North Sydney, they strangely fail to record that he was subsequently forced to resign his preselection. The farcical circumstances of the North Sydney preselection are detailed in Ian Hancock's history of the NSW Liberal Party. Hancock notes "in choosing Solomon, the preselectors did not know that he had included inaccurate particulars in the dossier which accompanied his candidature." The inaccuracies related to Solomon's service in the Army Reserve and included him claiming to have been an officer. More serious were allegations of Solomon's strange behaviour and associations in defending himself. Hancock cites the Liberal State President, David Patten, a political ally of Solomon, concluding after an investigation of Solomon's candidature that "it caused him 'great distress' that Solomon had so compromised himself that he had to stand down as a candidate".

In fairness to Landa, a person unable to defend himself, readers should have been provided with more information about those making the allegation. The fact that the character and veracity of both men had been publicly questioned is relevant and should have been reason for rigorous corroboration of the allegation before reporting it unquestioningly.

The authors also failed to apply proper journalistic scepticism in evaluating the allegations. First, and most critically, is the question of why Landa would have taken the risky path of setting up an inquiry if he wanted to pocket $50,000. Despite the authors claiming the inquiry "would allow the mine to proceed", a favourable finding by Coffey would not necessarily have led to approval. The final authority was not the SPCC but the NSW Planning and Environment Commission (PEC) and the SPCC could not replace the PEC as the determining authority.

I sought the advice of John Whitehouse, one of Sydney's leading planning lawyers, remembering that these events occurred before the passage of the *Environmental Planning and Assessment Act 1979*, one of Landa's significant ministerial achievements. Whitehouse's advice is reproduced in full below:

> In July 1977 the NSW Planning and Environment Commission issued a direction under section 342V(3) of the then Local Government Act 1919. The direction required a Council to forward development applications for extractive industries to the PEC for determination.
>
> The direction was issued following an environmental investigation conducted by the State Pollution Control Commission into extractive industries in the Hawkesbury Region. The report was released and published under the authority of Minister Landa on 18 March 1977 (State Pollution Control Commission 'Extractive industries in the Hawkesbury Region', SPCC, Sydney, March 1977).

Under the provisions of the Local Government Act 1919 applying to a development application which was the subject of a PEC direction, the PEC was required to offer both the Council and the Applicant a right for a hearing before dealing with any development application under s. 342V(3). If the Applicant was dissatisfied with the decision of the PEC, it had the right of appeal to the Minister under s.243V(5). If either the Council or the Applicant requested, there was a right of a hearing under s.243V(5A) before the matter was reported to the Minister. The Minister had the final role to determine the application under s.342V(5B).

In the case of Diamond Hill, the Minister referred the matter to the SPCC for a public inquiry under s.23 of the State Pollution Control Commission Act 1970. A SPCC inquiry could not lead to an approval, nor could it substitute for the right of a hearing under s.342V(3) before the PEC determined an application, or before the Minister decided an application under s.342V(5A). The rationale for a SPCC inquiry was that the SPCC had just published a major review of extractive industries in the Hawkesbury region, and that report made no reference to any significant gravel resource at Diamond Hill, as was claimed by the applicant. But an SPCC inquiry could not lead to any approval.

If Landa wished to approve the Diamond Hill development application all he needed to do was let the statutory provisions of s.342V(3) occur and approve it at the conclusion of those processes.

Following the SPCC inquiry into Diamond Hill, it is noted that neither the Applicant or the Council sought a hearing before the PEC refused the development application, and the Applicant did not appeal to the Minister against the PEC's decision, as they could have.

The key allegation against Landa – that he set up the SPCC inquiry to approve the proposal – therefore does not stand up. If Landa had been bribed, he had no need to establish an inquiry and Landa would have known that holding such an inquiry would not "allow the mine to proceed". Indeed, setting up the inquiry was counterproductive if the objective was to approve the application. The public and political reaction of a ministerial approval, following an adverse finding by Coffey, would have been immense. If Landa had been bribed, a ministerial approval under section 342V(5B), without the risk and glare of a public inquiry and finding, would have been a far more sensible approach.

The amount of the alleged bribe should also have led to scepticism on the part of the authors. For most people $50,000 is still a lot of money but in 1978 it was a huge amount, the equivalent of over $300,000 in today's dollars. The median Sydney house price in 1978 was only $37,000. Kurrajong Aggregates had nominal share capital of $40,000 and paid-up capital of only $1,000. We are meant to believe that Kisrwani was prepared to hand over more than the value of the company in a bribe. This smells like someone in 2014 inventing a story, and an amount, about events he claimed had occurred in 1978 and forgetting to discount the figure for 40 years of inflation.

Kisrwani claims he handed over the cash, in a bag, in May 1978 and that Landa returned it to him after Coffey reported in February 1979. There was an easy way for the authors to check the veracity of Kisrwani's allegations. He told the authors he went to his local Westpac branch in Parramatta and withdrew the cash. If the authors had been reporting this allegation about a person with access to the defamation laws, they would have demanded from Kisrwani the record of the transaction, something Kisrwani could have obtained from his bank without trouble. There is no evidence they bothered to do so. Incidentally Westpac wasn't formed until October 1982, four years later.

Nor do the authors appear to have asked themselves: why would Kisrwani hand over such a substantial bribe simply to hold an inquiry, which he must have known from his legal advisers would not necessarily have led to an approval? Why not hold on to the money and wait until after the inquiry had reported? If he is to be believed, Kisrwani was not only corrupt but displayed a naiveté and level of trust not usually associated with Sydney developers. The allegation against Landa is simply not credible.

Kisrwani's account of the saga of Diamond Hill does not end there, however. Part two allegedly takes place five years later, in 1984, when Kisrwani, now linked in business with Obeid, claims he sought to resurrect the mining proposal. According to McClymont, Kisrwani said he handed over $100,000 to Obeid, supposedly for the purpose of bribing Bob Carr, who was now Minister for Planning and Environment, and Labor Senator Graham Richardson. Kisrwani claims he was told by Obeid that Carr was to get $35,000 and Richardson was to get $65,000. Both Carr and Richardson have denied receiving any money from Obeid and their denials are reported by the authors. The obvious inference in the book is that the $100,000, if indeed it was paid, was pocketed by Obeid.

In considering the credibility of these further allegations, it is necessary to examine the findings of the SPCC's Diamond Hill inquiry. The authors touch only briefly on these findings.

The environmental impact statement by Kurrajong Aggregates estimated there was a proven quantity of 14 million tonnes of basalt and possibly as much as 20 million tonnes. The company later revised down its estimate to 10.6 million tonnes of extractable rock, of which 7.1 million tonnes would be sold as first quality road sealing aggregate and the remainder as road fill. Coffey found that estimate far exceeded other assessments, including those by Farley and Lewers and Pioneer Concrete, both of which had expertise in quarrying, unlike Kurrajong Aggregates. Farley and Lewers estimated there was only 2.3 million tonnes of basalt and concluded, according to Coffey, "that the viability of extracting the reserves was marginal and therefore did not proceed." Pioneer Concrete estimated the deposit totalled 5.4 million tonnes but, according to Coffey, the reserves "were definitely not great enough to permit economic exploitation of the deposit".

Coffey found that far from being a substantial deposit of basalt,

Diamond Hill would yield little and extraction would be uneconomic. He reported: "If the Commission had regard only to the firm data brought before the inquiry, it would assess the deposit as unproven beyond a total quantity of basalt and brecciated material of 5,100,000 tonnes, of which 4,670,000 tonnes would be capable of extraction. The likely maximum yield of first quality rock in these circumstances would be 3,100,000 tonnes. In either event, the deposit is so small in relation to total reserves elsewhere as to be inconsequential and, probably, uneconomic. This conclusion corroborates the earlier judgements of major companies such as Farley and Lewers and Pioneer Concrete, who, after detailed investigations, did not regard Diamond Hill to be a viable source of hard rock aggregate."

Coffey concluded that "even were the most optimistic assumptions regarding the practicality and economic viability of its extraction accepted the deposit would have very little importance as a natural resource". He recommended, instead, that Diamond Hill be rezoned for residential subdivision "to ensure prohibition of all activities and developments that would be incompatible with such preservation, including the extraction of hard rock and other minerals or material".

Coffey's thorough critique of the economic viability of the proposal undermines Kisrwani's later claim he sought to revive the project and paid Obeid $100,000 in bribes. Why would Kisrwani, with no expertise or experience in hard rock quarrying and no potential marketing contracts, seek to revive a mining proposal when Coffey had found there was "no evidence to show there is other than a minor deposit of hard rock"?

Under Coffey's recommendation the land was to be rezoned residential. The authors report that "the company's land at Diamond Hill was later subdivided and sold off for $2 million" and that Kisrwani was a beneficiary. With the prospect of a profitable residential subdivision on offer, why would Kisrwani seek to pursue an uneconomic and environmentally unacceptable mining proposal? There is no evidence that the authors asked this question of Kisrwani or of themselves.

Kisrwani's claim that in 1984 he sought to revive an uneconomic mining project, and forked out another $100,000 in bribes, is not credible. A more reasonable conclusion, based on the evidence, is that Kisrwani's claims about Obeid (and about Carr and Richardson), like his claims about Landa, are fanciful. It is astonishing this conclusion was not reached by the authors.

In her Andrew Olle Media Lecture in November 2014 Kate McClymont said: "The death threats I receive are not nearly as horrific as those nasty little white envelopes, with the law firm's address in the corner, which generally arrive by express delivery the day after your story." McClymont's revelation that it is the threat of defamation action which terrifies her the most perhaps explains why she was so careless when writing about Eric Bedford and Paul Landa. The relatives of dead people do not have the right to arrange "those the little white envelopes".

11

WE OWE THE DEAD THE TRUTH

"Despite gossip to the contrary, no persuasive evidence exists to support the view that Wran was corrupt in the sense of seeking personal financial gain. Nor is there persuasive evidence that Wran directly or indirectly sought to advance any criminal interests or had any direct or indirect relationships with such criminals." Rodney Tiffen.

"I don't think [Wran] was corrupt in the sense that he was taking money from business figures or colourful Sydney identities." Gary Sturgess, adviser to Liberal Premier Nick Greiner.

"They agree that Wran is not a crook, not game, Wran worked out a deal with Murdock (sic) for his support." Police summary of an illegally recorded telephone conversation on the phone of solicitor Morgan Ryan, 6 April 1980.

Rodney Cavalier, whom Wran appointed as Minister for Education in 1984, has one of the most extensive private libraries in NSW, a collection accumulated through more than 60 years of compulsive purchasing. In September 2021, Cavalier found in his library a copy of *George Freeman, an autobiography*, a book he could not recall buying or reading. On the front page, below Freeman's dedication to his wife and sons, Freeman had written in a child-like script and devoid of punctuation: "Neville I'm sure you will Enjoy chapter 17 as much as I liked writing it best wishes to you and your wife on your coming happy occasion G.F." Cavalier turned to chapter 17 which was an attack on crime writer Bob Bottom, who had been responsible for providing the transcripts of the illegal police wire taps to *The Age* newspaper. Wran had been outspoken in his criticism of the illegality of these recordings.

Cavalier provided me with a copy of the inscription, knowing I was researching this book. We were both puzzled. Neither of us was aware of allegations or gossip that Wran knew Freeman, a notorious Sydney SP operator and underworld figure, who died in 1990. Freeman had testified at the Street royal commission that he had never met Wran and this was not disputed. None of the books and articles on crime in NSW, including a book on Freeman, had ever mentioned or hinted at a connection between Freeman and Wran. Would this now require another chapter of this book?

Brian Dale, another bibliophile, solved the puzzle. The Freeman memoir had arrived unsolicited in Wran's office on its publication in 1988. This was after Wran had retired from parliament and just before the birth of his and Jill's daughter, Harriet, which was the "coming happy occasion". Jill's pregnancy had been widely publicised. Wran had put the book in the rubbish bin from which it had been retrieved by staff and passed to Dale for his own library. When Dale and his wife Sandra downsized from their family home, he passed some of his books, including Freeman's, to Cavalier. We all joked about what might have been the consequences if the book had landed instead in a second-hand bookshop and had eventually found its way into the hands of a sensationalist journalist. No need to rely on the word of a gangster's consort; here was evidence in writing of Wran's criminal connections.

This was not the first occasion Freeman had sought to create mischief. Wran had been forced to sit through each day of hearing of the Street royal commission in 1983. His days were broken only by the gratuitous advice he gave, during recesses, to his barrister, Alec Shand QC, on how Shand should be conducting his case. David Hurley, who had recently joined Wran as press secretary, accompanied him each day, always positioned one row behind Wran, who in turn sat behind Shand. Freeman had been called as a witness to explain his relationship with Murray Farquhar. Freeman appeared to treat his involvement in the commission as a joke. Hurley noted that Freeman was edging closer to him each day until one morning he found Freeman sitting beside him. Hurley, conscious that media eyes in the court room were constantly on Freeman, initially ignored the gangster's attempts to engage him in conversation. When that had no effect, Hurley curtly told him to "shut up." Freeman took the rebuff well: "I suppose if you talk to me, you will be next in the witness box". He then left the court. Wran, who had witnessed but could not hear the exchange, admonished Hurley in the luncheon break: "Why did you speak to that dreadful c**t?" Freeman's ploy had been observed by the press gallery. Evan Whitton, who wrote a daily sketch of proceedings for *The Sydney Morning Herald,* noted the next day, 25 June 1983, that Freeman "was in court yesterday in a dark blue suit, a light blue shirt, a red tie and a very dark tan and sitting, by chance, next to the Premier's press secretary, David Hurley." Whitton was unaware that this seating arrangement had not occurred "by chance".

I had no intention of including this anecdote in this book until one day I sought by telephone an interview with a person known to be a critic of Wran and free with his views that Wran was a crook. He refused my request for an interview but gave me parting advice: "I hope you include in your book the fact that Wran sat with George Freeman throughout his royal commission." When I pointed out that the royal commission had received extensive daily media coverage, none of which had included this very newsworthy fact, there was no response. I did not get the chance to relay David Hurley's anecdote or the fact that not even Hurley had been able to sit with Wran during his ordeal. If this person wants to fact check his assertion, and that is unlikely, he could look up Whitton's sketch published on 23 June 1983. Whitton accurately observed that throughout the royal commission Wran "sat shoulder-to-shoulder" with magistrate Kevin Jones and that neither man exchanged a word.

This anecdote illustrates how, in Sydney, one fact – a newspaper report of Wran's press secretary sitting next to Freeman – becomes, over time, a mythology that Wran sat with Freeman. It also illustrates one of the difficulties when examining allegations about Wran or any other prominent figure. Too often gossip passes for fact. This is exacerbated by journalists reporting gossip without any attempt at fact checking or corroboration. Examples of this journalistic laziness – journalistic malpractice is a more correct description – have been given throughout this book.

Rodney Tiffen has written that "the sheer number of controversies and allegations involving Wran has persuaded some people that he was corrupt". A "sheer number" in a city that thrives on malicious gossip means little but it is true that this has a corrosive effect on reputations. Wran admitted in 2000 his "residual bitterness" about malicious rumours spread about him during his time in politics. These included "that I was separated from Jill, that I paid her to appear on the political platform, that Jill had affairs with a whole range of people, people who were pretty notable around town." He also spoke of rumours "that I had a joint venture with Alan Bond to develop land at Tuncurry" and that "I had a half share in the Watson's Bay Hotel." Wran had previously noted that "refutation after refutation of false claims becomes itself evidence of 'a log of allegations of corruption'".

At the risk of adding to this "log of allegations of corruption", what has this book's examination of the corruption controversies found? Wran died a wealthy man, although not as wealthy as reported by the media. There is no evidence his wealth was accumulated during his period in politics, other than a healthy superannuation entitlement, and much evidence to the contrary. Wran built his wealth after leaving politics when he joined a merchant banking business founded by Malcolm Turnbull. Chapter seven has shown that it is Turnbull who, by legitimate means, made Wran a wealthy man.

Chapter three concludes there is no credible evidence of criminality in Wran's long-standing friendship with the controversial bookmaker, Bill Waterhouse. He was a beneficiary of the cut in the bookmakers' turnover tax in Wran's first budget but Wran's pledge to do so was an opportunistic election commitment which benefited the bookmaking industry, not just Waterhouse. Bookmakers still ended up paying more tax under Wran than they had for many decades. Waterhouse did not achieve from Wran his long-held ambition to hold a casino licence and the illegal casino he did operate for around a year was shut down by the actions of Wran's police minister with Wran's approval. Allegations that Wran financially benefited from this illegal casino are based on uncorroborated allegations and hearsay and one party to this hearsay denies it.

The allegation by an ABC television program that Wran handed the lease for Luna Park to crime boss Abe Saffron has been demonstrated in chapter five to be without foundation. The ABC ignored evidence the relevant decision was made by a committee of senior public servants. The Corporate Affairs Commission, after a lengthy investigation, found no evidence of Saffron having an ownership interest in the relevant lessee companies. Similarly, no evidence was produced for the program's claim that Wran interfered with the police investigation of the Luna Park fire to protect Saffron, a person Wran had previously told Parliament he had never met. This claim was quickly disavowed by the ABC's managing director.

Allegations by a retired chief magistrate that the Street royal commission got it wrong and that Wran had perverted the course of justice have been shown in chapter four to be implausible. The same magistrate has admitted that he was never asked to do anything illegal or improper by Wran or by any member of his government.

Chapter nine has shown there is no evidence that Wran, or anyone else in his government, were implicated in the prisoner early-release scheme which led to the jailing of the Minister for Corrective Services, Rex Jackson. The delays in the police investigation of Jackson's involvement were caused by a commitment given to the Federal Police not to expose the existence and identity of a police informer. The delay in bringing Jackson to justice did not prevent the government quickly suspending and then terminating the scheme once it became aware of possible wrongdoing. The claim that the government paid Jackson's legal fees, after he was charged with offences, is misleading. The payment was authorised by the independent Legal Services Commission and only after Jackson had exhausted his own financial resources.

Claims that Wran, in his dealings with media proprietors, was "happy to use the government's prerogatives to advance Labor's interests and that he wouldn't be inhibited by procedural niceties" have been shown in chapter eight to be without foundation. There is no doubt that Wran's motives were to assist the re-election of his government. That doesn't make him unusual as a political leader. In doing so, however, Wran did not ignore "procedural niceties" and it is difficult for anyone to argue those decisions have not been in the best interests of NSW citizens.

The transcripts of the illegal police phone taps did not implicate Wran in any wrongdoing. The only questionable action in which he was involved, according to *The Age*, was favouring a public servant, a former Labor candidate, in a senior public service appointment. Chapter six reveals this claim was discredited by a federal parliamentary commission of inquiry which found that all decisions had been made on public service advice. Neither Morgan Ryan nor Lionel Murphy had any influence on Wran, as had been alleged.

In hindsight, that most valuable commodity, Wran made mistakes in two critical senior police appointments, discussed in chapter two. The selection of Mervyn Wood as police commissioner proved to be a poor choice but is understandable since he had been recommended as commissioner by a selection committee of very distinguished Australians. The rapid promotion of Bill Allen to deputy commissioner, with the intention of him becoming commissioner, was also a mistake. This was not a case of promoting a policeman known to be corrupt. Evidence of Allen's corruption only became known after he was promoted to deputy commissioner. Claims that the government 'looked after' Allen by allowing him to retire are wrong. If the government had not negotiated Allen's demotion, and consequential reduction in superannuation, Allen could have retired soon after with the full entitlements of a deputy commissioner.

The failure to force Murray Farquhar off the bench when chief magistrate was also, in retrospect, an error although this would not have prevented Wran's ordeal before the Street royal commission. Chapter four reveals this was a decision by key ministers, not just Wran, and Farquhar's reputation in the community at the time was high. An investigation by very senior public servants found there were no grounds to remove him or to prevent him returning to bench duties. The consideration shown to Farquhar was later found to be undeserved.

Just why Wran has attracted such gossip and unfounded allegations is difficult to explain. I was struck by the contrast with former Labor prime minister Bob Hawke, following the publication in 2021 of Troy Bramston's substantial biography of Hawke. Bramston revealed the financial support provided to Hawke prior to him entering parliament by business friends, particularly transport magnate Sir Peter Abeles. Bramston, who had Hawke's full co-operation in his biography, reports they "paid his hotel bills, picked up the tab at the Boulevard Hotel … provided him with drinks, cigars and women." Abeles also paid Hawke's mortgage and his children's private school fees, as well as bailing him out of gambling debts over the years.

Abeles had significant influence on Hawke after he became prime minister, most notably during the pilots' strike in 1989 which obviously affected the Abeles-owned Ansett Australia. Abeles was able to veto Senator Graham Richardson taking the transport and communications portfolio because of personal animosity between the two men. David Hill, when appointed chairman of the ABC, had to overcome objections to him which Abeles voiced to Hawke. Hill had been a board member of the government-owned TAA and the two men had clashed during an official trade mission to China. Hill had objected to what he regarded as Abeles constantly pushing Ansett's commercial interests, rather than the nation's, during the visit.

Despite Bramston's revelation of Hawke's financial reliance on

Abeles and others prior to entering parliament little publicity has been given to these revelations. Sex trumps money in public appeal. Commentary on the biography centred on Hawke's frenetic sexual activities, even though this did not come under the heading of 'breaking news'. There is no evidence the financial revelations have impacted, or will impact, on Hawke's considerable reputation and popularity. Nor do I believe this is evidence of Hawke behaving corruptly in office. Such a revelation about Wran, however, would be regarded as 'game, set and match' by those who accuse him of being corrupt. I have spent several pages of this book addressing an uncorroborated allegation that Wran accepted $5,000 before becoming premier from his bookmaking friend Bill Waterhouse, which has been put forward as evidence of Wran being as "bent as a $3 note". I have shown that this transaction, if it indeed occurred, is most likely to have been an election donation, not a payment to Wran personally.

Graham Freudenberg advanced one theory about why Wran was singled out for corruption claims. He believed the accusations of corruption were a deliberate tactic by the opposition parties to put a dent in Wran's electoral dominance. Freudenberg wrote that in early 1980, "when our prospects seemed splendidly serene, I had said to [Wran] 'They'll never get you by normal means. They will develop a theory of corruption to explain your success and try to destroy you'". Wran also endorsed Freudenberg's claim. I have never been persuaded by this theory. An Opposition cannot sustain a credible campaign of government corruption without the necessary fodder. This was proved by the 'no holds barred' parliamentary debate on corruption which Wran called on 23 September 1980 and which left the Coalition scoreless. Not surprisingly, when Nick Greiner later succeeded John Dowd as Leader of the Opposition, he declared that the Liberal Party, under his leadership, would concentrate on 'bread and butter' issues. This was an implicit criticism of the corruption strategy that Dowd had pursued unsuccessfully against Wran.

Only after a few 'own goals' by the Wran government, such as

Murray Farquhar and Bill Allen, did the ammunition emerge for a credible campaign. All successful Opposition leaders must be opportunists and be prepared to seize any chance to expose weaknesses in a government. Greiner was no different and he took the opportunities that came his way. This was summed up in a reported exchange between Greiner and Liberal senator Chris Puplick at a function after the airing of the ABC *Four Corners* 'The Big League' program. Puplick is reported to have asked Greiner: "Is Murray Farquhar a bread-and-butter issue?" Ken Turner, in his comprehensive account of the 1984 NSW election, wrote: "In May [1983] the *Herald* reported [Greiner's] preference for playing down the anti-corruption crusade, in favour of treatment of bread-and-butter issues, where the voters' interests still lay. Still, he was able to take advantage when the breaks came his way on the corruption issue".

One of Greiner's key strategists, Gary Sturgess, has acknowledged the Opposition found no evidence Wran was personally corrupt. "I don't think [Wran] was corrupt in the sense he was taking money from business figures or colourful Sydney identities. Some of it was clearly a network of old friends who he continued to stand by as the years progressed, such as Lionel Murphy. Some of it was that he was caught in a shift of values – things that had gone on forever like phone calls to a public official about a mate's problems were no longer acceptable. Some of it was that by the middle of the 1980s, he was forced to defend actions and decisions that he had made, and which ministers and senior public officials had taken on his watch." Incidentally, the only alleged instances of Wran being involved in phone calls "about a mate's problems" – Murray Farquhar/Kevin Humphries and Lionel Murphy/Bill Jegorow – have been shown in this book not to be true.

Another explanation for Wran being singled out for corruption claims is said to be the way in which Wran responded to allegations of corruption. Brian Toohey, then editor of *The National Times*, when asked to justify publishing the initial report of the illegal police transcripts, said: "Denigration and denial have been the order of the day when corruption issues have been raised in NSW". Others have claimed the government was slow in responding to allegations of corruption made against key figures. David Clune wrote: "When confronted with evidence of widespread corruption, Wran made the serious error of trying to obfuscate and cover-up. Rather than admitting that there was a real problem that needed to be urgently addressed, he over-confidently assumed his political and parliamentary skills would enable him to defuse the situation." Clune has clarified to me that this criticism was limited to claims about the police and the judicial system generally. He cites the findings of the Wood royal rommission into the police in the 1990s as justification for his criticism.

Dennis Shanahan has claimed, with considerable exaggeration: "When an allegation was made there would be a denial, denigrating the 'alligators' and maintaining the innocence of all involved. If pressure was maintained and more evidence came out there would be a tactical retreat to an internal government inquiry, police inquiry or departmental investigation. Such internal inquiries could easily be controlled or limited by resources or terms of references and would often result in a finding which cleared the accused or could not substantiate the evidence. If new evidence emerged, or details of the internal inquiry came out which cast doubt on the original findings, there could be another government inquiry or finally an independent or judicial inquiry. Only when there was stark irrefutable and public evidence did the allegations lead to charges or a sacking." Shanahan's final sentence is particularly odd. Most fair-minded people would expect that "charges or a sacking" should only follow "stark" and "irrefutable public evidence."

The claim that the Wran Government often dragged its feet when investigating allegations of corruption does not stand up to examination. Ron Mulock immediately commissioned an investigation into Murray Farquhar's links with George Freeman as soon as the first newspaper report appeared. Peter Anderson wasted no time in arranging for the President of the Police Tribunal to investigate allegations against Deputy Commissioner Bill Allen, after the police commissioner alerted him to the possibility of wrongdoing and after Allen had been interviewed by the commissioner. The delay in the tribunal beginning its work was caused by a court challenge to the tribunal's authority. Wran, following the ABC *Four Corners* 'The Big League' program, immediately requested the attorney general refer the transcript to Crown Law officers. He agreed to a royal commission on the same day the crucial statement by magistrate Kevin Jones was received. The legitimate reasons for the delays in the investigation of allegations against Rex Jackson were outlined in chapter nine. Nevertheless, it is correct that a perception developed that the government was tardy or reluctant to investigate allegations of corruption. This was mainly the result of police investigations of allegations, then the proper course of action, which were slow moving and, in some cases, clearly inadequate.

Wran was rarely presented with evidence of widespread corruption. He was usually presented with allegations of corruption which were rarely backed up by evidence. Wran never deviated from insisting that those who were the subject of allegations were entitled to the protections of the rules of natural justice. In Wran's words: "In our attempts to deal with corruption allegations, we relied upon the legal principle commonly referred to as the presumption of innocence – a principle of law which in recent years has been increasingly ignored to the detriment of the rights of every individual in our country." Rodney Cavalier recorded that Wran told the Labor Cabinet, at the meeting that farewelled him, "his greatest failure was being unable to resist the reversal in society's acceptance of the presumption of innocence." After he had left politics, in an address to the Evatt Foundation in 1994, Wran said: "It seems that each week, in some parliament in some state of Australia, a law is passed reversing the onus of proof. We may well ask what's happened to that golden thread that was supposed to run through our system of justice, the presumption of innocence. All too often it has been converted into a presumption of guilt."

This "golden thread" has now been totally abandoned in NSW politics. This was shown by the treatment of a Labor MP, Steven Chaytor, (referred to in chapter nine) and, more recently, the treatment of a Liberal MP, Gareth Ward. He was expelled from the Liberal Party, and suspended from the Parliament, after being charged with historic child sexual offences. At the time of Ward's suspension, he had not faced a trial or been convicted. Ward's constituents demonstrated a greater commitment to this fundamental principle when they re-elected him, as an Independent, in his seat of Kiama at the March 2023 election.

No NSW premier since Wran has sought to defend the principle of the presumption of innocence. Electoral considerations now trump the proper application of the justice system. One can easily imagine a political adviser today telling a premier required to deal with the Rex Jackson matter: "Ignore the Federal Police's concerns. Don't wait for the police investigation. We are bleeding votes. Sack Jackson and get on with it." The existence of ICAC has provided some shelter to political leaders when serious allegations are made, an avenue that was not available to Wran. The unconscionable delays by that body, however, can still leave an accused MP or minister in a political deep freeze for an intolerable period. In other cases, former MPs have been left with a corruption stain which has never been proved or removed.

A further explanation for Wran having been singled out for corruption allegations is his initial reluctance to 'clean up the cops'. This gave rise in certain quarters to a suspicion that the police had a hold over the government or over Wran personally. This was certainly the judgment of crusading crime journalists but it was not confined to the crusaders. Max Walsh wrote in *The Sydney Morning Herald* after Wran announced his resignation: "It was the failure to move [to reform the police] at the outset of his administration which fuelled speculation of underlying corruption within the ranks of the Wran government". Walsh was an influential journalist and a respected former editor in the Fairfax organisation and this became 'group think' among some senior Fairfax journalists. Wran acknowledged this perception in 2006, after he had left politics, when he spoke of being "vulnerable in respect of the way in which we tackled corruption allegations relating to the police".

There is no doubt Wran inherited a police force riddled with corruption. There is also no doubt, as the later Wood royal commission demonstrated, that the police force which Wran, and his successor Barrie Unsworth, passed on to the Greiner Coalition government was one still riddled with corruption. This was despite NSW, from 1979 onwards, having had a succession of honest police commissioners. The reasons for the government's electoral caution in attempting to clean out the Augean stables were outlined in chapter two. Even the minister who urged Wran to "clean up the cops" later conceded that the police force was far more popular than politicians in the eyes of the electorate.

It is naïve to have expected Wran, early in his premiership and with a one-seat majority, to have tackled police reform. A more reasonable criticism is that the government was slow to take this on when the political environment became more amenable to reform. Although I can find no public opinion polls to back this up, there seems to have been a shift in public attitudes about the police in the early 1980s following repeated scandals. One of Wran's great strengths as a politician was his sense of political timing. As he later told one of his ministers, Rodney Cavalier: "Get the timing right and you can do anything in politics." Wran's sense of political timing let him down on this occasion. He failed to detect when public attitudes began to shift in favour of a desire to reform the police. When he moved it was with characteristic decisiveness, assisted by a reformist police minister Peter Anderson who, as a former policeman, had credibility within the force. By then, however, it was something that the government was seen to have been forced to do and for which it has received little credit.

This shift in public opinion away from a very favourable reputation of the police force should not be exaggerated. The campaign conducted by the police union and senior police officers against Wran's decision in November 1983 to appoint a Police Board, with power over senior appointments, showed the police force was still very resistant to change and believed it could carry public opinion. The refusal of the Fahey Coalition government in 1995 to support a royal commission into the police force shows that a reluctance to 'clean up the cops' was not confined to the Wran government.

The main reason, however, why Wran's name has been singled out for claims of corruption has to do with the media. Wran had a complicated relationship with the fourth estate. On one hand, he dominated political journalism, particularly those who reported out of the Macquarie Street press gallery. As we noted in the Wran biography: "Wran was all that political journalists find irresistible – intelligent, articulate, adroit and victorious." Away from Macquarie Street, however, there was a cynicism about Wran among many journalists. This was partly a reaction to what these journalists saw as Wran's domination of their Macquarie Street colleagues and partly a belief or suspicion of underlying corruption within the ranks of the government, as the Max Walsh quote shows.

There was also an overwhelming cynicism about the actions or motives of all NSW politicians, not only Wran. Jonathan Holmes acknowledged this when explaining why the 'Big League' program (discussed in chapter four) did not concede that Farquhar may have been using Wran's name for his own purposes. Holmes was frank: "in the climate of the times, it did not seem especially unlikely that Wran would have done what Farquhar alleged he did." By "climate of the times", Holmes alludes to the "recurring themes" of corruption in NSW, which we referred to in the Wran biography and mentioned in chapter one. The "climate of the times", however, was also one of extreme cynicism by journalists about NSW politics. This was exacerbated by Wran, himself, who could also be cynical in how he practiced politics. Wran also had a healthy cynicism about the practice of journalism. For many journalists, cynicism is regarded as a necessary quality in their own profession but is seen as an unattractive trait in their politicians.

Margaret Simons, now a veteran journalist but then a self-described "junior journalist" in *The Age* newsroom, has given a vivid description of the journalism environment of the early 1980s. She recalls when "Bob Bottom, a journalistic refugee from Sydney, arrived in 1984 [with the transcripts of the illegal police phone taps] in a cloud of glamour, righteousness and zealotry." Simons rightly acknowledges some of the ground-breaking journalism of the era. "But among some of the journalists, the zeal was sometimes excessive, and the shades of grey too often depicted as black and white," she observed.

The excessive zeal which Simons recorded in Melbourne was even more evident among the Sydney media. An observer from outside journalism, historian Frank Bongiorno, after rightly dismissing claims of a Fairfax/ABC conspiracy against Wran, noted that "some journalists, particularly in the Fairfax press, had little regard for the Labor government of New South Wales and believed that it was implicated in the continuing problem of organised crime.... Especially at Fairfax, journalists also influenced by the radicalism of the 1960s and 1970s were instinctively hostile to the machine politics of the NSW Labor Right, with its conservative Catholic strain, its cynicism about power and its culture of mateship." Wran, despite not being a product of this Labor *milieu*, was nevertheless a focus of this hostility. This is not to denigrate the work of individual Fairfax journalists in exposing corruption. Simons is right, however, in suggesting that "shades of grey [were] too often depicted as black and white". Thus, a failure to tackle reform of the police force is seen as evidence of underlying corruption, not a sign of understandable electoral caution.

The "climate of the times" has taken on a new meaning in parts of the media following Wran's death. Conviction of corruption has replaced suspicion. Inconvenient evidence to the contrary is now blithely ignored. Hearsay has become acceptable evidence of guilt.

Journalists no longer explore the background and motives of those making allegations. The requirement for allegations to be corroborated by an independent source, let alone multiple sources, is now considered old fashioned. This reached a low point when a senior ABC editorial executive wrongly told the Senate that there was no need for corroboration of corruption allegations the ABC made against Wran because he was not a focus of the investigation.

The defamation laws have become a convenient excuse for journalists for not having sought to establish the truth or otherwise of allegations while Wran was alive. Those same journalists have taken advantage of the defamation laws to declare open season on Wran's reputation after his death. 'Bring out your dead', the infamous summons during the Black Plague, has become a rallying cry. This is not confined to journalists. A senior book publishing executive told me, when I pointed out there was no evidence for a published defamation of Wran: "Clearly there has been no defamation of Wran given Wran is deceased." The fact that a publisher does not understand the distinction between the act of defamation and the law that prevents actions for defamation being brought on behalf of another person, seems typical of the climate of the times.

Journalists, when conveying allegations about Wran, no longer worry about multiple sources or independent evidence. In death Wran has been accused, without evidence or corroboration, of nobbling two police investigations, first to protect Abe Saffron and then to protect Bill Waterhouse. He has been accused of being a friend of Saffron, also without corroboration, despite Wran having told Parliament, without challenge, he had never met Saffron. Wran has been accused of corruptly delivering a lease to Saffron despite overwhelming evidence this did not occur. He has been accused, again without evidence or corroboration, of taking bribes from an illegal casino.

The freedom from legal consequences of defaming the dead is a legal privilege for journalists. Multiple examples in this book have shown that it is a privilege that is now routinely abused. Many journalists no longer accept that with legal privilege comes moral responsibility. Still the media wonders why parliaments are so reluctant to liberalise the defamation laws.

Andrew Rule, who has reported several allegations of corruption about Wran, has justified waiting until after Wran was dead by saying: "All we owe to the dead is the truth." This is a noble sentiment but allegations, without evidence or independent corroboration, do not establish guilt. Gossip and hearsay are not truth. Those who hurl allegations are automatically accepted as virtuous even though they rarely do so with purity of heart. Allegations about the dead should receive the same care, corroboration and scrutiny as allegations about the living. The character assassination of Neville Wran is mainly attributable to the media abandoning the moral responsibility which once went hand in hand with legal privilege.

Notes

Chapter 1. A Few Whacks On The Coffin Lid

The quotations which begin the chapter are from, in order, the *Herald Sun* 27 April 2014 and *The Australian* 22 April 2014.

Full accounts of Wran's career and achievements can be found in Mike Steketee and Milton Cockburn *Wran: An Unauthorised Biography* Allen and Unwin 1986; David Clune *Neville Wran* Connor Court Publishing 2020; Troy Bramston (Editor) *The Wran Era* Federation Press 2006; Graham Freudenberg *Wran, Neville Kenneth* in David Clune and Ken Turner (Editors) *The Premiers of New South Wales, Volume 2, 1901-2005* Federation Press 2006; and Brian Dale, *Ascent to Power* Allen and Unwin 1985.

David Clune's comment about the Wran model is from *Neville Wran* op. cit. Paul Kelly's comment was reported by Graham Freudenberg *Wran, Neville Kenneth* op. cit. The quotation by Rodney Tiffen about the "sheer number of controversies" is from 'Was Neville Wran Corrupt?' *Inside Story* 31 August 2021.

The claim that the Wran Government was "a byword for graft" was made by Richard Cooke in the *Sydney Review of Books* 8 December 2017. The claims that the Berejiklian Government was "the most corrupt government since the Wran years" and the Wran Government was "riddled with corruption" were made by Bernard Keane *Crikey* 15 March 2021 and 1 October 2021. The claim that Wran "was as bent as a three-dollar note" was made by Andrew Rule in the *Herald Sun* 3 May 2021.

Wran's comment about the fabrication of allegations was reported by Graham Freudenberg in his memoir, *A figure of speech* John Wiley & Sons Australia 2005. The claim about Wran and the CSIRO is from Kate McClymont, with Vanda Carson, *Dead Man Walking: The Murky World Of Michael McGurk and Ron Medich* Vintage 2019. The claim by Andrew Rule about the alleged luncheon at Bayswater

Brasserie and the cordless phone were reported in the *Herald Sun* 3 May 2021. The claim by Andrew Rule about Phillip Adams and Kerry Packer was reported in the *Herald Sun* 27 April 2014 and 3 May 2021. The actual version by Phillip Adams was reported in *Crikey* 17 February 2006. The claim by Andrew Rule about Wran and mineral licences was reported in the *Herald Sun* 3 May 2021. Bob Bottom made the claim about legislation allegedly to fine and jail him in an interview on the website *Democracy's Watchdogs*. Andrew Rule's comment about Wran's nickname was made in the podcast *Life & Crimes with Andrew Rule* 1 May 2021.

David Clune's comment that "there was not much competition" is from *Neville Wran* op. cit. The comment by Bob Carr about Wran's three distinct errors was reported by Rodney Tiffen 'Was Neville Wran Corrupt?' op. cit. The quotation from Dennis Shanahan is from his chapter 'An Assessment from the Outside' in *The Wran Era* op. cit.

Chapter 2. Minister for Corruption

The first quotation beginning this chapter is from the podcast *Life & Crimes with Andrew Rule* 1 May 2021. Andrew Rule also reported this in the *Herald Sun* 3 April 2021. The second quotation is from *Wran, Neville Kenneth* op. cit. The third quotation is from Hansard NSW Legislative Assembly 23 April 1979.

Frank Walker's confirmation of his advice about reforming the police force, and his acknowledgement about the popularity of the police, is from his chapter 'Social Policy and the Reform Agenda' in *The Wran Era* op. cit. Wran's comment about rusty razor blades was reported by Phillip McCarthy *The National Times* 13 September 1981.

Ron Mulock's comment about a 'Catholic push' is from his memoir by David Clune with John Upton *Inside The Wran Era: The Ron Mulock Memoirs* Connor Court Publishing 2015.

Andrew Rule's comment about Bill Allen being known as a 'bent cop' is from his podcast, op. cit.

The private letter to Bill Allen from John Dowd was reported in *The Sydney Morning Herald* 6 November 1981.

The Sydney Morning Herald report on the promotions of Abbott and Allen was on 15 November 1979.

All quotations from Peter Anderson are from telephone interviews with the author conducted in 2021 and 2022.

Andrew Rule's allegation about Roger Court QC was reported in the *Herald Sun* on 3 April 2021 and 3 May 2021.

Rodney Tiffen's comment about Bill Allen is from 'Was Neville Wran Corrupt?' op. cit.

The claim by Fia Cumming was made in her book *Sledgehammer Beck: One honest cop vs Sydney's Crime Bosses* Inspiring Publishers 2023.

The quotation from Evan Whitton about Superintendent Merv Beck is from his book *Can of Worms II* Fairfax Library 1987.

Gerry Gleeson's comment about the Police Board is from his chapter 'The Public Service' in *The Wran Era,* op. cit.

Chapter 3. Nifty and Watery

The quotations which begin this chapter are from, in order, the *Sunday Herald Sun* 1 December 2019 and *The National Times* May 1978. The second quotation was also reported in Paul Kennedy *High Stakes: The Rise of the Waterhouse Dynasty* Hachette 2014.

Wran's anecdote about Charles Waterhouse was reported in *The Sydney Morning Herald* 30 September 2009.

The relationship between Wran and Bill Waterhouse before Wran entered Parliament was recounted in *Wran: An Unauthorised Biography* op. cit.

Waterhouse's comments about Wran's advice on the handling of Charlie Waterhouse's estate, and the AJC hearing, are from Bill Waterhouse, *What Are The Odds? The Bill Waterhouse Story* Vintage 2010.

David Waterhouse's comments about his falling out with his family are from a television interview with Kerry O'Brien, ABC-TV *7.30 Report* 22 January 1996. His response to his father's claim about refusing to use a painting to guarantee the tax debt was made to Rick Feneley *The Sydney Morning Herald* 9 November 2012.

Andrew Rule's claim that Wran accepted $5,000 from Bill Waterhouse was made on his podcast op. cit.

The reference to Bob Askin raising and distributing campaign funds is from Ian Hancock *The Liberals: A History of the NSW Division of the Liberal Party of Australia 1945-2000* Federation Press 2007.

The anecdote by Gough Whitlam about Joe Cahill and Rex Jackson was reported by Rodney Cavalier in the *Southern Highlands Newsletter* No. 181 2012.

The claim by David Waterhouse about Bill Waterhouse sending Bill Allen to his illegal casino to collect bribes was reported by Andrew Rule in the *Sunday Herald Sun* 1 December 2019.

The ABC-TV *Four Corners* 'Horses for Courses' was broadcast on 10 November 1986.

The reference to the Palace casino in Kings Cross is from David Hickie *The Prince And The Premier* Angus & Robertson 1985.

Evan Whitton's comments about the meeting at the Taiping restaurant and the return of Merv Beck are from his book *Can of Worms II* op. cit.

The statement by Valerie Murphy to the NSW Major Crime Squad is from her transcript of interview dated 6 March 1987, a copy of which was seen by the author.

The reference to Merv Beck is from Fia Cumming *Sledgehammer Beck* op. cit.

Andrew Rule's comment about Wran nobbling a murder investigation was made in Andrew Rule *Chance* Pan MacMillan Australia 2021.

The author sought an interview with David Waterhouse, by telephone and email, on 21 and 22 November 2022. He insisted he would only be interviewed in the company of journalist Andrew Rule. This was declined in accordance with normal journalistic practice. I suggested both of us could each record the interview. This was also declined.

Chapter 4. "The Premier Is On The Phone"

The quotations which begin this chapter are from the *Report of the Royal Commission of Inquiry into Certain Committal Proceedings against K.E. Humphreys* July 1983.

Ron Mulock's account of the meeting of the Policies and Priorities Committee is from *Inside The Wran Era: The Ron Mulock Memoirs* op. cit.

Graham Freudenberg's comment about Sir Laurence Street's conclusion is from *Wran, Neville Kenneth*, op. cit.

Jonathan Holmes' defence of the *Four Corners* 'The Big League' is from *The Sydney Morning Herald* 24 April 2014 and 'Ghosts Can't Sue' ABC Alumni website 2 May 2021. His comments about whether the program should have acknowledged that Farquhar may have been misusing Wran's name were made in an email to the author on 14 October 2022. Chris Masters' comments are from an ABC video in 2011 celebrating 50 years of *Four Corners*.

Clarrie Briese's claims are conveyed in his book *Corruption In High Places* Noble Books 2021.

David Marr's comment about Clarrie Briese was made on ABC-TV's *Four Corners* 'The Murphy Scandal' 20 November 2017.

Chapter 5. The Ghost Train Fire Conspiracy

The quotations that begin this chapter are from, in order, ABC-TV *Exposed: The Ghost Train Fire* 30 March 2021; Hansard Senate Estimates hearing 26 May 2021; and 'ABC Editorial Review 25 *Exposed: The Ghost Train Fire*' August 2021.

An example of the advertisements by the Department of Services calling for tenders "to operate an amusement park" is given in *The Sydney Morning Herald* 18 August 1979.

The details of the lease negotiations for Luna Park were obtained from the report of the Parliamentary Commission of Inquiry *Allegation No. 27 Luna Park* released in 2017.

The reference to the NCA is from *National Crime Authority, Commonwealth Reference No. 1, NSW Reference No. 3, Interim report provided pursuant to Section 59(5) , National Crime Authority Act 1984, concerning certain matters arising out of certain fires in Sydney in the period 1979 to 1982, April 1989*. This was tabled in the NSW Legislative Assembly on 3 August 1989.

The report of the NSW Corporate Affairs Commission inquiry was tabled in the NSW Legislative Assembly on 27 October 1987. The report is titled *First and final report of the Inspector of the special investigation into Harbourside Amusement Park Pty Ltd, Sibaf Nominees Pty Ltd, Peak Nominees Pty Ltd, Peak Services Pty Ltd, Arcadia Amusements and Vending Pty Ltd and Marshin Holdings Pty Ltd.*

The comment by Andrew Andersons was published in *The Australian* on 15 April 2021.

Bob Carr's comment about the claim of Wran attending drinks at the home of Abe Saffron was published in *The Australian* 24-25 April 2021. Gary Sturgess' comment was published in *The Australian* 1-2 May 2021.

Wran's comment about Abe Saffron is from the Hansard NSW Legislative Assembly 30 November 1977.

The author sought interviews with the then ABC Chair Ita Buttrose and ABC Managing Director David Anderson about the program and, at the ABC's request, submitted in advance a list of questions. The interview request was declined.

Chapter 6. The Russian Tank And The Network Of Influence

The quotations that begin this chapter are from, in order, NSW police transcript of a recorded telephone conversation of Morgan Ryan on 31 March 1979 and the report of the Parliamentary Commission of Inquiry *Allegation No.18 Appointment of Bill Jegorow,* released in 2017.

Morgan Ryan's comments concerning his successful gambling on Dream King winning the 1961 Australian Cup were made in the 'Good Weekend' in *The Sydney Morning Herald* 2 November 1985.

The list of judges who, as barristers, had been briefed by the firm of Morgan Ryan and Brock was tabled by Wran in Parliament on 29 February 1984.

All details of the NSW police telephone surveillance operations are from the report of the *Royal Commission of Inquiry into Alleged Telephone Interceptions, Volume 1* AGPS 1986.

All material relating to the appointments of Wadim (Bill) Jegorow is from the report of the Parliamentary Commission of Inquiry *Allegation No. 18 Appointment of Bill Jegorow,* op. cit.

Ian Temby's conclusion regarding the Jegorow appointment allegation was tabled in the Senate on 28 February 1984.

The television interview Wran gave after announcing his retirement as premier was on Channel 9 *Sunday* 8 June 1986.

Frank Bongiorno's comments are from his book *The Eighties: The Decade That Transformed Australia* Black Inc 2015.

Chapter 7. The Mysterious Forty Million Dollars

The quotations that begin this chapter are from, in order, the podcast *Life & Crimes with Andrew Rule,* 1 May 2021; Hansard House of Representatives 14 May 2014; and *Wran, Neville Kenneth,* op. cit.

Brian Dale's comment about Wran knowing "the value of a quid" is from *The Sydney Morning Herald* 28 December 1991.

Andrew Rule's comments about Wran's success as a barrister are from the podcast, *Life & Crimes with Andrew Rule* 1 May 2021. Brian Dale's comment about Wran's earnings as a barrister is from *Ascent to Power* op. cit.

Gavin Souter's profile of Wran was published in *The Sydney Morning Herald* 12 May 1976.

Wran's comment that "he took it home in trucks" as a barrister was reported in *The Sydney Morning Herald* 28 December 1991.

Wran's comment in 1989 about needing to make money was published in *The Sydney Morning Herald* 11 November 1989.

Malcolm Turnbull's comment about Wran's lack of financial security when he left Parliament was made in the House of Representatives on 14 May 2014. His comment about persuading Wran to go into business with him was made in the same parliamentary speech.

Details of the commercial success of Whitlam Turnbull & Co. and Turnbull and Partners Ltd are from Paddy Manning *Born To Rule?* MUP 2016 and Malcolm Turnbull *A Bigger Picture* Hardie Grant Books 2021, supplemented by interviews with Malcolm Turnbull on 14 November 2022 and 13 March 2023.

Nick Whitlam's comments on Whitlam Turnbull & Co. are from his review of Malcom Turnbull *A Bigger Picture* op. cit. on his website.

Brian Dale's comment about Wran opening doors was reported in *The Sydney Morning Herald* 28 December 1991.

A copy of Wran's will, which is a public document, was obtained from the Supreme Court of NSW.

Chapter 8. Media Mates

The quotations that begin this chapter are from, in order, Brian Dale *Ascent To Power* op. cit. and Rodney Tiffen 'Was Neville Wran Corrupt?' op. cit.

A full account of the political controversy within the Labor Party over Lotto is given in *Wran: An Unauthorised Biography* op. cit.

Details of the financial return to the NSW government from Lotto were obtained from the NSW Parliamentary Library Research Service *NSW and Gambling Revenue* Briefing Paper No.16/96.

Rodney Tiffen's claim that Wran treated media proprietors as "targets of inducement" and ignored "procedural niceties" is from 'Was Neville Wran Corrupt?' op. cit. His statement that Lotto was "extremely lucrative both for the government and the companies running it" and that the Wran government overruled the SCG Trust are from Rodney Tiffen 'The Packer-Labor Alliance, 1978-95: Rip' *Media Information Australia* August 1995.

Andrew Webster's comment about Wran dissolving the SCG Trust is from his book *If These Walls Could Talk: A Celebration of the Sydney Cricket Ground* Stoke Hill Press 2021.

The account of the passage of the *Sydney Cricket and Sports Ground Bill 1977,* and Packer's reaction in *The Bulletin* to the Legislative Council decision to defer the Bill, is from David Clune and Gareth Griffith *Decision and Deliberation: The Parliament of New South Wales 1856-2003* Federation Press 2006.

A full account of the 1903-04 court case is given by Rodney Cavalier and Geoff Armstrong 'When only a court will do: resolving who was in charge of cricket at the Sydney Cricket Ground 1903-04' in the *Southern Highlands Newsletter* No. 243 July-September 2021. In summary the cricket ground at Moore Park came into existence as just that, a cricket ground. The Deed of Grant of 1876 created only a cricket ground. Almost from the beginning other sports and events were staged there but only after approval from the Executive Council as published in the NSW Government Gazette. A clause in the grant, unvaried as permissions grew, gave the NSW Cricket Association an absolute right to first use. In 1903-04 a group of SCG Trustees staged an event that prevented the playing of cricket. The NSWCA sued to have its rights affirmed. The court found in favour of the association.

Daniel Brettig's comment is from *Bradman and Packer – the deal that changed cricket* Slattery Media Group 2019. Arunabha Sengupta's comment is from 'The Birth of Day-Night Cricket Matches' in *Cricket Country*, available online. Sir Donald Bradman's comment is from 'Whither Cricket Now?' *Wisden* 1986. Andrew Webster's comment was reported in *The Sydney Morning Herald* 5 November 2021.

The agreement between the NSW government and James Packer over the Perisher Blue leases was reported in *The Sydney Morning Herald* 13 May 2009.

Frank Bongiorno's comment on the Lotto contract is from *The Eighties: The Decade That Transformed Australia* op. cit.

Chapter 9. Buckets Of Trouble

The quotations which begin this chapter are from, in order, Rodney Cavalier *Southern Highlands Newsletter* No.181 2012 and *Wran: An Unauthorised Biography* op. cit.

Rodney Cavalier's comments on Rex Jackson's performance as Minister for Youth and Community Services is from his chapter 'The Wran Cabinet' in *The Wran Era*, op. cit.

Jack Ferguson's comment about Wran appointing Jackson to the corrective services portfolio was reported by Graham Freudenberg *Wran, Neville Kenneth* op. cit. Rodney Cavalier gave a slightly different version of Ferguson's comment in the *Southern Highlands Newsletter* No. 181 2012. I have preferred to cite Cavalier's version since he was present at the gathering.

Details of Jackson's gambling losses are from David Hickie *The Prince and the Premier*, op. cit. These were revealed during the special commission of inquiry.

Details of the government's internal deliberations over the Jackson allegations were obtained from file notes, letters and minutes of Gerry Gleeson, copies of which are in the author's possession.

Evan Williams' account of the concerns of the Governor, Sir James Rowland, is from David Clune and Ken Turner (Editors) *The Governors of New South Wales 1788-2010* Federation Press 2009.

Terry Sheahan's comment about Jackson's support among Cabinet ministers is from his chapter 'Reflections Of A Minister' in *The Wran Era* op. cit.

Tom Kelly provided the information about the decision of the Legal Services Commission in an email to the author on 3 July 2021 and in subsequent telephone conversations.

Brian Dale supplied the author with the original letter typed for Wran accepting Jackson's resignation with the paragraph crossed out by Wran.

Richard Ackland's comment about granting legal aid to Jackson was made in his newsletter *500 words* July 2021 (paywall).

David Marr's comment on Jackson's death is from *The Sydney Morning Herald* 2 January 2012.

Chapter 10. Riddled With Corruption

The quotations that begin this chapter are from, in order, Bernard Keane *Crikey*, op. cit.; Richard Cooke *Sydney Review of Books* op. cit.; and Graham Freudenberg *A figure of speech* op. cit.

Kate McClymont's allegations about Eric Bedford and Paul Landa are from Kate McClymont, with Linton Besser, *He Who Must Be Obeid* Vintage 2014 and Kate McClymont, with Vanda Carson, *Dead Man Walking: The Murky World of Michael McGurk and Ron Medich* Vintage 2018.

Ian Hancock's comment on the North Sydney preselection is from his book *The Liberals: A History of the NSW Division of the Liberal Party of Australia 1945-2000* op. cit.

John Whitehouse is acknowledged as one of Sydney's leading planning and environment lawyers and is the author of *Development and Planning Law in New South Wales* CCH 2012. He is a former Director of the NSW National Parks and Wildlife Service and a former Assistant Director of the NSW Department of Environment and Planning. From 1976 until 1980 he was special adviser to the NSW Minister for Planning and Environment, Paul Landa and is one of the authors of the *Environmental Planning and Assessment Act 1979*. He was actively involved in the decision to establish the SPCC Diamond Hill inquiry and provided information for this chapter.

The report of the Eric Coffey inquiry into Diamond Hill is titled *Diamond Hill inquiry: report and findings of the environmental inquiry into a proposed extractive industry at Diamond Hill, Kurrajong* State Pollution Control Commission, February 1979.

Chapter 11. We Owe The Dead The Truth

The quotations which begin this chapter are from, in order, 'Was Neville Wran Corrupt?' op. cit.; *Neville Wran* op. cit..; and report of the Parliamentary Commission of Inquiry *Allegation No. 27 Luna Park.*

Evan Whitton's daily sketches of proceedings of the Street royal commission were published in *The Sydney Morning Herald*. The references are from 25 June 1983 and 23 June 1983.

Rodney Tiffen's comment about "the sheer number of controversies" is from 'Was Neville Wran Corrupt?' op. cit.

Neville Wran's comment about his "residual bitterness" is from an interview for the National Library of Australia Oral History Section on 25 August and 6 October 2000.

The reference to Bob Hawke's financial reliance on Sir Peter Abeles before entering Parliament is from Troy Bramston *Bob Hawke: Demons and Destiny* Viking 2021.

Graham Freudenberg's comment about corruption claims being a deliberate tactic is from *A figure of speech* op. cit.

Ken Turner's account of the 1984 NSW election is from Michael Hogan and David Clune (Editors) *The People's Choice: Electoral Politics in 20th Century New South Wales Volume Three* Parliament of New South Wales and University of Sydney 2001.

Gary Sturgess' comment was reported by David Clune in *Neville Wran* op. cit.

David Clune's comment about Wran's approach to corruption claims is from *Neville Wran*, op. cit.

Dennis Shanahan's comment about the handling of corruption

claims is from his chapter 'An Assessment from the Outside' in *The Wran Era*, op. cit.

Rodney Cavalier's report of Wran's regret over his greatest failure is from his chapter 'The Wran Cabinet' in *The Wran Era* op. cit.

Max Walsh's comment was made in *The Sydney Morning Herald* 9 June 1986.

Jonathan Holmes' comments were made in an email to the author on 14 October 2022.

Wran's comment about being vulnerable in the handling of corruption claims is from his 'Forward' to *The Wran Era* op. cit.

Margaret Simons' comment is from 'The premier, the crime boss and the ABC' *Inside Story* 2 September 2021.

Andrew Rule's comment is from his podcast *Life & Crimes with Andrew Rule*, 1 May 2021.

www.ingramcontent.com/pod-product-compliance
Lightning Source LLC
Chambersburg PA
CBHW070345240426
43671CB00013BA/2408